GO-BOY!

Roger Caron was sixteen when he was first convicted for breaking and entering. Since then he has spent his life behind bars. He has tasted almost all the bitter fruits that such a life has to offer: the violence, the hate, the hard labour and the solitary confinement, the twisted friendships and the naked, deadly quarrels.

His is a grim tale, but one which it is impossible to leave aside. For he describes the life inside Canadian prisons with a horrifying realism.

Pierre Berton writes in his foreword: 'As a bank robber Roger was a dismal failure. I suspect that it is as a writer that his real future lies.'

GO-BOY!

The true story of a life behind bars

ROGER CARON

Foreword by
PIERRE BERTON

Nelson

Copyright © McGraw-Hill Ryerson Ltd., 1978
© Thomas Nelson & Sons (Canada) Ltd., 1979
81 Curlew Drive
Don Mills, Ontario
M3A 2R1

ISBN 0-17-600786-5

Original paperback edition published
under the title of Go-Boy by the
Hamlyn Publishing Group Limited

Printed and bound in Canada

890   89876543210

ACKNOWLEDGEMENTS

It is with intense pleasure that I take this opportunity to express my sincere gratitude to those individuals who have aided and encouraged *Go-Boy!* to see the light of day; as for those who have done their best to discourage me I can only thank them for spurring me on.

I am especially indebted to Mr Pierre Berton who is truly one of this country's greatest men, past and present. I will never be able to find the proper words to thank him enough for his generosity and the personal interest he took in *Go-Boy!* May you always walk tall.

My gratitude is no less to my wonderful family, in particular to my sister Sue who has stood by me all these years no matter what, and whose life has been a positive and sustaining source of inspiration to me. My thanks as well to my very good friend Roland Graser who is deeply involved in the field of penology in Cape Town South Africa. Thanks, also, to a former colleague of Mr Graser and a past Director of the John Howard Society of Quebec, Stephen Cumas, now a National Parole Board Member. Both of these men were a moving force behind the writing of *Go-Boy!* in its early stages. Nor could I forget the young lawyers Gunter and Nadia Vordemberge for supporting me in court and, most of all, for their ardent encouragement and aid in the writing of my autobiography. Charging to my rescue at this period in time – a time when I was ready to give up living – was Professor Desmond Morton of the Law Faculty of the University of Toronto, a bona fide genius.

My everlasting appreciation goes out to an unnamed school teacher who rescued my book manuscript after it had been forcibly taken away from me at the point of a bayonet during the 1971 Kingston riot in which two prisoners were killed. Gratitude also goes out to Doug Tait, my classification officer at Collins Bay Institution, for his patient co-operation in facilitating communication between my publisher and myself, and so much more. To Jane Allison, one of the resident psychologists in Collins Bay, and the first person to help me truly understand why I robbed banks. To the Visits & Correspondence staff in both Millhaven and Collins Bay for being understanding; to those few guards along the way who have won my respect; and to Judge Charles F. Doyle whose condemnation spurred me on to prove him wrong and who later 'tipped his hat' to me for doing so. Thanks also to Linda Florence, a very fine reporter and writer.

My strangest source of inspiration comes from a complete stranger, a beautiful and intelligent lady who works on the staff at Collins Bay Institution. Whenever my morale was sagging I would make it a point to observe her moving gracefully down the 'strip' to lunch, a heart stopping vision that never failed to send me hurrying back to my typewriter and *Go-Boy!* For me, she embodies what lost freedom is all about. Thank you Connie . . .

Finally, a very warm thank you to the staff at McGraw-Hill Ryerson Limited for without their trust and support there could be no book. Special thanks goes to Marilyn Gray, the Rights and Permission Representative, for her continued encouragement and to Arthur Gale, the Product Manager, for his early vote of confidence. But more than anybody, anywhere, and at any time, is my giving of thanks more profound than to my wonderful editor Elizabeth Hemsworth who laboured long and weary hours on *Go-Boy!* in her office, at her home in the living-room cutting and patching, and right inside the walls of two grim penitentiaries while struggling to conquer her fear of the slamming gates.

ROGER CARON
Collins Bay Inst
October 14, 1977

FOREWORD

I have read a good many books and articles about life behind prison walls, but this document by a multi-time loser is far and away the best I have yet encountered. It ought to be, for the author has been in and out of all the major prisons in Eastern Canada – Guelph, Kingston, Collins Bay, Millhaven, Stoney Mountain, the infamous St Vincent de Paul, Dorchester and even Penetanguishene, which is reserved for the criminally insane.

I have called him a loser because that is what he is – or at least *was* until he started work on the present manuscript, an act of therapy as well as an act of creation. He wrote me at that time, enclosing a first draft, which I found compelling. We have corresponded ever since.

For most of his life Roger Caron has been a loser because he has refused to conform and also because, until recently, he has neglected to learn from experience. A feeling of impotent rage suffuses his narrative. Defiant, rebellious and burning with anger, he would not knuckle under to the wardens, the screws, the tough cons or the world at large. His story emerges as that of a man banging his head, again and again and with utter futility, against impervious barriers.

In the half-world of the prison, he was a survivor and even a winner. He won the respect of his fellows by the strength of his will and of his fists and – here is the irony – by conforming to the unwritten convict code. Within the penitentiary walls, Roger Caron was able to adapt to the society around him – something he was not able to do whenever he stepped outside.

There are moments of real horror in this book. Incidents,

officially sanctioned, have taken place within Canadian penitentiaries that are as terrifying and as repellent as some of those we have read about in the Soviet Union or the various dictatorships around the world. Caron's graphic description of his two sessions with the 'paddle' – that euphemistically named instrument of official torture – is mind-chilling. It is not good enough for Canadians to say that they did not know these things were going on inside our prisons. They did know. They were told about it over and over again. Some of us have tried over the years to protest; but the Canadian public, in spite of the clear knowledge that physical torture of the most painful kind was part of official policy, continued to accept it, and indeed, in some cases applaud it. One of the reasons that the Canadian penal system has yet to emerge from the dark ages is because the people continue to demand revenge rather than rehabilitation. It is my hope that this book, with its detailed accounts of legalized beatings, will change at least some minds.

The physical battering of the naked human body in the name of punishment is appalling; but I personally find the author's description of solitary confinement, and what it does to the human spirit, infinitely more dreadful. We have heard similar stories of the treatment of war prisoners by the Chinese and others; but this is twentieth century Canada that Roger Caron is detailing. No country that can, as a matter of official policy, confine nearly naked men in concrete boxes under bright lights without human contact for months on end – I say no such country can properly be called civilized. It is necessary to read the author's own account of what this does to the mind and the soul to appreciate the true dimensions of our brutality.

One of the things that struck me, when reading this document, was Roger Caron's lack of self-pity. He knows that he has been a damn fool – not once, but many times. His various attempts at bank hold-ups, none of them successful, would have a comic opera quality were the circumstances not so serious. Although society and the prison system have not always served him well, he has himself been the instrument of his own downfall. We can understand the rage that boiled up within him, often at the most inopportune moments; but we must admit that his inability to control his hair-trigger temper has been his undoing. The newspapers dubbed him 'Mad Dog Caron' and the description was apt enough; but it is clear from his own story that behind that wild-man image there lurks a remarkable human being.

One cannot help but admire his persistent attempts, foolhardy though many of them were, to escape from the various institutions in which he was confined. In other circumstances – a German POW camp, for instance – this kind of demoniacal perseverance would have made him a legend. Only in recent years, however, has he come to understand that the real method of escape is through a fundamental change in himself. As a bank robber, Roger was a dismal failure. I suspect that it is as a writer that his real future lies.

Unlike so many tyros, he has a great deal to write about: after all he has completed more than twenty years of research. This is his first book but certainly not his last. He has the narrative gift; he knows how to describe events and people so that the reader feels himself present among the cons in the yard or on the run from the police. It is pleasant to be able to report that, although still confined, he has already commenced a second book. I am confident that long before that manuscript is finished, the parole board will have given him his freedom. When that happens and he and I meet at last, I will already have known him well enough, through his letters to me and through this remarkable book, to call him friend.

PIERRE BERTON
Kleinburg
December 23, 1977

PREFACE

The writing of this autobiography has been a voyage of self-discovery for me. At no time, no matter how adverse conditions became, did I doubt that my goal would eventually be realised. The compulsion to tell my story was as compelling as the act of breathing, as urgent and encompassing as the evolution of life itself. Through it all I was reborn: I found out all about myself, not stretched out on a shrink's couch but rather through the inner therapy of writing my life story. I can look back on all those wasted years with a fresh perspective. The effect of this is that I am able to dismiss from my mind some of the more crippling memories and yet retain what is useful and rewarding. In this way I find it easier to view the future and to formulate what I want to do with what remains of my life.

The completion of my autobiography has also provided me with a sense of dignity and self-worth that I never had before, the opportunity to discover my true self and to expand, but, most important of all, I hope that this account of my disastrous career in a life of crime will vividly illustrate the futility of trying to buck the odds for, as one sage put it, 'the hours are great, but the pay is lousy'.

R.C.

I wish to dedicate *Go-Boy!* to my three
perfect little nephews, Todd, Kurt and
Tate, who will always be able to count
on me to make sure that they never
encounter my mistakes. Also to Kim,
my Vietnamese angel whose dream shall
not be in vain. Finally, to all my
numbered friends, be you ever so few.

CHAPTER ONE

October 17, 1954: Because it resembled an oversized hearse, the reformatory bus with its armed guards and barred windows was called the Black Maria. On the last leg of a two-day round-up of convicted prisoners from provincial jails, it stood poised like a bird of prey beside the grey wall of the Cornwall City Gaol.

Shuffling through the early morning fog in shackles and handcuffs three of us felons boarded the bus under the close scrutiny of uniformed guards. At 6 a.m. the inside of the Black Maria was dark and those already aboard were either dozing or wrapped deeply in their own shells. Sleepy-eyed ourselves, we groped along the cluttered aisle dragging our chains and stumbling over personal belongings and feet, flushing up a flurry of ill-tempered curses and grunts, until finally we were able to seat ourselves. With the shotgun guards locked securely away from us inside their screened compartments at the front and rear of the bus, the ponderous vehicle lurched off and soon my home town faded from sight.

As a sixteen-year-old leaving home for the very first time, I was frankly scared, but because I was being transported to a notorious prison where I was told weakness was preyed upon, I was grimly determined not to show it.

In a while a hazy sun revealed countryside that was as blustery as my thoughts and further impressed on me that I was now an outcast, something to be shunned or feared. Hours earlier, Hurricane Hazel had struck and the Black Maria was gingerly picking its way through the wreckage, making endless detours. The devastation formed a natural background for the prison on wheels and for the convicted within.

'Want a TM?' asked this strangely gruff voice in my ear.

Startled, I turned to stare at an impish-looking, redheaded kid about my age with a mug full of freckles. He was holding out a package of cigarettes in a hand so small that the cuffs looked like leg irons around his tiny wrists. I smiled and shook my head.

'Go ahead, man. Take one. This is going to be your last chance for a tailor-made.'

Again shaking my head I said, 'I don't smoke.'

'Boy! You're lucky. Wish I could say the same; shitty weed is stunting my growth.'

About ten minutes later the gruff voice sounded off again, 'Got a name, pal?'

'Sure, my name is Roger and I'm shaking fourteen months for B & E.'

He grinned. 'You don't have to tell me you're in for Break and Enter. You don't have to tell anybody what you're in for. Not even the screws. Besides, the guards never believe anything we say; they'd rather look it up in our records – makes them feel important.'

I knew I liked him. 'Thanks, I'll remember that.'

'Wanna know my name?' he asked.

'Sure.'

'It's Red. Everybody calls me Little Red. But don't get me wrong!' he growled, sticking out his jaw. 'I'm no push-over.'

His disgruntled humor was starting to undo the knot in my guts. I got to know him pretty well before the end of the 300-mile trip to the Ontario Reformatory at Guelph.

He was born in a prison for women where his mother was serving a year for her part in a robbery. He stayed right there with her until the day of her release. At the age of four he was placed in an orphanage after his mom had been pushed down an elevator shaft by a jealous lover. From the orphanage he graduated to one training school after another. He laughed a lot telling me this so that I'd think it didn't bug

16

him. Later, when he was older, he took to stealing cars every chance he got. He confessed to me that he was a teenage alcoholic.

'I don't much care what happens to me; nobody cares. Still, where we're going, it's a jungle. A guy needs at least four eyes just to hold his own. I only got two and that's no good. Same for you, too, Rog. Look here, waddya say we team up? We'll have four eyes and twenty knuckles between us. We can be each other's right arm. Leastwise, that's how we worked it in training school.'

So it was that we touched chains and sealed the bond.

About a mile and a half from the town of Guelph we got our first look at the hellhole that contained over a thousand prisoners from all walks of life and of all ages. The first glance was deceiving because all the exterior ugliness was masked with ivy and lush green lawns. There were attractive flower beds, large stately maple and fir trees, two beautiful miniature lakes with little corrugated ripples playing to and fro, even apple orchards and red barns with cattle grazing in the open fields. Farther in the distance over the tree tops rose the splendour of blue mountains.

As the Black Maria drove closer, some of the veneer peeled away. A spine-tingling chill took root. Materialising through the ivy-covered concrete administration building and sprawling cellblocks were thousands upon thousands of steel bars, barbed wire fences, and at intervals the white watchtowers with peaked roofs and revolving searchlights. Seated on high stools within were uniformed pickets armed with sawed-off pump shotguns and revolvers.

Behind the main buildings, paved roads led to large clusters of industrial buildings: shops like the 'Markers' where vehicle license plates were punched out by huge presses and also, where fingers were lost on a routine basis. Farther back was the large slaughterhouse where prisoners bled as often as the animals they were instructed to kill. Way out in the fields was the quarry, a sixty-foot pit where the legendary Bull Gang toiled year-round under heavy guard to supply the material for the man-made landscaping.

Guelph was a provincial institution which meant that only those serving a sentence of two years or less would serve their time there. Peering through the bars of the Maria were two goggle-eyed delinquents, very pale and more than a little scared.

Unable to contain himself a second longer, Little Red exclaimed, 'Man, oh man! Gives me the creeps to think I gotta be buried in there.'

A gale force wind was still blowing. The skies were grey when the guards herded us off the bus, through the main entrance and into the administration area of the prison. Inside it looked a little like an old hospital. In double ranks we shuffled across the highly-polished marble floors, our chains jingling.

At the far end of the hallway we were brought to a halt by an armed guard at a locked barrier. Words were exchanged by our keepers; a large key was produced and with a loud click, the barred gate swung open on well-oiled hinges.

Finally our group stood in the centre of the reformatory. Here the cellblocks branched off and led to a maze of similar wings and tiers. Prison byways have many names known only to prison dwellers. It's a community with its own code of morals, customs, and vines carrying information. To the left was Gunsos Alley where the stoolies slept under the paternal vigilance of the staff. To the right was Torpedo Lane where the security risks were also closely guarded. Straight ahead was Lovers' Lane, the sleeping quarters of the drag queens who were only too willing to spread their wares around. For obvious reasons they were never permitted to sleep in one of the dormitories.

Our shackles were removed and we were paraded down Torpedo Lane towards the basement Receiving Room at the far end.

'C'mon! Button up your shirt, boy. And keep it that way! Do you understand?' shouted a corporal to a fat prisoner who immediately began to stammer incoherently. A crack on the shins with a nightstick, a surprised yelp, a growl, and the double rank began moving again.

At one point we had to step around a small group of disgruntled prisoners scrubbing the marble floor with toothbrushes. Overlooking the denim-clad figures was a skinny corporal polishing his sunglasses.

18

From the side of my mouth I asked Little Red, 'Hey, buddy, you sure this ain't the loony farm?'

'Shit! I wonder where they hang guys up by the thumbs?' retorted Red.

'Goddamn you lugs! Quit the yacking and straighten out that goddamn line or I'll run you both into the goddamn cooler,' shouted a grizzly old sergeant, bearing down on us.

We dummied up but somebody at the front of the ranks made a rude noise with his mouth and immediately the sergeant changed his course and waving his club in the direction of the insult, he started spewing out threats. 'The bastard that did that will be walking bowlegged for a long time if I find him out. We tame lions in here, too!'

His words were laughable and yet none of us doubted the deadliness of his threat. Getting crippled might be the gentlest thing that could happen to a guy here. To further hammer home the sinister effect was a sign posted on the wall in the Receiving Room which read:

> Always keep your words soft and sweet
> As you never know from day to day
> Which ones you may have to eat!

Nineteen of us were now seated on a long, wooden bench facing a bank of open showers. In the centre of the floor was a desk and seated behind it with an air of swaggering importance was a burly sergeant smoking a cigar. Beside the desk stood a tattooed trusty. Standing off to both walls were five guards dog-eyeing our every move.

One by one we were called to attention before the desk to answer a battery of questions. Our weight and height was recorded. We were fingerprinted and photographed, and finally, given a towel and a bar of lye soap and ordered to take a cold shower.

What an assortment of physical shapes! An old guy in his sixties with a huge belly; another with a wooden leg; and this sad looking prisoner with no jaw (having failed in a suicide attempt after killing his wife was the rumour). Most astounding of all was the transvestite in our midst. This blonde had fully developed breasts and as a result was a sure bet for Lovers' Lane. When the trusty handed 'her' the bar of soap, the cigar-smoking sergeant wisecracked, 'Don't drop it, sweetheart.'

Damned if 'she' didn't start to cry.

After we towelled off, the trusty handed us our clothing issue: blue jeans, blue shirt, denim jacket, cloth belt, peaked hat, woollen socks, heavy boots, and our bedroll of three blankets and one towel. Our toilet articles: safety razor with one blade, shaving soap, brush, hand soap, comb, toothbrush, ground-up chalk for toothpowder. Finally, we were given a stubby pencil to scribble our one letter a week. These worldly possessions were placed in a cloth sack that would be tied to the end of our bunks.

We were separated into two groups: Repeaters and Fish. A fish is a newcomer and a target for ridicule by the hardliners in the prison population.

We were then marched off to Reception where we would remain isolated from the corrupting influence of the repeaters – at least, for two or three weeks, until a selection panel stamped us 'salvageable' or 'unsalvageable'. If, after the interviews with classification officers, psychiatrist and other specialists, their recommendation was thumbs down, we would be tossed into the cauldron of the main population. Out there one learned to stick by the inmate code at all times or be crushed. It was an environment where might was right and an act of kindness regarded as weakness.

On the other hand, if the decision was thumbs up and a spark of goodness was detected, well then it meant a transfer to a small reformatory called Brampton, some forty miles away. The emphasis at Brampton was on rehabilitation and learning a trade; it had better recreation facilities.

To get to Reception from Receiving we had to pass along endless corridors and through at least a dozen locked gates, each manned by a guard with a long key. Finally we were passing cells that were occupied and from which faces peered out at us, hands gripping the bars so tightly that the knuckles turned white. Some of them stared with undirected hate smouldering from squinted eyes. Others stared with a cynical smile as if they were withholding some huge joke on society. There, too, were the ones who stared with open-eyed wonder because some do so right up to the day that they are sprung back into the free world. It started me thinking: when my fourteen months were up, what kind of look would I be displaying? Luckily I didn't know what was in store.

Reception consisted of a closed tier of cells on the bottom floor of the north-west cell-block which housed approximately two dozen of us fish waiting to be processed. This was the newest part of the institution; the cells were airy and spotless. Everything seemed to be made out of marble, concrete and steel. The front of the cell had an open network of bars and a few feet away was the corridor wall with barred windows, through which you could see fields and trees in the distance. The interior of each cell was as bare as a slab in a morgue: a metal bunk; combination table and stool firmly anchored to the wall; the sink and lidless toilet; and a stainless steel mirror riveted above the sink. No pillow, mattress, or sheets. The three army blankets issued had to be neatly folded at the head of the bunk each time we left our cells, or else. The cell was approximately five feet wide and eight feet long. A man six feet tall could lie down full length only in one direction. The ceiling light was turned off at 10 p.m. and on again at 6 a.m. Two minutes after the morning light came on a guy was out of bed or he got the bum's rush to the cooler. The radio system was a squawk box fastened to the corridor wall and turned off at 10 p.m.

I lived in No. 17 and Little Red in No. 19 and so after being deadlocked for the night at four in the afternoon we could talk to one another and even play chess by numbers. Red was the smallest guy on the range but he soon became the biggest in popularity. Red had a girlfriend whom he liked a lot and during our first evening in Reception their favourite song started playing while we were in the middle of a conversation and he suddenly went deathly quiet. Afterwards I could tell that he must have been crying and for that reason I've never forgotten the song. It was Kitty Kallen's, 'Little Things Mean a Lot'.

In charge of Reception was a small, Napoleonic sergeant by the name of Turner; however, Turner was better known by the prison population as 'Mother Goose', because it was his job to herd us fish around and away from the influences of the hardened prisoners. Of course, no one was foolish enough to call him Mother Goose to his face. Ironically every inmate at one time or another had been a fish led around by Mother Goose.

The mess hall could seat a thousand prisoners at one crack and was considered the hot spot for trouble within the institution. There were four gun turrets up by the high ceiling as a precaution against riots or attacks on the guards. The silence rule was in effect throughout the institution and especially in the mess hall. No talking was allowed. Not one word. Or else. Club-swinging guards patrolled unceasingly along the rows and rows of tables searching for whispered conversations or a lighted cigarette. We got the impression that they begrudged the food that went into our bellies.

Whenever we fish were paraded down to the mess hall for jug-up we would do so self-consciously because we were acutely aware of the repeaters eyeing us up. Somebody was sure to give out with a wisecrack and that would stir up the guards patrolling the floor. There was nothing we could do but wait for the day when we too became repeaters and could show off by catcalling some dude. A lot of these wise-acres liked to play the role of studs and give the 'sweet kids' sly looks and remarks. Poor Mother Goose's vigilance was sorely taxed. Some of the guys could disguise their voices so well that they would be the envy of a professional ventriloquist.

Passing through the meal line with a heavy metal tray and blunted eating utensils, we silently accepted the food ladled out by the grumpy cooks and made our way to our own reserved section.

There was one eating rule. Whatever amount of food you took, you had to eat it, every crumb, or else. When the meal was over, everybody would remain seated and mute while a lieutenant moved slowly along the aisle systematically signalling each table to move out by tapping it with his club. Near the exit a guard would carefully scrutinise each prisoner to make very certain that he had deposited his utensils in the basket. No one was allowed to take any food with him.

Stealing from other prisoners in the reformatory was

looked upon as an artistic achievement. It was also an initiation rite for newcomers. Lighters and trinkets such as medallions, pens, plastic combs, all have an exaggerated value on the black market and have to be closely guarded. However, there are some jailhouse thieves who are downright inventive.

Red and I witnessed the performance of a little old shrivelled-up prune of a man who sidled up to the locked barrier leading into Reception. He cast his eyes about nervously as he shouted.

'Okay, boys, Mother Goose sent me over to collect your blocks for refuelling. If you don't do it now, you'll go dry for the next ten days. C'mon, c'mon, let's go. Drop your lighters in my hat and I'll bring 'em right back filled.'

I didn't have one to give because I didn't smoke and Red was too suspicious to throw his in; nevertheless, that old geezer made off with sixteen lighters!

Just three weeks after our arrival, Little Red and I were mildly surprised to see our names listed for a transfer to the medium security reformatory in Brampton. Later that same day our classification officer informed us that all the tests we had taken indicated we had the ability to learn a trade. We would be transferred. I thought to myself that maybe, just maybe, everything would turn out Okay.

CHAPTER TWO

November 8, 1954: Again Red and I were aboard the Black Maria racing through the autumn countryside at a furious pace. It was as if the Maria was anxious to disgorge the handful of prisoners it held gawking through its barred windows. Suddenly the Maria veered off the main highway on to a winding gravel drive and, still rolling along at high speed between two rows of trees, it came to an abrupt sliding halt before a locked gate. A heavy touch on the horn brought an elderly guard hurrying from a grey guardhouse. There was an exchange of papers and the gate swung wide allowing the Maria to roll triumphantly in.

Brampton Reformatory is about three miles from the town of Brampton and about forty miles from Toronto. During the Second World War the buildings and grounds were used as a training base for the air force: the huge hangar and rows of barracks were still there. The hangar was converted into a well-equipped gymnasium; the huts remained relatively untouched except that the regimented men inside were prisoners, not soldiers.

In many ways it resembled a military base. The entire area was enclosed by a high fence topped with barbed wire. As a show place with an inmate population of only around a hundred, there was no open display of guns, but they were there. So were the pickets' shacks and the spotlights. Beyond the perimeter of the reformatory were nothing but deep fields of wheat and, farther back, heavy bush.

A large brick house stood near the entrance: the superintendent's residence. The gymnasium, baseball field with a backstop, and two identical rows of white barracks separated by an asphalt driveway was all of it. One row of barracks contained trade shops, chapel, hobby shop, library, school and barber shop. The opposite row housed the kitchen, mess hall, and dormitories.

Each of the huts was named after an animal: Cougar Hall, Tiger Hall, etc. In less than six months a prisoner could theoretically obtain a valid trade diploma and walk out of there with his head high. But that wasn't in store for me; fate had something else in mind.

'Toe the line while you're in here, boys, and you'll be treated well. However, if any of you step out of line, just once, you will be shipped back to Guelph so fast you'll think Brampton was just a dream,' warned the superintendent by way of a greeting.

Red and I were bunked down in Cougar Hall, a rather barren barracks with two long rows of army beds. We had a locker each. Near the entrance was an office for the guard watch. All the huts were joined by a narrow passageway which also led to the shower room.

It was mandatory for new fish to spend half a day in a shop learning a trade and the other half doing general maintenance work around the grounds. It was just our luck that when we arrived the need for a ditch six feet deep and forty feet long was acute. Five of us were put to work on it. A grizzled corporal called the Scotchman had been incensed over Little Red's wisecracks about the guard's wife balling the night shift while he was at work and so he assigned Red to be pick man. The earth was hard and it was a heavy, old-fashioned pick and so it was that Red spend most of his time teaching the rest of us a whole new style of cursing.

During the afternoons Red and I worked just as hard in our efforts to absorb the trade of tinsmithing. The two of us spent our evenings and week-ends inside the gym playing floor hockey and doing gymnastics in an attempt to neutralise our frustration level. It was in this locked and closely-guarded building that all our problems started.

Our very first evening in the joint we decided to just float around and check things out. We were standing around the boxing ring watching this big muscular guy punching his way through opponents with obvious glee. About thirty years old, his barrel chest and huge biceps were covered with exotic tattoos. (He was an ex-navy man and former boxing champ serving time for manslaughter.) Weighing in at two hundred and thirty pounds, with his bashed-in nose, blond brush cut and eyes bulging inside cavernous sockets, he looked mean. As it turned out, he lived up to his image.

Climbing out of the ring, he spotted Red lighting a cigarette with the beautiful lighter that his girlfriend had given him. On one side the lighter had a picture of a very sexy broad, on the other was inscribed: 'Be nice to me; good friends are hard to come by.' Boner, as his name turned out to be, immediately developed a burning desire to possess the lighter. He made a grab for it.

'No way!' retorted Red, as he backed away from the big ape. 'Nobody even gets to touch this block. Not you! not nobody.'

By now quite a few prisoners had gathered around expectantly. Boner was the big shot in the joint and a natural born bully, accustomed to having guys knuckle under to him. But even Boner couldn't justify slugging a kid less than half his size, although Little Red was standing right up to him.

'If you weren't such a little pip-squeak I'd give you something to go with your freckles!' shouted Boner in rage.

Little Red gave a nasty laugh, stuck his chin out, and made tight fists. 'Watch these freckles don't jump down your throat, fat man!'

By the time I dragged Red away, Boner was fit to be tied, waving his hamlike fists and stammering.

'That big creep is power-tripping, Rog!' Red complained. 'You let that kind climb up on your back and they never wanna slide off again.'

'Okay. Case closed, Red! All right?' I said trying to cool him down.

Suddenly he gave me that big, stupid, friendly smile, and said, 'All right. Case closed. C'mon, I'll buy you a drink of water.'

But it wasn't closed because from that night on they kept sparring with each other in verbal attacks until one night, almost two weeks after we arrived, I got caught in between.

Red chose that evening to stay in the hut and write a letter to his girl. Boner decided to get at Red through me by taunting me to climb into the ring with him. For me, such a move meant suicide. Not only did he outweigh me by eighty pounds, but I had never worn boxing gloves in my life.

'Well, well, if it ain't little peckerhead's silent partner,' Boner taunted, leaning over the ropes and brushing sweat away with his glove. 'You gonna climb in here and defend your friend's honour? He's too much of a runt to be bothered with, so I'll just show you who's boss instead. Why don't you tell peckerhead that, eh? Ha, ha, ha.'

Like a prize fool I let him make me angry. I tore off my shirt while two guys slid the boxing gloves on me. Boner blocked every blow and chewed me to pieces for three rounds, until the PT instructor leapt into the ring and broke it up. Boner had knocked me down so many times I felt like a yo-yo, but I had the satisfaction of not giving up and not

26

getting knocked out. The instructor chewed him out for taking advantage of me even though I said it was all my idea, climbing in the ring like that. As a result of the fracas I ended up with a black eye, a bloody nose and a fat lip.

'I'm gonna murder that big punk!' roared Red when I returned to Cougar Hall all patched up. 'Oh, sweet Jesus, just see if I don't spread his guts all over the gym floor, the big pig!'

Boner and I lost five days of gym privileges as a cooling off precaution, which I was glad to see because I figured by then Red would have got over his anger.

The first night back in the gym – I had Red's promise that he wouldn't fight with Boner – I involved myself in a furious game of floor hockey while Red and Larry wandered over to the basketball court to work out. The auditorium was always a beehive of activity and noise. Apart from the PT instructor who was usually refereeing a floor hockey game, there would be three or four guards grouped together near the exit drinking coffee and talking among themselves. With the boxing ring, weight-lifting platform and gymnastic equipment, there were numerous blind spots where the guards couldn't see what was going on unless they were right there on the spot. And normally, if there was going to be a fight, it would take place in the ring with gloves on.

The evening rolled along smoothly until the last ten minutes when Larry rushed over to the players' bench where I was resting and whispered excitedly in my ear that Boner and Little Red were fighting!

Gripping my heavy floor hockey stick, I burst into the area between the boxing ring and the weight-lifting platform just in time to see Red go reeling backwards, arms flailing and mouth gushing blood, to land sprawling on the steps leading into the boxing ring. His eyes were glazed over so he couldn't see Boner drawing back his heavy boot in order to kick him in the face.

Without thinking I raised the hockey stick high over my head with both hands and brought it down with all my angry strength on to the back of Boner's skull! The stick splintered in half with a sickening, crunching sound, very much like

27

squashing a rotten pumpkin. Then to everybody's astonishment, Boner slapped both hands to the back of his skull and pivoted slowly around in a weird pantomime until he was facing me. A look of disbelief spread across his face as he extended his left hand and slowly opened the palm to display Red's lighter. Then with a low, whimpering sound he collapsed to the floor.

'Holy Mother of Christ, Roger,' exclaimed Red in a hushed voice, as he shook the cobwebs from his numbed brain, 'I think you just croaked the big moron!'

'He looks just like my Uncle Bruno did when my pa hit him over the melon with the soapstone and Uncle Bruno was dead!' When Curly said that everybody looked at him with respect as if he were a doctor telling a patient's condition.

Shaking like an old wino, I decided, 'I'm going for the man; maybe he isn't dead, maybe he's just knocked out.'

'No! Don't be nuts,' protested Red as he staggered to his feet, wiping blood from his mouth. 'No way, you did this for me and I ain't gonna let you put your head in a noose. Let's tuck the big punk under the ring and we'll make it look like he fell out on his head or something.'

Larry, who was older and wiser than we were, interrupted Red. Pulling us off to the side, he whispered, 'Forget the accident bit. Look around you; there's at least a dozen guys taking in the scene and by tomorrow everybody in the joint will know what went down, including the screws. Your best bet is to jackrabbit, and I mean tonight!'

Red and I exchanged solemn glances and slowly nodded our heads.

We'd make our break while parading back to our huts at the termination of gym activities, which would be in ten minutes. Frantically everybody pitched in, grabbed Boner's body and dragged him under the canvas aprons of the boxing ring. We were all too spooked to see if under all the blood there was a pulse. He looked dead and that's what counted. We had one big break in so far as Boner was a trusty and always remained behind in the gym to clean up and put away the sports equipment. For that reason he wasn't included in the head count. If we had a five minute

28

start away from the gym before Boner was discovered we'd have a fighting chance we thought.

When the whistle did blow at 10 p.m. we nearly jumped out of our skins we were so on edge. Everybody rushed over to the exit to line up smartly, four abreast. Routinely Sergeant O'Connor moved slowly along the ranks confirming the count.

'Sixty-four, sixty-five, sixty-six, sixty-seven. Count's in! Roll them out.'

The door swung open to reveal more guards standing outside, ready to escort us back to our huts. A flock of blue denim moved out into the moonlight and was immediately surrounded by the guards like so many sheepdogs.

'Hup, one-two-three. Hup, one-two-three,' they chanted in a sing-song voice over and over again while barking at anybody who got out of step. The beam from a powerful spotlight stayed with us every step of the way. In the centre of the athletic field stood the patrol jeep, lights out, motor purring menacingly, ready to run down any would-be Go-Boy.

Five hundred yards separated the auditorium from the double row of white barracks; the asphalt road terminated ten yards beyond the last hut. Each hut was joined by a passageway and so this area was very much like a slot. At the end of that slot stood a human barrier in the form of three guards, legs spread wide across the narrow roadway, nightsticks tapping menacingly against the palm of one hand. One hundred yards behind them was a high chain link fence topped with rows of barbed wire; beyond that were tall wheat fields and darkness.

Red and I had placed ourselves in the front ranks for a speedy departure keeping one another's morale up with slow winks. The five hundred yards stretched away in front of us like five hundred miles as we steeled ourselves for the break. Finally Sergeant O'Connor barked out the order: 'Left turn'.

Two swift forms broke from the marching ranks, ran straight ahead, and smashed into the human barrier. Behind us sounded the shrill blast of whistles and loud shouts of 'GO BOYS! GO BOYS!' shattered the stillness of the night.

29

There wasn't enough room to squeeze past without being latched on to by the guards and that's what happened to the two of us. One guard had a firm grip on my hair, another had me by the jacket. I tried to twist loose before more of them got into the act. I glanced in the direction of Little Red in time to see him clubbed to the ground. With a bellow of rage I kicked the guard who was holding me by the coat in the belly and watched with satisfaction as he sagged slowly to the ground. Another violent lurch left the second guard with nothing but a handful of hair. I then pivoted defensively towards my friend and was stricken to see him obviously hurt and unable to run. Again the guards reached for me but like a frightened deer I bolted for the distant fence amid rising hysteria and shouts of 'Go Boy! Go Boy!' Most of the guards had to remain behind to watch that none of the others made a break for it.

Reaching the fence I leapt up high and, getting a firm grip, I started to pull myself up hand over hand just as the jeep slid sideways into the fence in a shower of gravel. A guard then stood up on the jeep and swung at my legs with a heavy club, narrowly missing me. By then I was all tangled up in the rolls of barbed wire which grasped at my clothing, ripping and tearing both cloth and flesh, until I was fairly screaming in pain. The guard below me was all set to swing his club again from a higher vantage point and this gave me the strength and determination to tear free of the restricting wire and tumble over on to the outside.

Dizzily I staggered to my feet and as I was stumbling into the wheat field I faintly heard my friend's voice, 'Go Roger! Go, go, go!'

Shaking off the spotlight I veered towards some heavy bush about two miles from the reformatory. Half a mile from the trees I was unable to run any farther. The blood pounding through my veins and lungs sounded like a riotous waterfall in my ears; my vision was blurred, and my heart felt like it was going to burst from the strain. I stumbled on for another short distance and then with my breath coming in short jerks, I collapsed in the grass.

It took long minutes for my breathing to slow down and for my vision to clear. It was only when I raised my arm to wipe the perspiration from my brow that I realised that my hands and chest were caked with blood. My torn clothes had taken the brunt of the punishment from the barbed wire. Even so I was badly hurt, particularly my chest where the barbs had sliced a furrow six inches long and almost an inch deep. I was still too shook up to feel any pain and deeply distressed that Little Red was not with me.

I was convinced that by now I was wanted for murder and if I didn't at least get shot, well then I'd surely hang. I rolled over on my back and stared up at the black clouds scudding across the face of the moon and I thought, 'Jesus, now it's going to rain.' Hanging around my neck was a very old silver chain with a medallion of Saint Joseph given to me when I was seven by Father Lebrun. He hoped it would banish the nightmares that had been plaguing me in my father's house. Whenever I was in serious trouble, Father Lebrun had advised that I should think of Saint Joseph and rub the medallion. I did so now, even though I wasn't a deeply religious person. To me the medallion was a talisman, a charm that averted evil and kept me alive, and so it meant a lot to me.

The jeep! I had rested too long and so here it came, roaring like the devil, into the field where I lay hiding. Its sudden appearance startled two horses that had been grazing quietly a few feet away and now they came galloping directly towards my place of concealment! I only had time to raise my arms when the squealing animals thundered right over the top of me! My right knee received a terrific wallop that spun me like a top. I almost bit off my tongue stifling the scream that built up in my throat. I curled myself into a ball and kept telling myself that it didn't hurt.

Cackling laughter came through to my ears and I heard the Dutchman say: 'By Golly, O'Connor. It wouldn't do for you to shoot a horse just because you're mad.'

'You just watch your tongue, man. You're just as responsible for that Go-Boy as I am and don't you forget it.'

Still gasping in pain I raised my head slightly until I was able to observe the sergeant standing upright in the jeep. He wasn't hard to distinguish with his mane of white hair and beer belly. There were six of them in the jeep and they looked like they were loaded for bear.

'Sy,' bellowed the sergeant. 'Let's see if we can flush us a rabbit. Put this thing through its paces.'

With a groan of despair, I burrowed deeply into the tall grass wishing I could make myself as small as an ant. With an angry roar the jeep came alive and took off at full speed with the guards hanging on like Keystone Cops, shouting, 'Pour the coal to it, Sy. YAAHOO!'

The jeep tore up and down several acres like a demented maniac in the hope of flushing me out into the open. I'd hear it coming, the roar of the engine getting closer and closer and the sound of the grass rushing under it. A couple of times I thought I could feel it coming straight towards me. Fervently I rubbed my medallion, wishing that maybe the jeep would strike a hidden rock and do a headstand, but no such luck. It combed and combed the field endlessly before it finally left for another pasture.

Just over one hour later I limped painfully to the outskirts of the town, looking like something out of a nightmare. My clothes were in shreds and I needed some tape to pull the lips of the wound on my chest closed. A couple of dozen stitches would be better but I wasn't in a position to answer a lot of questions. My face was dirty and still showed the bruises from the beating Boner had inflicted on me the week before. And apart from all that, my knee was stiff and grotesquely swollen. Fortunately I've always been very tolerant of pain; I've had a lot of practice.

I had listened closely to some inmates bragging and so I had no trouble breaking into a parked car and hot-wiring it. When the car obediently growled to life, it gave me a solid feeling of power and the happy knowledge that I would no longer have to walk. Finally, I was getting my share of luck.

Knowing instinctively that there would be roadblocks I spun the car off on to a side road and gunned her along blindly until it threw us once more on to the main highway, some thirty miles beyond Brampton. I was now driving in a thunderstorm charged with brilliant lightning bolts that lit up the countryside, followed by ear-splitting peals of thunder that sent shivers up and down my spine. I was really getting spooked. It seemed as if somebody up there was mad at me for killing a man and escaping from prison. Bone-tired, very cold, and very sore, I was driving with my one good leg and I had the car blanket wrapped around my shoulders for warmth. The windshield wipers were labouring at full speed and still my vision was practically nil; it was as if I was travelling in a submarine. Most other vehicles had pulled over to the side of the highway, but I was now a fugitive and I had no choice but to keep on running and running and running.

Three days later, at the hour of midnight, in the city of Hamilton, I was arrested in a restaurant by two detectives who recognised me from a wanted poster. My first two nights of freedom had been spent sleeping in the back of wrecked cars, freezing and nursing a knee which had swollen to twice its normal size. After being fingerprinted, photographed, and paraded through line-ups, two cops took me to a nearby hospital and had me fixed up. It was too late for stitches and as a result I still have a wide scar running across the left side of my chest. Thinking that I was a murderer, I refused to open my mouth or even acknowledge my name, and so for the first few hours I was on the receiving end of some rough handling from the police. Nor would I admit to stealing the car from Brampton that was found abandoned outside Hamilton, out of gas. I had learned my lessons well in the reformatory – Always tell the cops that you know 'nuthin from nuthin'. No fingerprints could be lifted from within the car because I had left the windows open, having been advised that by this manoeuvre, the morning dew would turn any prints to mush.

I spent the first two days after my arrest in a filthy, steel-riveted, drunk tank, full of slobbering, snivelling drunks and tough-looking hoods. It was a large bullpen that stunk of vomit and fear and overflowing toilets. A beehive of activity around the clock, men were crying, screaming, cursing, begging, making lewd suggestions, spitting racial bias, fist-fighting over cigarettes, over sandwiches, over who was going to take the beef. It was an evil place littered with prostrate bodies, some of which were covered with blood and gore, having been brought in like that by the police.

Tired, lonely, and suffering from so much physical pain, I dragged myself into a corner and stayed there awake, eyeing suspiciously anyone who came near me.

CHAPTER THREE

November 26, 1954: This time I entered directly into the mainstream of Guelph reformatory, not as a fish, but as a repeater. I did so cautiously as any man would if surrounded by pockets of quicksand. I was beginning to acquire the art of looking without seeing, of mental evasion, of staying adrift in a sea of mysterious shadows, and yet still being alert to the dangers around. It was a state of mind where a laugh or a smile was simply a sheathing for true emotions.

The name of the game was to stick to the prisoners' code at all times or else be crushed. In this environment if you weren't tough, you at least put on a tough front; otherwise you would find yourself muscled out of your new boots and everything else of value. Your best bet was to observe the twist and tricks of doing easy time and if you didn't wind up as a 'wheel', you'd at least learned a lot about crime. I found myself in the midst of a mind-boggling array of specialists who helped educate us in life's finer vices.

It was never long before a newcomer was lured into contraband and gambling. A kind of gambling fever gripped the institution from dawn to dusk: 'Who's going to win the boxing match?' 'Who's going to get to the mess hall first?' In place of cards or dice, the games of chance were played with packages of tobacco. They also served as stakes. One side of the package was heads, the other, tails. The players threw them down in rapid succession, calling: 'You come to me!' or 'I'll go to you.' The only sound, the soft clunk, clunk, clunk as the bales hit the floor. Always there would be a six-man to stand watch. If you were caught gambling, it was a sure trip to the cooler. Often pills were used as stakes: the stronger the pill, the greater its worth. Gambling more often than not fomented fights.

Unlike federal penitentiaries, the reformatory had no inmate canteen; consequently, there were no such things as tailor-made cigarettes, or candy bars and gum. That is, legitimately there were none; but on the black market such items were worth twenty times their street value. For instance, a package of gum was worth a dollar. Money came into the institution by way of the visiting room or else through a guard for a 20 per cent rake-off. Naturally there were always guards who brought in cigarettes and other contraband and made a good living at it too!

Every four days we were issued one bale of weed and those who didn't smoke exchanged this tobacco for choice desserts in the mess hall, or simply gambled with it. The more weed you owned, the more prestige it gave you. Everything in that place had a price tag on it, from tailored clothes on down to a nylon comb. The only personal items a prisoner could retain upon admission were his lighter and whatever religious article he had hanging on a chain around his neck. Ironically the most valued item was a cross and chain – the more delicate, the greater its worth. Uniqueness in a lighter made it more treasured than its actual price tag. In a way we were like primitive savages who idolised exotic trinkets and used them for barter. The most bizarre curio I saw hanging around a guy's neck on a chain was a glass eye won on a bet from some unfortunate inmate who had nothing more to wager.

The so-called wheels with their convoy of followers were easy to spot around the institution by the way they dressed. They always reminded me of sharks with their escort of pilot fish. Each wheel had half a dozen close buddies, including one sweet kid and one village idiot. It was a matter of prestige for the wheel to dress up his kid in tailored clothes, fit him out with a fancy lighter, cross and chain, and a nylon comb. In a way the kid was a walking bankroll. For instance, if the wheel lost his bankroll during a gambling session and needed more stakes, he'd just strip them from the kid, one item at a time to throw in the pot. A new pair of boots were worth twenty-five bales and a nylon comb fifteen.

The local tattoo artists did a landslide business with their primitive equipment. It's a small miracle that I did not cut any on. Being marked with five dots in the web of the left hand was considered the password into the underworld and since we were all there to increase our skills and acquire self-images as crooks, most everybody had themselves marked. By running a continuous line through the five dots the letters ORG would emerge (Ontario Reformatory Guelph). It was a sort of graduation certificate to prove that you were skilled in the ways of piracy. Another mark that was popular was to have the fingers of both hands lettered to read LOVE, HATE.

The inmate code was really a guidebook on how to succeed in prison by not really trying to reform. By turn the code is humorous, pathetic, and vicious. Whatever category the administrators place a newcomer in, it will not mean very much. His true standing comes from fellow prisoners, who will classify him as a wheel, a solid guy, a tough guy, a goof, or, if he is thought to be an informer, a rat. In order to gain acceptance one must follow the code to a fine degree.

I was celling in the old part of the institution on the second floor. Here the heavy doors were slid open and closed by a metal lever at the head of the range. The twenty cells in a range could be shut all at once or separately. Whenever the guard at the control box shouted: Lock-up! and pulled the lever down, it was wise to keep your fingers clear. Either that or lose them.

I was now serving a sentence of twenty months, having received an additional six months from the courts for escaping custody. I was greatly relieved to learn that Boner had suffered little more than a mild concussion and that nothing further was being said on the subject. As for my friend Red, I learned through the grapevine that he was being held in solitary confinement in Brampton Reformatory pending the outcome of an investigation. The fact that Red had not succeeded in getting off the prison property saved him from being tried in court of law; instead his case became an internal disciplinary problem. It was a sure bet that he would eventually be transferred back to Guelph and, unpleasant as that would be, at least we'd be together again.

The cell-block where I lived was four storeys high and honeycombed with tiny barred windows. There were four such blocks in that area and, placed as they were, they formed a boxed-in yard that became known later as the Badlands. During the warm months when everybody kept their windows open these cell-blocks crackled with whispered and shouted conversations in at least a dozen languages. In the evenings, when the cell lights were on, it was like observing a hundred television sets all tuned to the same picture.

It was also a rather cheerless sight. If the guys weren't arguing over some point, making bets, or baying at the moon, then you could at least count on them to be dealing in contraband articles. These items would be passed on to buyers by means of a ball of string and a little bit of expertise at swinging your weighted line into the right window. There was one guy called Bigfoot who owned a contraband library of pornographic books; he made a killing loaning them out at three bales a crack. Of course all these back window activities were not permitted – not even talking was permitted – so a guy had to be constantly alert not to get pinched in the act.

The Badlands was considered a highly sensitive area within the institution and so it was heavily patrolled by club-swinging guards with armed pickets on the roof tops. When a thousand prisoners were milling about, almost shoulder to shoulder, scheming, dealing, and horsing around, a guard needed a keen eye to detect something going on. Most of the guys were past masters at the art of diversion and camouflage, whether it was zapping a stoolie or screening a crap game. Here the guards patrolled in pairs and were quick to blow their whistles whenever a rumble developed, but usually it took a blast from a shotgun to break up a determined fight. The reason being that the prisoners traditionally formed tight circles of blue denim around combatants, a circle that not even the bravest guard dared to break through. There were simply too many shivs and too much animosity in that prison, so a guard had to train himself to stay away from shadows and tight spots like that or else end up with a knife in his back.

To describe the Badlands as a miniature jungle is no over-statement. It was a proving ground for muggers in which newcomers never failed to become the unwitting victims. At least on the street if you were being mugged you could yell for a cop; in prison the code forbids such an unmanly manoeuvre. The way we saw it, the natural thing to do was to stomp your own snakes. There was no such excuse as not being big enough or tough enough; a shiv or an iron bar was considered the equaliser.

My fourth day in the joint saw me leaning against one of the cell-blocks in the Badlands, my hands thrust deep into my jeans, a peaked hat pulled low over my eyes and a blue denim jacket pulled tightly around my neck to ward off an icy wind. I was just idly toeing the hard earth with the new boots I had worn when I escaped from Brampton and I guess I was lost in thought when suddenly I became aware that one of the wolf packs was stealthily encircling me like hungry vultures, ready to pick me clean if they judged me to be weak enough. Alarmed, I slowly removed my hands from my pockets and without looking up I balanced myself for whatever was to come.

'That's a nice pair of kicks you're wearing buddy. Ain't none in here like that.'

Slowly I raised my head to look at the guy and the first thing I noticed about him was the two gold teeth he had and the hungry way in which he was sizing me up. He had dirty blond hair and a good build – about twenty years old. He also had five goons flanking me and gunning me off from under their peak hats. I got the feeling that without their leader they would be from nowhere. I also remembered that Little Red once said, 'You let that kind climb up on your back and they never wanna slide off again.'

'Why don't you try them on for size, Art?' egged this bony little jerk standing farther back than the others.

'OK Blade, why don't I?' this Art guy asked his crony. Then turning to me he added: 'You don't mind if I do, huh?' Without looking at Blade he snapped his fingers and said menacingly, 'Help the man off with his kic ...'

38

There was just no way he expected that kind of angry reaction from me as I kicked him in the balls! I must have scored real good, because his eyes and mouth got as big as saucers and with a horrified expression he sank to the ground all rolled up into a ball, gurgling and gasping for air.

I then shoved my right hand inside my coat like I was gripping a knife and backed myself up against the cell-block wall, all the while eyeing the pack to see what their next move would be. I wasn't too surprised to see them slowly melt back into the gathering crowd until they were out of sight. Art was still squirming and trying hard to catch his breath and some of the more blood-thirsty guys in the crowd then started hollering at me to put the boots to him.

Suddenly the shrill blast of a guard's whistle brought me back to my senses so I leapt into the crowd and the guys immediately closed up for me. However, the roof picket had spotted the whole play and keeping me under observation he pointed me out to a goon squad of club-bearing guards who immediately latched on to me.

The following afternoon, handcuffed behind my back, I was hustled from the basement cooler up to the superintendent's office. The office had no windows, just a large desk that reminded me of an altar for pagan sacrifices. Standing upright on either side of the desk were two large flags, just the way the President of the United States has flags in his office. Seated behind that desk was the assistant superintendent known as Marble Mouth. He was a burly, short man with a balding pate and a harsh and gravelly voice. His love and joy in life was a fat bulldog which answered to the name of Gusher. He took the dog everywhere, even to the court. In addition to the two guards who had ushered me into this inner sanctum, there was also a male stenograper to record the minutes of this mini trial. Last but not least was Sergeant Dum-Dum guarding the door. Dum-Dum was a massive giant who tipped the scales at more than 300 pounds and towered somewhere up around seven feet – he looked like Goliath to a sixteen-year-old kid. He had craggy features and shaggy black hair. He had absolutely no sense of humour and when he spoke it was very hard to understand him because he stuttered to an extreme degree. He was the joint's bully and trouble-shooter.

At least the bulldog didn't bark at me when I entered to plead to a charge of 'fighting and creating a disturbance' in the yard. Just the same, the mutt did give me a baleful stare, which in turn made me very nervous because some of the guys had said that Marble Mouth judged guilt or innocence according to whether his dog growled or wagged its tail. So I tried smiling at it. That's when Sergeant Dum-Dum cuffed me on the side of the head with one of his meaty paws. It was a hard blow that slammed me up against the desk and almost on top of the bulldog!

'P-p-p-pay at-t-t-tention p-p-p-punk!'

By the time he pulled me back up on my feet the dog was going into hysterics, running around the desk, knocking over the flags, and growling like crazy. I guess the mutt thought that I had attacked him or something.

'Quiet, Gusher! Quiet!' grumbled Marble Mouth. Then directing his anger at the sergeant he yelled, 'Out of here you idiot and take the prisoner with you!'

Embarrassed and frustrated, Dum-Dum took off down Gunsos Alley and left me in the company of the two screws who had big smirks on their kissers. They locked me in the bullpen on Torpedo Lane where I nursed a sore head for the next hour, all the while wondering what had happened.

I was still handcuffed behind my back when the steel door slid open and one of my two escorts said that Marble Mouth found me guilty as charged and that he sentenced me to 'ten days on bread and water and twenty days good time. OK, let's go.'

The cooler is reached by descending an old creaky cargo type elevator in the tower. It was a spooky ride that took us deep into the catacombs. When the elevator jolted to a stop, we stepped out into an eight foot concrete tunnel that snaked around under the institution for about a mile. It was very damp and chilly down there and it felt like we had de-scended into an Egyptian tomb. The gloom was feebly illuminated by a series of tiny light bulbs, which in turn distorted our shadows into grotesque shapes. Our footsteps

40

sounded hollow and eerie as we tramped along down a series of tunnels. Down there were other sounds, too, of rats running along the overhead pipes and water dripping down the walls and forming puddles on the concrete floor.

We must have tramped along for a distance of two city blocks before we came to a halt in front of a green metal door with a peephole. One of the guards flanking me gave it a sharp rap with his key and we waited silently until an eye peeked out at us. Beyond the green door was a small concrete room that contained a scarred desk and a dozen cubby holes used for storing clothes. The walls were painted battleship grey.

Here the handcuffs were removed, my clothes taken away and, in return, I was given a heavy pair of socks and a white baby doll outfit. The days I had to serve were noted in the record book. Then I was ushered to another green door, also with a peephole. It swung open on well-oiled hinges. Straight ahead lay a dimly-lit corridor with a row of wooden doors numbered from 1 to 12.

No. 9 would be mine for the next ten days. It was a brick cocoon in which even at that age I could touch both walls by stretching out my arms. The single piece of furniture was an iron cot embedded in the cement floor. The surface of the bunk was designed in such a way as to give the prone victim the impression that he was lying on a bed of spikes. Steel slats criss-crossed the frame leaving a pattern of open squares, all of which curved up and down like a roller coaster. On the ceiling by the door a strong light shone night and day, burning down into your eye sockets until you were ready to scream and beg for darkness. The toilet consisted of a hole in the centre of the floor, a hole that gurgled and flushed once every sixty seconds, night and day.

Here it was cold and damp and the baby doll outfit did little to keep me warm, nor did the socks keep the cement floor from chilling my feet. Our bedding consisted of three blankets issued at 6 p.m. and then cruelly snatched away again at 6 a.m. just when they were needed the most. Our food ration was three slices of brown bread, three times a day, plus a quart of water. Each dissociation cell was provided with a Bible; when I managed to fall asleep at night I dreamed of angels and devils struggling for possession of my soul.

It was a long and tedious ten days and when I emerged back into the population I felt like I had withstood an initiation ceremony. At least no one thought of me as an easy target anymore.

I was now working in the prison cannery and just before Christmas I got into a brawl in the washroom after catching another prisoner stealing a nylon comb from my jacket. This time around they gave me twelve days in the cooler. It was while I was logging hard time down there that Little Red was admitted to the institution and immediately put to work in the kitchen. This was exactly to his liking because he'd be in a position to gather the material needed to make a prison brew. With the help of three other inmates he put together a powerful cherry brew in some kind of metal container, and stashed it in an air vent to sit and age for a few days. It didn't take long for it to ripen nor did it take long for them to get roaring drunk in the kitchen dormitory. In the middle of the night all four of them came down with extremely severe cramps and Red, being the smallest and the weakest, was rushed to the city hospital in critical condition. He was poisoned by the lining of the metal container they had used. I got sprung two days later from the cooler and was struck dumb to learn that my friend Little Red was dead! Just him. The others recovered.

That same evening when the cell doors cranked open and a guard shouted: 'Showers up! One to six, let's go,' I was still in a battered state of mind as I stripped off my clothing, grabbed a bar of soap and paraded naked to the end of the range to join my neighbours in a row of open showers.

I was soaping up when this bowlegged guy showering next to me pointed out that I was still wearing one of my socks. The guys – not aware that I was nursing an unhappy mood – all laughed. As usual when the guys found something funny they were reluctant to give up on the subject.

'Man, you're stupid!' piped in Greyhound, having overheard. 'Jimmy, can't you see he's wearing that sock for a good purpose. Roger always wears a sock like that just in case the shrink shows up, spots the play, and decides to cut him down to size. Ha, ha, ha.'

'Now that you bring up the point,' says Jimmy, 'I should be wearing one too. I ain' had no toys to play with when I was a kid neither.'

'Aw shit!' exclaims Jay who was a black guy and a friend of Jimmy's.

'Waddya mean, "aw shit"?' growled Jimmy puffing out his chest. 'For a little guy, I'm well hung,' he added peevishly.

'The only thing that's well hung about you is your ears,' cracked Greyhound amid loud peals of laughter.

They were all laughing and throwing water around when the guard shouted that we had to get out of the showers and into our cells. Still laughing everybody ran naked down the corridor and slid into their drums, including me, just as the man threw down the big lever and shouted: 'Stand clear! Going on dead-lock.'

For some strange reason I wanted to hurt myself and I did so by leaving my fingers in the track just as the iron monster slammed home with a loud crash – I gasped, gurgled and screamed!

Much later that night in a hospital cell I stood at my open window staring over the barbed wire fence at the twinkling city lights in the distance. I had a broken thumb and three severely bruised fingers. But I felt better now that I was hurting so much, that way I figured Red wouldn't be mad at me anymore for having led him into all this mess. I just couldn't help thinking that if I hadn't slugged Boner none of this would have happened. Even the icy wind and wet snowflakes that lashed my face were no match at the moment for the wild state that my emotions were in.

For the next two months I continually locked horns with the custodial goon squads and received punishment after punishment until finally one day the Kangaroo Court saw fit to banish me from the inmate population as being too rebellious to live and associate with normal prisoners. I was then sentenced to serve an indefinite period of time on the legendary Bull Gang, a segregated unit within the institution that harboured fifty or sixty of the toughest and most desperate prisoners in Canada.

CHAPTER FOUR

February 1955: Toiling on the Buller at this time of the year was enough to make a guy wish that he had never been born or at least that he had never committed a crime. However, in the long run all it really accomplished was the production of hard and bitter men anxious to have their turn up at bat to even the score.

The gang existed for one reason, we felt, and that was to break our spirits through hard labour and lots of cell time. We were given absolutely no privileges other than a hard bed and three meals a day. Segregated on the top floor of 3-D, our cells were perhaps a little more spartan than usual. This was one of the newer wings and the cell doors were locked and unlocked electronically. We had absolutely no contact with the guys in the general population. Our meal trays were shoved under our doors three times a day, to be eaten with a spoon.

Often when we trooped in from work we were so indescribably exhausted that we didn't have the strength to eat, although we were ravished with hunger. Being the youngest member of this close-knit group of rebels was doubly hard for me because my mind and body were less mature than those around me. Weighing heavily in my favour was my inborn stubbornness to overcome obstacles and that usually bulldozed me through bad times.

Bossing the Buller at that time was a legendary guard by the name of Sergeant Tracy; he was better known to us as The Dick. A strange and gloomy sort of man in his early forties, with dark and rugged features, his muscles bulged under his

44

brown tunic like football pads. He spoke with a heavy English accent and his favourite word was 'bloody'. Not that he spoke that much, but when he did it was soft and deadly. Everything about him was threatening, even the way he moved – catlike. For a big man The Dick could run faster and farther than anybody in the joint. If three Go-Boys made a break from his gang, Sergeant Tracy would be hot on their trail and never failed to capture at least one would-be escaper, punch him out too!

The Sarge had no use for the rule book and operated the gang by his own code of justice which wasn't too different from our own and that was probably why we had such high respect for him as a man. The Dick often got into jackpots with the brass, but they gave him a lot of leeway; they were acutely aware that only he could handle the Buller with a minimum of mayhem. Handle it he did, with an iron fist and if anybody disputed his leadership over the gang, be it screw or con, he'd peel his tunic off and fight the guy with a quiet fury, no holds barred.

Sergeant Tracy always won his fights because he used every dirty tactic there was. In return a prisoner could butt him, knee him, or kick him in the balls, that is if he was fast enough and man enough. Mercy or squeamishness certainly was not one of his strong points. But he did sincerely care about his gang, maybe a lot more than we appreciated. He'd slap us around if he caught us doing something wrong rather than turn us over to the Kangaroo Court for punishment; he just didn't believe in that rule book justice. He also didn't tolerate a guard from any other detail bothering one of his boys; pity the screw that tried it. We guys on the gang were mixed up on the question of whether we liked him a lot or hated him a lot. I guess it just depended on the day.

Sergeant Tracy's assistant on the Buller was a lanky corporal whose face was beet-red. For that reason we referred to him as Tomato Face, behind his back of course. He was the sergeant's flunky and was always kissing his ass with, 'Yes sir! Right away, sir! I'll get them off their lazy butts, sir!' We hated him because he was always bad mouthing us. If he wasn't shouting or spitting, then most likely he would be chewing soda crackers to feed his ulcer.

45

The guards would have us out of our bunks by 6 a.m. by running their clubs along our cell bars and blowing their goddamn whistles. I'd wash up (cold water only), throw a blanket around my shoulders to ward off the morning chill and stand shivering at my cell bars waiting for our breakfast (hot coffee and mush).

At 7.30 a.m. all the doors would swing open simultaneously and we'd step out and stand at attention while Tomato Face worked his way down the line of blue denim, expertly running his hands over each body for hidden weapons, such as hardwood shivs that wouldn't show up going through the metal detector. Nobody talked and nobody smoked. Overseeing all this would be a captain and a handful of guards who still retained authority over the gang while we were within any of the cell blocks. The Dick would busy himself shaking down the drums for hidden contraband and especially checking for neatness. Each bedroll had to be done up in a very precise manner and even though we had no mattress, pillow, or sheets, some guys could never quite master the art.

If somebody goofed up, the sound of an open palm striking hard flesh would smack in the stillness and some sleepy-eyed prisoner's jaw would go slack, his face register shock and indignation, and he would grumble, 'Aw, Sarge. Whaddya do that for?' (As if he didn't know.)

After the inspection we would file down three flights of stairs, pass through a series of locked barriers, and in the auditorium-sized basement we would spread out, five paces apart, and pass through a narrow passageway in which electronic beams scanned our bodies for hidden metals. From there we would exit into a snow-covered courtyard and line up four abreast in our usual spots. To take someone else's spot would get you an instantaneous punch in the face. The first four prisoners at the head of the rank were the leaders on the gang and/or the best fighters. They would set the marching pace.

When everything was in readiness the wire gate would swing open with a crash and the Buller would march out on to a paved roadway in perfect formation. If by chance an inmate was out of step the Sarge would let him know with a sharp command, if that didn't do the trick, a swift kick to the shins would. Guarding the Buller was a permanent detail of eight pickets armed with pump shotguns and .32 revolvers. They would ride herd on us from a distance of a hundred yards while remaining fifty yards apart. As for The Dick and Tomato Face they would tag right along with us.

The roadway we marched along led us straight through the industrial area where all the work shops were and eventually to the quarry five hundred yards beyond the last building. This notorious area was known as Migs Alley because of the mass escapes that took place there during Go-Boy season (April to October). The goal was always the dense bush half a mile distant. The roadway was patrolled by a black scout car and a paddy wagon and, farther out in the fields, by mounted outriders. Although the majority of escapes were doomed to failure and sometimes even death, Go-Boys still persisted, year after year, in desperate attempts to regain their lost freedom by braving a heavy volley of gunfire and the pursuit of angry posses.

The most spectacular mass escape I ever witnessed took place along Migs Alley on a beautiful April afternoon. Spring fever had set in and a lot of guys were itching to go. On that particular day there were at least a dozen gangs parading into jug-up, fifty feet apart, and with a guard detail of from one to three pickets apiece, depending on the size of the unit. The Buller as always was about three hundred yards away from the closest gang when suddenly three Go-Boys darted like arrows from the tailor shop gang and took off into the field in a wild effort to squeeze past their pickets. The excitement was contagious what with all the whistles blowing and hysterical shouts of, 'Go-Boys! Go-Boys!' And so what happened then was contrary to the rules and training of pickets: they all cut loose at once with tremendous firepower! Included in this crazy Waterloo were our own pickets firing away, although a sawed-off shotgun was only effective up to seventy-five yards. Two of the escapers went down in a hail of pellets from their own guard detail while the third Go-Boy hightailed it out of range and made for the bush.

Meanwhile a few guys from each gang had been carefully

counting the shots and when it was determined that most of the pickets were now holding empty guns a second wave of Go-Boys, as many as a dozen more, darted from their units in as many directions and away they went!

Again there was the sound of piercing whistles, shouts of, 'More Go-Boys!', and the odd blast from a shotgun (most of the firepower now came from pistol shots). It was commonly believed that the average picket couldn't hit a car at fifty paces with his revolver; nevertheless, there was so much shooting that half of the escapers deemed it wise to fall to the ground and stay right there in surrender.

Among the seven Go-Boys still going strong, four of them were from the Buller and Sergeant Tracy was hot on their trail! Two pickets on horseback were tearing up the muddy field after a couple of Go-Boys with thunderous hoofbeats, twisting and turning their mounts like cowboys bulldogging steers at a rodeo. A third rider, galloping full tilt with the reins gripped in his teeth, was pumping away with his shotgun like he was on a buffalo hunt and once more a couple of Go-Boys punctured with buckshot threw themselves to the ground to indicate surrender. Meanwhile, The Dick had collared a Go-Boy called Mongo and was wrestling with him in a thick patch of mud as the paddy wagon hurried to pitch in. An Indian kid had had his leg broken by a pistol shot aimed from the scout car which was now in full pursuit of the last remaining Go-Boy who showed no sign of giving up.

'Go man, go!' boomed the voices of hundreds of prisoners lying down on the roadway. It all seemed so futile as the vehicle closed in with a vengeance on the lone figure. A screw was leaning out the window as far as he could in order to fire his shotgun . . . once, twice, three times! Still the target kept running and was now within fifty yards of the trees. Just when it seemed a sure bet that the next blast was going to tear a hole in the prisoner's back, the scout car suddenly swerved on the wet grass and the screw flew through the window as if shot from a cannon! By the time he hit the ground in an awkward tangle of limbs, the Go-Boy was safely in among the trees. All our cheering was rather deflated by the sight of the paddy wagon driving around the field like a hearse, collecting both the wounded and the dejected.

All who attempted to escape had been wounded in varying degrees, certainly enough to keep the hospital staff busy for several days probing for shotgun pellets. The escaper who made it into the bush later stole a farmer's tractor to continue his headlong flight and the darn thing tipped over and pinned him underneath and that was how the posse nabbed him.

The last few hundred yards to the rock pit was uphill along a well-beaten footpath. The quarry was an enormous pit some two hundred feet square and about sixty feet deep. It had been excavated by pick and shovel and human misery over a period of decades. The Buller's project, day after day and year after year, was to haul all that rock and gravel from the pit in long caravans of wheelbarrows down a narrow trail known as the Last Mile, to dump the stuff over the steep embankments in the so-called lakes in an effort to reclaim useful acreage from the swampy lowlands.

On most days the wind swooped down through the mouth of the pit like a banshee and echoed and re-echoed off the steep walls like demented spirits wailing for the souls they had lost, the limbs they had lost, and the lives they had lost, here in the pit. It was really very spooky.

Each prisoner had to load his own buggy by chipping away at a vertical wall of frozen earth with a heavy pickaxe, crying out in pain and rage each time fragments of rock rifled upwards, cutting and stinging, the blood turning into an instant icicle. While we laboured in a pit so deep that the rays of the sun were unable to touch us until early afternoon, the shotgun pickets encircling the rim stamped the feet and drank steaming coffee from Thermoses provided by their wives. Our only source of liquid was water provided by the runner on our gang in a milk pail that always had a thick layer of ice over it. The bleak winter chill ate away at us like cancer and even our furious labour didn't keep our teeth from chattering in a fearful manner.

Our clothing was primitive to the point of being a cruel farce. Our jo-jos and mitts were made in the tailor shop from discarded blankets. When things got really bad down

49

there in the pit we couldn't help hating the guards for their warm clothing and for having thoughtful wives. Shifting their shotguns from the crook of one arm to the other, the pickets would stare down on us like predatory hawks as we drove our pickaxes into the wall with a fury. Always their image would be in our mind.

If a guy found himself going stir crazy and unable to keep it bottled up any longer, he'd toss his tools down and, throwing his head skywards, let out a series of blood-curdling screams so full of anguish and venom that it chilled more than the cold. Every time that happened or if a guy refused to work, the paddy wagon would come and get him and take him away to the Limbo Room and just thinking about that would always give me the strength not to lose my cool and end up in the same boat.

I was in a bullpen once with a guy who was waiting to be strapped and the thought so scared him that he swallowed three razor blades and ten sewing needles buried in bread dough. When I next saw him, his upper torso had been so carved open in order to fish out all that hardware that he looked like some kind of Frankenstein monster. If what happened to a guy inside the Limbo Room was worse than that, I thought, it was surely a place to shun.

With the spring came the mud – oozy, sticky, muck – that gripped the wheels of our buggies and slowed the caravan down to a muscle-tearing crawl. Somedays it felt like I was pushing the world uphill in my buggy, but always I somehow found the determination to go on and on. I was now seventeen years old and the Buller was proving to be my initiation into manhood.

The Buller had a fleet of sixty antiquated wheelbarrows with long wooden handles and iron wheels. Very heavy and cumbersome to push when empty, when loaded down with rock it was like pushing a Volkswagen uphill. That was the reason each guy had his own personal buggy which he cared for like a mother grizzly. We would even sacrifice our short afternoon rest period to tinker with our buggy, greasing it and smoothing out the bugs, anything at all just so that we could get it to roll with a little less friction. Each buggy had a name painted on the side to indicate ownership. Mine was

'Voodoo'. One sure way for a prisoner to get his melon caved in with a rock was to make a play for a neighbour's buggy. Some buggies were more souped-up than others and so when a guy got sprung from the gang he deeded his buggy to a friend, with the clause that he could have it back in the event he was shanghaied again.

With the spring thaw upon us we had to watch out for falling rocks inside the pit, and that brings to mind the extremes to which some of the guys would go in order to be admitted to the joint hospital, including breaking their legs with heavy sledgehammers. This one guy in his forties just couldn't hack it anymore and so he made up his mind to twist the situation of falling rocks into his favour. His name was Smokey and he had a lot of guts (he could also be a lot of fun). At one point, he was determined to have a friend bust him over the head with a rock in order to become an accident casualty. This cold-blooded decision inadvertently led to the strangest freak accident anybody on the gang ever saw. Smokey had the buggy position just ahead of me and as we were loading rocks into the wheelbarrows he looked up at me from a stooped position.

Nervously he asked, 'Dick looking this way?'

'Naw, he's yakking with Tomato Face on the rock pile.'

'Okay, Rocko,' he said to his friend, 'don't miss you bastard.'

Rocko, who was a muscle on the gang, grinned wolfishly and zapped Smokey with a rock the size of a football.

With a sharp cry of pain Smokey fell to the ground holding his hands to the top of his skull which we thought was split wide open. Not long afterwards we watched him placed into the back of the paddy wagon on a stretcher and spirited away. Silently the guys cursed themselves for not having the guts to do the same stunt.

However, in less than three days Smokey was back on the gang looking like a Turk with all those white bandages wrapped around his melon.

'A couple of days is better than no days,' was his ready answer when the guys ribbed him about not being able to swing a longer stall.

'You would've been better off letting Mongo pound you

just once with that big ham of his, it would've fractured your skull for sure!' wisecracked some egg.

Mongo was a big, hulking black man with no front teeth who was laid up with eighteen months for (would you believe it) cattle rustling.

Now for the ironic twist. Smokey was back on the gang less than two hours when the whistle blew to end our fifteen minute smoke break.

'C'mon, c'mon, get the lead out of your ass and get those buggies on the road!' cracked Tomato Face in his tough guy act.

'Christ!' exclaims Smokey, 'I gotta water my horse,' and with those fateful words he hurried over to the east wall which was out of bounds because of its steep walls and started doing his thing just as a bunch of rocks broke loose and tumbled over the edge, the biggest of which struck him smack dab on top of his injured head. This time the guy went out like a light and ended up in the hospital with a fractured skull. He never did return to the Buller.

With summer upon us, there was no escape from the broiling sun which roasted our bodies brown and beyond. The rays of the sun also bleached our denims almost white, while we squeezed our eyes to narrow slits. Grimly we slogged back and forth along the Last Mile pushing our buggies along in silent formation. I guess we looked a lot like pirates – half naked, no shoes, no shirt – just jeans and red bandanas wrapped tightly around our foreheads to keep the burning sweat from our suffering eyes. Shadowing us like hungry buzzards ready to pick our bones clean should we break ranks were the shotgun pickets, carefully observing our every step. This was Go-Boy season and both sides were on red alert, for it was expected that a certain number of attempts would take place on the Buller each year. That was why Sergeant Tracy always positioned himself not far behind the last buggy man. That way, he could observe the mood of the guys and jump off when they did.

There were inmates in our gang who were on the alert for that freak opportunity that would give them a chance to jackrabbit. The key to that sort of success was guts and the ability to make snap decisions. In July of that year a unique opportunity was afforded to four Go-Boys. One hot steamy afternoon the Buller was marching past the front of the old slaughterhouse on the way to the pit when the quietness was rent by a series of spine-chilling squeals, spooky enough to set a guy's hair on end. In a pen at the side of that ominous building were some longhorn steers, about two dozen in all. Whoever was doing the botched pigsticking inside the slaughterhouse was responsible for the wild stampede that suddenly erupted.

The three pickets flanking us on our right-hand side were just a few feet away from the fence penning in the animals when the fence burst and out poured these snorting, flaming-eyed beasts, heading straight for them! Disorganized, they leapt aside and ran in every direction. Taking advantage of the opening left by the pickets' flight, four Go-Boys burst from the marching ranks and ran along with the thundering herd!

Regrouping themselves the pickets had time for only a quick volley of shots and immediately two large steers plunged to the ground! One ceased moving, while the other sat on its haunches, bawling in terrible anguish. Through the dust we observed The Dick thunder down on one Go-Boy with short legs called Marty and poleaxe him with a looping haymaker, 'Wham!' By then the remaining three escapers and the crazed steers were fast disappearing downhill towards the apple orchard.

The pickets had regrouped and were surrounding us, pointing their revolvers at the gang as a whole. Just then The Dick, looking like a caveman returning from the hunt, trudged in with Marty's still form draped across his power-ful shoulders. While Tomato Face was yelling into the walkie-talkie, calling for help, badmouthing us, and handcuffing the guy, Sergeant Tracy armed himself with a revolver and a moment later two sharp reports echoed across the shallow valley and the two wounded steers ceased to suffer.

From where we were all gathered, it was about half a mile to the main highway. That was the direction our buddies were headed – a very poor escape route. By now the three Go-Boys had veered away from the stampeding cattle and were jogging along a single set of tracks nestled in a deep ravine between the two lakes and the rambling apple orchard. Two minutes later they emerged on to the highway and were almost run over in their desperate attempts to flag down passing vehicles. Observing that a score of scout cars was pouring out of the reformatory parking lot, they abandoned their efforts to commandeer a car and took off for the hills leading up to the blue Mountains where there was some heavy brush cover. It was an additional two miles and they didn't have a prayer of making it in time. There was some more shooting until one by one they were all recaptured, including the runaway steers.

Not everybody wants to escape or has the guts to, whether it's a prisoner of war or a criminal. Half the guys will think about it and talk about it, but it goes no farther than that. Being pursued like a fox before the hounds isn't something a normal guy wants to jump into. As for myself, I didn't want to escape because I was going up for parole within three months.

It was true that the Sarge was sometimes seemingly cruel with us, but he did show concern for our welfare in other ways. Like the time the gang trooped into the clothing depot after a particularly wet and muddy day only to have a tough-talking, burly sergeant refuse to give us dry clothing. In the blink of an eye Sergeant Tracy had him pinned back against the counter, his steel fingers digging into the jerk's shoulders.

'Give the lads their issue you bloody fool!' The Dick's voice hissed, low and deadly.

We got our change of clothes. I guess if we hadn't got it, the depot sergeant might have met up with an accident in the parking lot.

Sergeant Tracy may also have taken perverse pride in being in charge of such a notorious gang of cut-throats as we were. I recall one day when half a dozen of us rebels were tramping ahead of The Dick down long corridors and though a series of locked barriers to visit the hospital. Sick parade was held during the noon hours for those of us on the Buller who were ailing, and either the Sarge or Tomato Face would escort us to the joint hospital to be tended to. Our

54

bleached denims all dusty, faces hard and cold, peak hats pulled low over our eyes, fists clenched at our sides, our boots made thump, thump, thumping sounds.

The guys in the population feared and looked up to us while we held most of them in contempt. Those who met us in the corridors squeezed out of the way to let us pass, watching us with big eyes. It was little wonder that they reacted in such a manner, with Big Mongo and Rocko in the lead. Trooping into the last corridor leading up to the hospital barrier, we noticed that there were about a dozen inmates sitting around on benches waiting to be called in to see The Croaker.

The Buller never waited; we were always ushered straight through, the officials not wanting us to rap with anyone. Blocking our way that day were four toughs deep in a boisterous conversation. Rocko stopped and laid his hand on the shoulder of the biggest guy who, in turn, spat on Rocko's hand, snarling, 'Bugger off!' without looking up. Mongo and Rocko swung at the same instant and that tough guy went down and out. We all had our dukes up by then, spoiling for a fight, when Sergeant Tracy jumped in front growling,

'You bloody idiots! Can't you see that the lad has fainted? Help him on the bench.' Turning to the three screws standing around he added, 'Keep your charges away from my boys, understand?'

'Yes, sir!' they echoed together.

When it came to power struggles, the Sarge would always let the problem resolve itself by permitting the two combatants to slug it out in the centre of the pit during a rest period. We would create a large circle by joining hands and then we'd cheer the warriors on. Everybody would wager on the outcome, even the pickets up above would bet among themselves. One of the most memorable fights that I witnessed took place between two evenly matched light heavyweights vying for the position of lead buggy man.

A good-looking guy by the name of Eddie was defending his title for the third time in six months. Challenging him was a new guy on the gang known only as Fisher, who claimed to have some ring experience. For twenty minutes they slugged it out in a stand-up shuffle fight until finally Fisher was knocked down for the umpteenth time and couldn't find the strength to get up again. Eddie retained his title with barely a mark on his face. As for Fisher, he was a bloody mess; both his eyes were so swollen shut that he couldn't see. Nevertheless the Dick ordered him to resume his position on the buggy line! The poor guy had to be guided along the Last Mile by his buddies. The Sarge just didn't believe in pampering us.

One day in July The Dick lost his cool at something big dumb Rocko had done, and called him a 'bloody simpleton'. Sulking, Rocko later sneaked up behind The Sarge and hit him over the head with a shovel. Immediately a picket overhead fired a pistol shot into the ground and everybody froze, watching as The Dick charged around the pit holding his sore head. Shaking the cobwebs from his numbed brain he roared, 'Form a bloody goddamn circle!'

The fight was quick and vicious, ending in less than three minutes, when The Dick smashed Rocko's head against a big stone! Had he been any other guard, charges of assault with a deadly weapon would surely have been laid. But not The Dick; he believed in stomping his own attackers.

One sweltering summer day on the 'pit to the lake' run a gutsy guy called Maxie lost his head at the sight of all that cool, clear lake water and while dumping his load of rocks over the edge of the steep embankment both he and his buggy 'slipped' and fell in! According to plan, he started splashing, sputtering and bellowing like a wounded buffalo that he was drowning.

'Hey, Maxie is croaking!' sombody shouted the alarm.

'Yeah, quick, let's save him.' With those words five of the bravest jumped in feet first and laughing and yelling made like they were rescuing Maxie.

'Corporal!' roared The Sarge. 'Go get me a bloody revolver. On the double!'

Tomato Face ran off to the nearest picket and rushed back with a pistol, saying breathlessly, 'Here you are, sir. Don't blame you if you shoot them, sir.'

The way those clowns clawed their way up that muddy embankment you'd have thought that crocodiles were snapping at their heels. The Dick kicked their asses and doubled their loads for the rest of the day.

Late one evening in September I was sitting on the floor of my cell with my ears close to the bars, hungrily absorbing the whispered conversations of my neighbours. They were talking about the bread that flowed through their fingers after each caper and their near scrapes with the law and the women they had loved. To a small town kid like me who was still a virgin it was spellbinding. I was a quiet kid who hardly ever said a word, preferring to listen and to learn. When the lights went out at 10 o'clock everybody was supposed to dummy up; talking was strictly taboo. Just after midnight somebody suddenly uttered a hissing sound. Next thing I knew a strong light was blinding me and this guard known as The Worm was badmouthing me,

'Aha! I caught you talking and now you've got a ducket!'

I hadn't said a word!

He pushed the long flashlight through the bars at me and with his hawkish face not far from mine he sneered and snarled, 'So you think we're all a bunch of farmers and cowfuckers, eh?'

I didn't say that!

'Don't you be giving me that look, punk!' His spittle flew in my face and suddenly I broke my silence with a low moan that got louder and louder until it was a scream! I took his flashlight from him and smashed it against the bars with all my strength; bits and pieces flew past his head as he covered up and staggered back against the wall, amazed at my sudden fury.

I continued, concentrating all my resentment on the flashlight, until it was practically disintegrated. By now there was a great uproar on the range as my neighbours cursed and threatened The Worm and banged their beds and rattled their bars until finally the goon squad arrived with gas masks and clubs. I was wrestled out of my cell, handcuffed, and carried struggling down to the cooler. It took me a few hours to cool down and by then I knew that I was in deep trouble.

The following morning I was taken up before the superintendent, Good-Time Charley. He was so called because he

57

took delight in forfeiting a portion of a prisoner's earned remission. He was a tall, well-built, distingushed-looking man, who carried a gun in a shoulder holster and jogged a mile in the gym every morning before he started his work day.

I had four duckets, the most serious being assault on a guard. I pleaded Not Guilty and the court found me Guilty as charged and this time sentenced me to ten strokes of the Paddle. I would visit the Limbo Room after all.

Adhering to formality in the case of corporal punishment, two guards escorted me in handcuffs to the shrink's office for him to judge if I was mentally fit to undergo such severe punishment. All the prisoners in the joint considered him to be slightly off-centre himself. 'Take him away, gentlemen,' said the doctor, displeased at my tart reply to his weird questions. 'Just the therapy he needs.'

Our next visit was to the joint hospital where the Croaker checked out my heart, pulse, temperature, and my buttocks to see if I could physically withstand the punishment that was in store for me without having a heart attack or something like that. What an unfeeling bastard he was.

It was shortly after one o'clock in the afternoon by the time the elevator descended into the catacombs with me still in handcuffs and a dozen witnesses escorting me to the Limbo Room, just like I was going to the electric chair. It was cold and damp as our solemn procession moved slowly along down that long stretch of spooky nothingness. I was shivering visibly because I was cold and scared, and only seventeen years old. I had heard so many grusome stories about the paddle, how it castrated one guy and how it crippled another. In my heart was also the fear of displaying fear.

By the time we came to a halt before a metal door my teeth were rattling and my knees were weak but I was determined to be brave. A long key was inserted, followed by an audible click; next, two locking bars were withdrawn, sounding shockingly loud in the deathly silence. Finally the imposing door squeaked open and I was shoved into the centre of a large whitewashed room that had a naked light bulb dangling from the ceiling on a cord. A sudden breeze swayed the light causing our shadows to dance eerily about the room as ripples of terror ran up and down my spine. Anchored to the far wall I saw a mass of metal tubing contoured to embrace a human form and, affixed to it, shackles and restraining straps. Hanging from pegs on the left wall were three leather straps with wooden handles, so thick and coarse as to barely sag. Each one was perforated with hundreds of tiny holes designed to trap and rip the flesh from the buttocks.

The cuffs were removed and the gravelly voice of Marble Mouth ordered me to 'Step right into it, boy.'

Shivering, I did as I was told.

'Now drop your pants . . . all the way down!'

My shirt was pulled over my head and so was a black hood. My ankles were firmly shackled as were my knees. A wide metal band encircled my waist and was locked into place to protect my kidneys. My arms were pulled straight out ahead of me and cuffed. Naked from head to foot – securely anchored in an upright position – I was totally at their mercy.

Everything was in readiness. The doctor stood on my right monitoring my pulse throughout the ordeal. A guard stood on my left gripping the wooden handle of the strap waiting for the signal to begin. I was cold and terrified and shivering and trying to brace myself for the blow.

The eerie ritual began when the dozen witnesses ominously scraped the soles of their shoes on the floor in unison, deliberately done to confuse my sense of direction.

'ONE!' I clenched my teeth and my body went rigid as the strap sliced through the air, 'CRACK!' Like a pistol shot, it made solid contact with my buttocks, my head snapped backwards, while violently driving my shackled body forward. White searing pain exploded throughout my being and blood gushed from my lips as I struggled to stifle a scream. It was brutal and it was horrible. My whole body vibrated like a band of tempered steel and my mind filled with nightmares as I awaited the next blow.

'Two!' swish, crack! 'Three!' swish, crack! 'Four!' swish, crack! 'Five!' swish-crack!

Over and over again I heard the scraping of the shoes, the

sharp command, the long seconds, the strap cutting through the air, the explosion and then the crazy-out-of-this-world pain that struck terror into my very soul. Finally it was all over. Ten strokes of the paddle and I didn't scream or beg as so many did. That was very, very important to me.

When they pulled the hood from my head I stared at them with blood dripping down the corners of my mouth, angry and yet proud, asking myself how they would have fared in my place. They just stood there in their gestapo like uniforms talking among themselves and not looking at me. The Croaker squirted white foamy stuff inside my mouth to stop the bleeding and then rubbed salve on my mutilated buttocks as the blood trickled down my legs.

Coincidentally, as I emerged on the main floor of the tower flanked by two guards I was advised that the Provincial Parole Board had been patiently waiting to interview me – that my eligibility date was on this very day. Painfully, I limped into a magnificently designed room, decorated with elegant ornaments and artistically-designed fireplace, just like a Governor's mansion. Seated around a curved, black mahogany table were five well-dressed men and one elderly lady.

When I walked out half an hour later I was in excruciating pain, because the numbness had worn off. I guess the parole board members understood my silence, because my mouth was full of bloody cotton. The lady had told me that Sergeant Tracy had dropped in to speak on my behalf, also informing them that I had actually done nothing wrong. The chairman seemed to think otherwise.

'The fact that you reacted in the way you did indicates, at least to me, that you are harbouring some very dangerous hostilities. All of which is not healthy to yourself or to society in general. It does not indicate rehabilitation on your part. Nevertheless we are going to defer judgment for ten days. Perhaps corporal punishment will have been a rewarding lesson to you after all.'

Lying on my belly much later that evening I thought about what the chairman had said, about that bizarre paddle and rack being a rewarding lesson to me. In my heart I wondered what type of person could feel rewarded through

60

that kind of discipline and retribution. My thoughts turned to the letter on my pillow. My kid sister, Susie, always stuck by me and was very dependable. With the letter was a group picture of Susie, her classmates and their teacher, a nun, who smiled benevolently beneath the arch that announced that the place was a French Academy for girls. Susie spoke of her piano lessons and the fact that Dad was going to drive them all down to visit me at Christmas, if I didn't make parole. I deliberately flexed my muscles and squeezed the pillow in agony not want to think anymore. How could I explain to them that the Roger they once knew so well no longer existed?

Ten days later to my great surprise I was granted a parole, but I was feeling much too empty to rejoice. My buttocks were still horribly discoloured and welted, although I was no longer limping or hurting very much. But deep down, where it really counted, I was aching real bad.

At 9.30 every morning of the week a little toylike milk train, belching huge clouds of smoke, would come chugging between the apple orchards and the two lakes hauling one passenger car, one mail car, and a red caboose. Whenever the engineer spotted the Buller silhouetted on a high ridge, he'd give a sharp blast on the steam whistle and we would shake our fist at him in mock anger. We all dreamed of one day being a passenger on that shuttle line which would carry us out to a little way station in the middle of a wilderness from which we could board an express travelling to points east and west.

The very next morning after receiving my parole notice in the mail, I was on that train, a dream come true. Outlined on a high ridge along the Last Mile was the buggy line, looking for all the world like a caravan of smugglers plodding across a sandy desert with their booty. They were all standing, looking down at the little milk train puffing along the lower valley with a long streamer of toilet paper fluttering far behind the caboose. This time when the engineer let go with a blast on the steam whistle the guys all waved, a wave that was directed at me inside the tiny washroom where I was signalling to my friends. I could make out Sergeant Tracy standing there stolidly and just looking and I couldn't help

61

wondering what he was thinking. Nobody ever knew what The Dick was thinking. Soon they were gone from sight and sadly I went out and took my seat in the passenger car and closed my eyes.

In my pocket was a twenty dollar bill, my parole papers, a train ticket, and a telegram from my father telling me that the family would be awaiting my arrival at the train station in my home town. I clenched my teeth and stared down at the parole papers anxious to get to Toronto where I could exchange them for a gun.

CHAPTER FIVE

October 19, 1955: Twelve days after my release from the reformatory and with a warrant out for my arrest as a parole violator, fate had me cruising along a main drag in Toronto behind the wheel of a V-8 Ford. Tucked inside the waistband of my jeans was a .32 calibre Belgian automatic. My partner Ralph and myself were about to pull off our third hold-up in less than one week. It was a cool and sunny autumn afternoon and Ralph who was a tall, good-looking, red-headed kid had the radio up full blast while Fats Domino was belting out a song called 'Blueberry Hill'.

Things were not panning out quite the way I had planned it from my prison cell. I was still living in a cheap rooming house in a sleazy district and worst of all I was still a cherry. Although I had come close to balling a nurse that I met at a rollerskating rink, at the last minute I chickened out. My friends on the Buller had filled my head so full of bogus, fearul tales of sex that they brainwashed me out of having a good time.

It was one of those situations where Maria and I were kissing and squeezing and after a while I started getting

62

these real sharp pains and right away I recalled what the guys had told me, about how my groin would swell up until it would burst, and then I would die. I quit fooling around right there and then and made a hasty retreat back to my pad only to find that everything was quite normal. I told Ralph about the pains and he laughed and said that my problem was waiting too long and that I should have gone all the way earlier. The problem was I was shy around girls and I was lucky I had the nerve to go as far as I did. I made another date with Maria thinking, tonight after the score, this time I was going to go all the way. Bad enough that I didn't smoke or drink.

I had first met Ralph in a pool hall called the Dug Out a few days after I got sprung. It was one of those cellar joints where you had to wind yourself down a spiral staircase; immediately your senses were assailed by clouds of tobacco smoke, muffled voices and the click of cue balls all blending into the distinctive atmosphere of poolrooms everywhere. I was looking for a partner because I was discovering that the spacious, frantic, seething city of Toronto was turning out to be more of an adversary than I had bargained for.

Here I was, a small town hick trying to dominate it with my puny strength and I couldn't even get a gun. To me the city was an implacable and awesome concrete jungle and I wanted a guide and friend who would back up my play. When I saw the five dots in the web of the hand holding a cue stick, I knew I had my man. Neither of us had ever gone on an AR before but I was determined to try it and he was willing to follow. He armed himself with a blank pistol that made a big bang when it went off and I had this big automatic that looked scary but was harmless in so far as the mechanism was broken and it had no clip. So I guess you could say that at that stage we were all bluff. Two kids playing Dillinger and riding high after our first two hair-raising stick-ups.

'C'mon Ralph, turn that chatter down, I wanna make sure that everything is straight . . . aw.'

'Hey! don't do that, I like the guy. Besides I'd rather not think.'

'And why not?'

'Because he's a big strap, that's why, mean too.'

'What are you sweating about? I'm the one that's going to make the entry and this piece ain't even got bullets to shoot.'

'Yeah, but I'll be right behind you, you know. He just won't open the door if he sees the two of us. Besides you don't look like a crook.'

'You don't exactly look like a killer either. You ain't even shaving yet.'

'Neither are you!'

'Yeah, well if I didn't shave, I'd end up with a moustache.'

'Balls! I'm gonna listen to Fats.'

The heist was a combination post office and grocery store. According to Ralph the hulking proprietor, who lived in the rear of the place, picked up a small fortune every second Wednesday at a nearby bank and locked it away in a large safe behind the post office wicket. The money was used to cash the cheques of employees from a nearby factory when they got off their 5 o'clock shift. The man charged the workers two bits apiece for his service.

We ran into a snag even before we reached the block we were looking for when the tinsel paper came loose and fell from the back of the ignition switch and the motor conked out, just as a traffic light was turning green at a busy intersection! We were now blocking a long line of homebound traffic and they wasted no time honking their horns.

'Let's split!' gasped Ralph, as he reached for the door.

'No, damn it. I can fix it; look cool.'

Even under the best of circumstances hot-wiring a car with tinsel paper took steady nerves and patience but I was determined to give it a go. I crouched under the wheel and did some sensitive fiddling around with my fingers as Ralph nervously urged me to hurry up. 'Ouch!' I received a nasty burn to the tip of one of my fingers when I touched a red hot electrical connection and I cursed Ralph out loud while continuing to probe, amid a growing pandemonium of horns and shouts.

'Let's go, Rog; we'll get another one later, the cops are sure to show up.'

'No, hang on; we won't make it to the score on time

unless we ... aha!' I pulled myself upright in the seat, pressed the button starter and the Ford roared to life. Trembling, I floored the gas pedal and we tore out of there in a loud squeal of tyres. Heaving a great sigh of relief, Ralph reached over and flicked the radio back on.

It was exactly 5 o'clock when we pulled up to the kerb across the street from the store which was only a few doors away from a very busy intersection. The entire area was a beehive of frantic activity as people scurried home. This was the old business section of town and on this block all the buildings were joined together; not even an alleyway separated them. However, on our side of the street and looking like an oasis in a sandy desert, was a small park with trees, park benches, swings and sand boxes. In a few minutes that park would materialise through the mist of a very real nightmare.

Getting out of the car, I told Ralph to wait for me while I scouted around on foot first – a preliminary precaution that I always insisted on. Skipping through the traffic, I crossed over to the opposite sidewalk and, acting as if I was window-shopping, I slowly worked my way towards the heist. As Raph had said, I just don't look like a crook. The store windows reflected a tall, slim youth, with tousled black hair and healthy complexion, wearing dark jeans, a black turtle-neck sweater, and corduroy jacket.

Looking through the large display window and into the store I could see three long counters piled high with food stuff. On the extreme right-hand side was a shorter counter completely enclosed with a grillwork of tiny bars, which was obviously the post office. Everything inside looked cluttered and murky. At the rear of the store a door led to the proprietor's living quarters. Ralph said he was a bachelor or a widower or something. I saw no one inside and so I stepped into a small alcove around the door to see if I would have enough privacy from the sidewalk, and when I did I was suddenly struck numb, as if I had just fallen into a river of ice! Overcome with a feeling of such stark horror, I had to shake my head violently. I almost ran back to the car.

Sliding behind the wheel. I said in a voice filled with emotion, 'It's all off Ralph. We're getting out of here.'

'Are you crazy? Why would you wanna do that for?'

'Because I've got this weird feeling that something very, very bad is going to happen to me if I go through with the play. I've had these feelings before and I know.'

'I told you you're acting crazy! We're here and we're set and you know we need the dough. If we don't hit that joint now, we won't get another chance for two weeks!'

'We can cruise around until we find another score.'

'No! This is a gold mine and we're never going to find a better spot. Maybe you're just chicken.'

I squeezed the steering wheel and rested my head on it as crazy thoughts rushed through my mind and after a minute I raised my head and said, 'Okay, I'm going to do it, but don't you ever call me chicken again.' I took off my glove and rubbed my holy medallion in the hope that the eerie feeling would fade. It did not. I then started the car and leaving the motor running we both got out and crossed the street.

A minute later Ralph leaned against a mail box about twenty feet away from the entrance to the store, ready to rush over as soon as I got the door to open. Gripping a phony cheque in my left hand, I rapped sharply on the glass partition and immediately the proprietor lumbered into view from the back room looking like something out of a scary movie. Sucking in my breath I watched as he approached. He had a huge, shaggy head, a craggy, unsmiling face, and big gnarly paws – three hundred pounds of solid bulk. He looked like a quarrelsome old giant. Upon reaching the door and dwarfing over me, his harsh German accent confirmed that he was a most impatient man.

'Yar fellar?'

Smiling meekly I replied, 'Will you cash my cheque Mr Gorman? The foreman at Clark's said you would.'

Raising his meaty hand he jabbed a clublike finger in my direction and growled: 'I nevar see you befar.'

Gulping down my apprehension, I answered, 'I only started working three weeks ago and this is my first paycheque.'

He studied me closely from under shaggy brows and suddenly he unlocked the door and hauled it open for me to

66

enter. Pulling the gun from my belt I took two quick steps inside and rammed the big automatic in his belly, threatening him with, 'This is a hold-up! Do as I say and you won't get hurt.'

I don't know where he got the bottle from. I saw him swing and was unable to duck in time. It smashed against my forehead and shattered in a million pieces! It felt like he had caved in my skull as I screamed in pain and fell back against the door jamb. Crazed fear gave me the strength to fight back the waves of darkness and nausea that threatened to overwhelm me. Knowing that my bluff had failed and still standing on my feet, I desperately wanted to flee the scene (as Ralph obviously had).

Bellowing like an enraged bull the man charged at me with what remained of the bottle in an effort to bury the broken shards of glass in my eyes! I was just able to pull my head aside and still dazed I started backing out of the store when he again lunged and this time grabbed me in a mighty bear hug. He started to squeeze. Instinctively I lashed out with the barrel of the automatic catching him violently across the top of his big head and slashing him to the bone. That only made him bellow all the louder and squeeze all the harder! I yelled at him to let me run away, over and over again, but he wouldn't; he only wanted to hurt me and so I started defending myself by lashing out with the gun. By then he was crushing the life out of me. Everytime I brought the barrel down across his head he would let out a terrible scream of rage and butt me with his shaggy head, showing no sign that he was willing to let me go. It was becoming a very ugly scene with both of us bathed in blood.

By now we had backed out to the sidewalk and a streetcar crammed with passengers was watching the scene. Nobody made a move to intervene; instead the people passing by just stopped and watched us mutilate each other.

I continued smashing him with the gun and he continued grasping at me and butting me with his head until my nose and lips were bleeding and my left eye was drowning in blood from the cut on my forehead. It was macabre, a seventeen-year-old boy and a fifty-nine-year-old giant slashing and clawing at each other and none of the bystanders in the huge crowd stepped forward to break us apart. He wouldn't even let me give up, he only wanted to hurt me!

Finally, after I don't know how many blows, the man crumpled to the sidewalk and then tried to grab my legs. It was only with great effort that I managed to pull away. Free from him at last! It had to be a dream, a nightmare, it couldn't be real. I was almost out of my mind with terror. All those people encircling me were a sea of faces displaying a variety of emotions, like in a fog, so unreal. I stood there for a moment wavering and wiping the gore from my face. Then I thought that this was a mob and that they probably wanted only to hurt me. Like a wild animal at bay I lisened to the sirens, an angry wailing that seemed to be coming from all directions at once.

'Run, Roger. Run!' screamed my inner voice as I staggered towards the crowd waving the big bloody automatic before me. It had the effect of a magic wand. I was mildly surprised to see the throng split apart and an avenue of escape present itself. Dizzily I staggered into the middle of the street and tottering frantically through the congested traffic I searched for the getaway car only to find that it was gone!

Shaking the cobwebs from my numbed brain I decided to run through the small park. I was climbing over the spiked fence when a wave of blackness surged over me and I fell to the ground on the other side. While I was lying there, a large section from the crowd broke away and made a menacing move towards me, but stopped dead in their tracks when I staggered to my feet and aimed the gun at them. Images of hysterical lynch mobs flashed through my mind as I fled across the park towards a row of buildings. The crowd followed behind yelling and urging each other on.

One block from the scene of the crime I darted down an alleyway. Here it was already dark. I didn't slow down my headlong flight. Between the towering walls of two buildings, very suddenly, there appeared an illuminated basement window – a dead-end – but I was moving too fast and my legs were too wobbly to stop or to prevent my foot from crashing right through the window! A loud chorus of screams assailed me as I retrieved my leg from a kitchen table where a family were eating their supper.

Turning around and lurching back down the alley, I became more convinced than ever that some monstrous nightmare was happening and that it would be just a matter of time before I snapped out of it. Gathered around the exit like a bunch of gargoyles staring at me with wide-open eyes were the spectators. Not uttering a single word, just watching and waiting for me to fall so that they could conquer me and be heroes. I plodded towards them and again they opened an avenue of escape for me when I pointed the gun. A minute later, I was running down the centre of a tree-lined residential street. People were standing on their porches, staring at me. My head was filled with loud wailing and then I realised that it was only the sirens and that I was still being pursued.

Brushing away the blood from my eyes with the sleeve of my jacket I gasped mightily to draw oxygen into my lungs. I realised that I didn't have the strength to run any farther and so I darted into the first laneway. A hundred feet and once more I came face to face with a dead end! Hope flared when I saw that it was only an eight foot wooden fence and parked nose-up against it was a car. With my last ounce of energy I scrambled on to the hood and gripping the top of the fence I started climbing over when a section of it broke off and I fell over it on to a thick carpet of grass. I lay there stunned with my eyes closed.

After long seconds I rolled over on my back, my chest heaving and my throat filling with blood. When I opened my eyes I immediately closed them again with a loud groan of despair. I now had positive proof that it was all a terrible nightmare because staring down at me was the Grim Reaper in person! A very old man with a long, white beard and flowing gown held a six foot sickle. This time I kept my eyes open and studied him more closely and was relieved to see that he was a Japanese dressed in Oriental clothing who had been cutting the weeds in his enclosed backyard when I tumbled in so unexpectedly.

Spitting out blood I scrambled to my feet, showed him my

gun, took his sickle away from him, and motioned for him to enter the screened back porch. Meekly, the very ancient gentleman did as I requested. By now the wailing sirens had reached a peak of intensity that threatened to swallow me up as I entered the house.

Everything was spinning around. I leaned back against the wall and fought off the darkness that threatened to engulf me. The old man stood motionless in the centre of the room while an elderly lady, wearing modern dress, stood over a sizzling frying pan looking at me with sad, inquistive eyes. The only sounds were the sirens, the meat frying, and my tortured breathing. Just then the door leading from a long hallway swung open and in walked a very lovely Japanese girl about my age, wearing a sweater, skirt, and bobby socks. Her eyes and expression registered astonishment as I reached out and grabbed her wrist saying,

'Please don't be scared. I mean you no harm. I won't shoot anyone if you do what I say. I want to stay here for an hour and when the police go away I will also leave.'

The terrible fear in her eyes faded a little as she nodded her head and asked, 'Can I explain to my grandparents?' I nodded yes. She looked down at where I was holding her wrist with my gloved hand and I immediately released it and said, 'I'm sorry.' Speaking rapid Japanese to her grandparents, she wiped away the blood from her wrist where I had touched her.

I had her turn off the stove and then I herded them along the hallway towards the front living-room, where I encountered a little girl and boy watching Superman on television and a muscular guy about thirty-five-years-old, obviously the father of the children and the young girl. Upon seeing me he dropped his newspaper and spreading his arms out like a wrestler he made like he was going to get up and tackle me!

Holding my arm straight out towards him and pointing the big, bloody automatic, I said, 'No mister don't do it or I'll have to kill you.'

He sat back down and kept his silence. The little boy and girl went on watching television as if I wasn't even there. The man's wife, carrying a small baby, came down the stairs

70

and I asked her to join the others sitting around the living-room. My entering their home like that was obviously a very frightening experience but they seemed to be adjusting to it.

I stood point in the darkened hallway where I could keep an eye on my hostages and on the back door and the front door all at once. My head was hurting and I was still scared and very, very confused about all that had happened; the thought that I may have murdered the old man preyed upon my mind. Why did he do what he did? What would have happened if the gun had been able to fire?

The wailing sirens were driving me mad! There were so many of them and they sounded so near, maybe I did kill the man. At one point the hostages and everything in the room blurred before my eyes, spinning, and I suddenly crashed to the floor taking the phone stand with me. Still clutching the automatic I pointed towards the room through a white mist and there was the man shuffling towards me with both fists cocked! I drew back the chambering mechanism with a loud click and making my voice strong I told him to sit down and he did. After a while I got back up on my feet and seeing a spark of concern in the young girl's eyes, I wanted to leave. No sirens had been heard for the past few minutes. I asked the girl to go out in the kitchen and get me a pan of water and a towel so that I could wash off the blood, warning her that she must not flee the house for the sake of her family.

Just then there was heavy pounding on the back door! My heart stopped and my blood went cold and my breathing started coming faster and faster. I felt so trapped and so vulnerable. More pounding. I cocked my ear, poised for flight.

The kitchen door slammed open and heavy footsteps were approaching the hallway door. It swung open to reveal half a dozen big, rough-looking, uniformed policemen, all pointing revolvers in my direction. I jumped for the front door amid loud shouts and pulled the door inwards. I found myself inside a screened porch, pulled another door open and was about to leap down on to the lawn when powerful spotlights blinded me and a booming voice blared,

'Drop your gun! The house is surrounded and you can't get away!'

Pivoting wildly I bounded back into the hallway, intending to run upstairs, and collided with all those blue uniforms. Down we all went in a pile of thrashing limbs, everybody yelling and punching and kicking until finally I was securely pinned to the floor and somebody was grinding a revolver barrel into the side of my temple and cursing and threatening me until somebody else chimed in with a word of caution,

'Ease up, Al; he's just a kid.'

Emerging from the house with my hands cuffed behind my back and most of my weight supported by two big detectives I saw where all the sirens had been coming from. The entire block, from one end to the other, was thronged with police cruisers and motorcycles, their dome lights flashing while garbled radio messages crackled in the night. The sidewalk on the far side of the street was lined with curious onlookers. A cordon of police hustled me across the street, through the crowd, and into an unmarked squad car, whereupon the bystanders pressed their faces against the windows for a closer look at what the police had captured. With a mournful wail from the siren the powerful car surged ahead as the crowd gave way. My romp in the outside world had lasted exactly twelve days.

The following day, while I was sitting alone in a jail cell one of the jailers brought me a handful of newspapers along with a sandwich and some water. The *Star* and the *Telegram* had two page spreads of my misdeeds and photos of all the key witnesses, including their personal observations at the time. There was a picture of the proprietor being wheeled out of the emergency room by a nurse in a candy-striped uniform, his mammoth sized head completely swathed in white bandages. His rugged features made him look downright malevolent. I had also been hurt by him and stitched up and bandaged. Nevertheless, sitting there on a hard steel bunk in a damp cell, I was feeling really bad about the evil thing I'd done. There were also pictures of the family I had held hostage, including the little boy and girl whom the mother said were, 'more interested in watching Superman on television than a real live gunman in our own living-room.'

A photo showed me sandwiched in the back seat of a

squad car between two detectives and trying to hide my face with my manacled hands; blood could be seen streaming down one side. They described me as a clean-cut, mixed up youth, who didn't smoke or drink. A tabloid called *Hush* displayed a full-length front page photo of me entering the cop shop and over it was a banner headline that read, 'EASTERN ONTARIO GUNMAN.'

The police had grilled me for a long time, wanting to know among other things who was my accomplice, seen running away from the scene of the crime. After a few hours I laid a bogus snow job on them about having met the guy in a pool room the day of the crime and that I didn't know his last name or where he lived, only that his first name was Mako and that he spoke with a foreign accent. I then described a profile of Ralph opposite to his own, adding that the man was in his forties. This was all printed in the newspaper; the reason they believed me was because of my credibility and the fact that they figured I'd want to get even with him for leaving me holding the bag on the score. However, in the reformatory we learned to keep our silence and stomp our own snakes. I hope Ralph went straight after that fiasco.

I wanted to have a speedy trial and get it all over with. Everything weighed so heavily on me and it was all so hectic. My folks had heard all about my situation some 300 miles away in my home town and arrived in Toronto just in time for my sentencing by a judge four days after the incident. A jailer led me from the crowded bullpen, down a long hallway and into a small room and it was then that I saw my Dad, my sister Susie, and my half-sister Gertrude. It was the first time I had seen them since I was hustled away to the reformatory and they must have seen a big change in me because Susie stifled a scream by biting her knuckles and Dad's eyes filled with tears.

In our family we rarely displayed outward emotion, anger yes, but not much loving affection. Big, stern Dad with tears in his eyes – this was the first time he did that for me, mostly he used to beat me and made me cry. Obviously overcome by the magnitude of my predicament, they let a priest and a lawyer whom they had brought along do most of the talking. The little, grizzled lawyer obviously knew his way around the city courtrooms blindfolded and was responsible for the private visit. He said it had been arranged because my father and sisters had travelled so far to come to my side plus consideration of my youth. He thought that he might be able to keep me out of the penitentiary.

'Let's hope the judge is in a forgiving mood,' he told me.

'I will also reason with the judge and later you can reason with God,' said the young, scholarly-looking priest.

'I don't want my boy he go to penitentiary,' said my father in broken English.

'If you do go, Roger, I'll come to visit you,' murmured my kid sister, trying to act brave.

'Here, let me comb your hair,' Gertrude offered.

'Dad you shouldn't be spending your money like this, coming all this way,' I said.

The judge chewed me out for a long time with a wrath that made my knees tremble. He reminded me how I very nearly killed a man and how I was responsible for the largest police raid in two years and mentioned the grief I brought to so many people: 'Your counsel informs the court that you understand the enormity of your crime and that you are sincerely appalled by it. Consequently, I will not bundle you away to the penitentiary for ten years; instead I will give you this one last chance to redeem yourself: two years less one day in the Ontario Reformatory, where you will be able to absorb what is proper and what is improper.'

The following morning Dad arrived at the grim, fortress-like Don Jail to visit a few minutes before returning to Cornwall. The visiting arrangements were primitive and scary as was everything else about that notorious city jail. The guards were probably paid very low wages and seemed to take their frustrations out on everybody and my father was no exception. The visiting area was a tiny, white-washed room about ten feet square, partitioned by two waist-high counters and chicken wire. In a four foot space beween the counters sat a lantern-jawed guard on a high stool furiously chewing gum and monitoring the conversations. There was enough space for only three visitors at a time on either side and there was already two prisoners there when I arrived. For that reason Susie couldn't get in. I sat down on the hard bench and greeted Dad with a tired smile when he stepped into the room. I felt sad because he looked so haggard and nervous. Dad sat down and had just started telling me in French that he was in touch with Mom by phone when the guard sprang off the stool like he was stung and shouted in my father's face,

'Speak English in here or get out!'

The shock of his spiteful objection so astonished my Dad that he just staggered to his feet and hiding his face from me, he fled the room. I went berserk!

I brushed the two prisoners off the bench we were seated on and raising it high in my arms I started battering the screen. The sudden fury of my attack caused the turnkey to shrink to the floor and skulk along under the partition, shrieking at the top of his lungs for help! Within seconds so many guards showed up on the scene that I thought they popped out of the woodwork. Using their combined body weight they pulled me down to the floor and then worked me over with fists and boots. Afterwards they tied my hands behind my back with pieces of cloth ripped from my T-shirt and then half carried me to the office of the chief keeper, a big-boned man with a shock of white hair, a pot belly, and what appeared to be a nasty disposition. I believe he encouraged his men to vilify the prisoners from sunrise to sunset in the belief that this was the way to rehabilitate felons. A small portion of guards were believed to excel in such things as kicking over a bucket of soapy hot water on some skinny wino scrubbing the wooden floors or beating up on a prisoner bound up in chains.

'Trouble-making punk, huh?' asked the keeper, waving his fist under my nose. 'Wanna clobber one of my men with a bench, eh? How about if I bust that pretty face of yours with a bench or with this!'

The force of his slap nearly cracked my neck and then he fired his fist into my guts and I sagged between the two guards holding me, struggling mightily to drag air back into my lungs. It took long agonising seconds before I could pull myself erect once more.

'Tough little punk, eh?' My face rocked from more slaps and my guts convulsed from more punches until finally I could not stand up anymore and so the screws let me fall to the floor, where I lay gagging and gasping.

Vaguely I heard the order to toss me into solitary confinement for ten days' punishment on bread and water.

The way to the cooler was deep into the bowels of the large prison where everything was constructed from huge blocks of stone, just like in a medieval castle. This particular hole had long ago been condemned by grand juries and put out of official use, except for prisoners whose offence was attacking a guard. There was not even any electricity down there, just dust, decay, and cobwebs.

I don't recall my journey down there at all clearly, mostly because I was feeling sick and the last stretch was navigated by flashlight. I remember winding stone steps, a worn old door with a small barred window, a sort windowless tunnel in which the light briefly illuminated three heavy doors with large bolts and locks. One of these doors swung open on squeaky hinges and I was thrown into an abysmal inky darkness – a cavity which turned out to be my solitary cell.

Unable to straighten up fully because of the pain, I inched along the concrete floor searching for the slop bucket I knew had to be there somewhere. When I located it and removed the lid the powerful lime stench almost ate my eyes out, but not even that could prevent me from vomiting my guts out into the bucket. Afterwards, because there was no bed, I crawled into a corner of the damp cell and hugging my half-naked body I wept.

CHAPTER SIX

November 1955: I was struggling through my eighth day of darkness in the bowels of the old Don Jail when the Black Maria swooped down on the archaic prison with a stack of transfer warrants, one of them with my name on it. In a fog and still suffering from the beating, I was removed from the filthy hole, sprayed with DDT, steered through a cold shower, nudged into civilian clothing, and finally chained hands and feet for the bumpy bus ride back to the Ontario Reformatory.

Three hours later the Black Maria deposited its prisoners in Guelph Reformatory and shortly after that, while still in a daze, I found myself tagging along behind the corporal of the guards with my meagre bedroll, shuffling through one damning barrier after another, moving deeper and deeper into the mainstream of prison life. Arriving at 3-West we stopped next to a control panel; pointing down the range of locked cells, the guard intoned in a robot-like voice,

'You got cell No. 19, go on down there and wait 'till I throw the lever.'

In a moment the heavy door cranked open and I stepped into my cage. I just stood there, numbed, unseeing, unhearing, until the crash of the door closing jarred me back to awareness. Shaking my battered head I moved off to the tiny sink and splashed cold water on my face and neck in an effort to clear the cobwebs from my brain. Afterwards, running my wet fingers through my hair, I made my way over to the tiny barred window and glared resentfully upon The Badlands far below where the spotlights illuminated discarded tobacco packages and whirling dust devils. I could feel a tremble to the night air and it made me realise that soon snow would be covering the prison grounds. Gazing skywards at the mass of blinking stars and the mystery of a half moon, I fervently stroked my lucky medallion, vowing that somehow I'd find a way to escape the evil clutches of the reformatory.

Shivering from the penetrating chill I closed the window and resignedly undressed. Lying down on my hard bunk the thought suddenly occured to me that I was not alone after all, that the lone electric light glaring painfully from the ceiling was watching my every move, and that in some mysterious manner even my reaction would be reported. Soon I fell into a fitful sleep.

In what seems like an incredibly short time I was snatched

from unconsciousness by the shrill blast of a guard's whistle and my nerves, already quivering raw areas of anxiety, screamed out in a pitch which outdid the whistle itself. But I was awake now and the light that seeped through the barred window revealed a new day.

Before I'd been two weeks in the institution, I got myself into a very serious jackpot. It all started early one evening as I lay on my bunk reading my neighbour's newspaper. At first the fluttering sound was so faint that it barely tickled my consciousness, but it kept nagging at me until finally I got to my feet and peering through the food slot in the metal door I soon discovered the source. A small, pretty bird had fluttered down an air shaft and ended up a prisoner between two window frames on the far wall from which there was no escape. The sounds I heard were the fierce struggles it was making in a blind attempt to free itself. By morning it would be dead and thinking these thoughts my heart reached out to it for I knew only too well that the cruel environment of prison quickly destroyed anything beautiful and defenceless. I concluded that the only way to free the bird was to smash out two window panes and with nearly ten feet separating my door from the window, this meant that I was hardly in a good position to do so myself. Would the guard making his round do it? Fat chance, but I decided to ask just the same.

Not long after this Lieutenant Flashlight Freddy came along on his nightly inspection tour with his ever-present torch gripped in his right hand. He had been a guard for so many years that he was going stir crazy and getting meaner with every day.

'You got the gall to ask me to break a window just to free a goddamn flea-ridden peacock!'

'It ain't a peacock, sir, it's a chickadee.'

'I guess you should know, being a jailbird and all.' With that he stormed off down the range, muttering to himself.

My neighbour Butch, who had bent an ear in our direction, now whispered, 'What a dirty, lousy, stinking dog! Ten to one Flashlight Freddy has got at least three cats hanging from his clothesline right this fuckin' minute. You know Roger somebody oughta . . .'

Just then I let fly with a bar of soap that hit square on

target and two panes of glass exploded from their frames and clattered to the marble floor making a terrible racket. For a brief moment there was a shocked silence on the range, even the wall radio seemed to be holding its breath, then all hell broke loose! My neighbours all started applauding and cheering, square dancing music blared from the squawk box, somebody was blowing on a whistle for all its worth, and through all this came the sound of running footsteps. Quickly I leaped upon my bunk, snatched up a book, and pretended to read just as Lieutenant Flashlight Freddy stuck his pasty face up to the food slot in my door.

Trying to control his beating heart he screamed with indignation, 'You'll pay with the flesh off your ass for this! You, you, savage!'

Thinking it the wise thing to do I clamped my mouth shut real tight and carried on like he wasn't there. This lack of reaction caused him to blow three more times on his whistle, a signal which was supposed to summon the goon squad on the run.

His over-reaction to the situation excited my neighbours and they took to taunting him, 'Why don't you have a heart attack you old fucker?'

'Your wife drives a garbage truck and wears army boots!'

'Yeah, and stick that flashlight up your ass!'

'Get lost, you old fruit cake!'

If he wasn't stir-crazy before, he was now! Hysterical with rage and roaring like a demented bull the lieutenant charged up and down the range in a drooling, wide-eyed effort to catch one of his hecklers in the act of calling him names.

'You oughta be on the funny farm, you jerk!'

'Your wife is balling the day shift!'

Each time Flashlight Freddy would barrel down to one end of the range it would go silent but the opposite end would immediately start up again! By this time he was incoherent and bobbing up and down like a jack-in-the-box, waving his flashlight over his head like a tomahawk.

When the goon squad stampeded on to the range in Three-West he let out a shout of joy and pointing to my cell he roared, 'The bastard is in No. 19, go and get him men. If he struggles, kill him!'

As the door crashed open I backed warily into the far corner of my drum expecting to be clubbed unconscious by the blackjacks each guard was wielding. The grizzled sergeant leading them pulled up a few feet from me.

Extending a pair of handcuffs he growled, 'How is it going to be? With or without your co-operation?'

A bit worried about what they might do to me after they cuffed me I slowly held out my hands. Everything seemed to be going okay as the Sarge locked them in place and started leading me out of the drum. I had just started lowering my defences when Lieutenant Flashlight Freddy charged with a lunatic look in his eyes and grabbed me by the throat.

With a scream that was both rage and pain I gave a mighty lurch and breaking away from him, I burst into the hallway. Running amok, I started smashing out windows with my manacled hands until guards caught up with me and wrestled me to the floor. By then I was enraged and very, very unco-operative as I struggled to free myself. When the lieutenant calculated that I was again defenceless he rushed over. Thinking that he was going to choke me again I found the power to break loose for a brief heartbeat. Just as Flashlight Freddy was stooping over me, I was able to grasp the front of his blue uniform with my manacled hands as the goon squad beat at my arms with blackjacks. With a scream of horror he sprang back faster than at any time in his life and started brushing vigorously at the large bloodstain my hands had left on his tunic.

Just then the captain trotted on to the range with more screws wearing gas masks because the place was in an uproar with all the prisoners on Three West banging on their doors and threatening the guards. The captain, who was wielding a bulky gas gun, picked out Butch and another guy called Sonny as the prime movers and blasted them each with tear gas and then closed their food slots. The rest of my neighbours, realising that they were outnumbered and out-gunned, lapsed into an uneasy silence.

The captain, realising that Flashlight Freddy had flipped his lid, ordered him brusquely to return immediately to the tower. He then turned his attention to me where I lay on the floor.

'Interested in walking to the hospital to have those hands tended to or do we simply drag you all the way?' His voice was hard and cold and it was obvious that he thought ill of me.

Afraid that my voice would fail me I simply nodded and off we went with a guard holding me under each arm, arms that were as dead and listless as rolls of salami hanging in a butcher's window.

One hour later I was pacing the floor in the cooler wearing nothing but a baby doll outfit, a heavy pair of socks, and the bloody bandages the nurse in the joint hospital wrapped around my hands. Apart from all this I was cold, icicle cold, because nobody had given me any blankets as was my right.

There was one guard in charge of the hole on the evening shift, a screw known as the Road-Runner, a skinny, hyper-active character who was believed to spend most of his time sucking-ass to the brass.

To get his attention I rattled the locked grill which was three feet inside the wooden door and shouted, 'Guard up!'

This was followed by the sound of footsteps. Then an over-sized eyeball peeked in at me for a second or so, a key grated in the lock, the door swung open and lo and behold there stood the Road-Runner holding a key in one hand and a Donald Duck comic book in the other!

'Captain Langton says that you were supposed to give me two blankets a long time ago,' I said with chattering teeth.

'You ain't gonna have none!' The Road-Runner set his pointed jaw, clamping shut the slash he had for a mouth.

Surprised and disturbed I reported, 'You just call the captain and you'll see that he'll . . .'

Shaking his comic book at me he snarled back, 'You ain't getting none I tell you; besides it's the lieutenant's orders.' With that he turned around and walked out, slamming the door hard.

Thirsting for revenge against Flashlight Freddy and the Road-Runner I came up with a diabolical plan. Scooping up the roll of toilet paper from the cell bars I jammed it tightly into the round hole in the centre of the floor which was my toilet. If I calculated correctly, the very next time that the toilet automatically flushed water pressure would build up and at a certain level it would overflow like a broken fire hydrant and keeep right on spewing out water until somebody closed off the main valve. Sitting high and dry on my metal bunk it wasn't long before I watched the stunt work beyond my fondest dreams.

Ten seconds after the toilet flushed there was a loud, gurgling sound and suddenly the water started overflowing faster and faster. As it rushed out under my door and into the hallway I started visualising in my mind's eye its probable course of destruction. It would flow silently along the dimly-lit hallway, which was angled slightly downhill, and flow swiftly past a series of solitary cells, slither under a wooden door and then, finally, like some creeping fungus from a horror show, spill into a square concrete office and swirl around the legs of a battered desk, seen or unseen by the Road-Runner who more likely than not would have his long legs propped up on that desk and would be leaning back in the swivel chair reading his Donald Duck comic book.

With a satanic grin I waited with bated breath upon my dry perch for the shocking discovery. Colder than ever I was now shivering uncontrollably but I had the grim satisfaction of knowing my misery would be shared. Some twenty minutes later the water was still gushing forth when the tomb-like silence was shattered by the sound of a telephone ringing. Steeling myself I waited, heard the scraping sound of the chair as the Road-Runner reached for the blower, followed by a long, shuddering scream as both of his feet landed in a pool of cold water! Little shivers of satisfaction ran up and down my spine as the scream echoed through the hole and the water continued flowing from the toilet.

Soon there were sounds of somebody running through the water, a key nervously turning in the lock, the wooden door swinging violently open, and there stood a bedraggled Road-Runner with a plunger in his hand! Pushing it through the cell bars he shouted, 'Quick you idiot! Your toilet is plugged!'

As calm as can be I peered over the edge of my bunk and then with disdain I moved my eyes slowly up to meet his angry stare and shaking my head from side to side I replie softly, 'Can't do it, I'll get my feet wet.'

'You rotten fucker!' he screamed and poked the plunge in at me until I had to retreat to the far edge of my bunk.

Still unruffled I watched as the water hypnotically swirle around his ankles; when he stopped cursing me long enoug. to take a breather, I said, 'I'll do it if you'll give me tw' blankets.'

Realising that threats would get him nowhere he decide to be diplomatic and galloping through the water he re turned in the blink of an eye pushing two blankets throug the bars to me. I then reached down and pulled out the plug and the water pressure immediately dropped back down to normal. Giving me the evil eye the Road-Runner slammed the door and left to open the drain in the walkway and mop up what remained.

Gleefully I rolled up like a squirrel inside the blankets at the far end of my bunk and permitted the waves of sleep to roll over me.

It was about one hour later that a pail of ice-cold water hit me square on and I came out of my sleep, ranting and raving and pawing at the air like I was being pursued by a school of piranha fish! The dirty, double-dealing rat had Pearl Harbored me! Retribution bubbled inside my heart as I lunged for the soggy roll of toilet paper and, grasping it, shook it violently at the laughing Road-Runner and cried out, 'I'll get you good this time, you red-neck bastard!'

Furiously I rammed the bulky material tightly into the hole in the floor; wet and shivering like I was coming to pieces I sprang back up on my bunk and just squatted there, staring sullenly at the toilet, waiting for it to flush. Still cackling the Road Runner departed with his empty pail and when he returned a few minutes later he found me in a state of distress; the toilet would not flush!

'It ain't gonna either,' gloated my tormentor. 'I found the main valve.' With those mocking words he let fly with another pail of cold water and retreated.

A few minutes before midnight the door creaked open again and I was so cold, so miserable, so uncaring, that I never even looked up from where I lay huddled.

'Here, take these,' said the voice of the Road-Runner. 'I'm going home now and I don't wanna come back tomorrow and find you dead; too much paper work to fill out.' The door closed softly and when I looked up there were two grey army blankets draped through the bars.

The following afternoon, with my hands handcuffed behind my back and flanked by two hulking guards, I was escorted into Good-Time Charley's Kangaroo Court to face some serious breaches of prison discipline. Again I was bearing marks of a beating as I pleaded 'Guilty' to the charges.

I winced at the superintendent's tongue-lashing which ended with the ominous words, 'It seems that your first trip to the Limbo Room, when you were serving your first term in here, has been too quickly forgotten. Perhaps a refresher course will show you to respect authority once and for all time, and with that in mind I'm sentencing you to twelve strokes of the paddle. In addition to that, you will also be segregated on the Bull Gang for an indefinite period of time.'

One hour later I huddled in a corner of the barren bull-pen, still in handcuffs, trying vainly to banish from my mind the terror that awaited me in the Limbo Room. Just then the steel door slid open with a loud crash and I was greeted not by the goon squad, but by a rather cultured-looking gentleman wearing a dark, conservative suit. Middle-aged with sandy hair and a neatly trimmed beard, he gripped in his right hand a curiously shaped walking stick made of fine wood crowned with a fearful looking gargoyle. Big, lumbering Captain Nicholson followed him into my cage. I scrambled defensively to my feet, taking up a position in the centre of the bullpen, not knowing what to expect.

'Roger Caron,' boomed the authoritative voice of the Captain. 'This is Dr Bonin. He's going to be our new resident psychiatrist in charge of our new psychiatric ward. So happens that he has an interesting proposal to offer you, one which you can accept or refuse.'

Smiling amiably and speaking in a low, controlled voice, Dr Bonin mapped out his expectations of me. They boiled down to this: in a locked room on the psychiatric ward,

84

there was this experimental gadget of his and he needed individual personalities to try it out on. Twice a week the treatments would take place, for a period of two months. He already had selected a few guinea pigs who were regular patients of his on the ward, and he wanted a defiant rebel to cap off his brainchild – me!

Fearful of the unknown horrors that might be lurking for me at the hands of Dr Bonin, I backed off a few steps and muttered softly, 'You're not getting me on some bug ward so you can stick some wires in my head.' As always when I became emotional I could feel a red hot flush turning my cheeks a livid red, a cursed condition of the flesh which I considered a betrayal, because it made me look the seventeen-year-old that I was and an easy target. 'Besides why should I volunteer?' I added belligerently.

'Ah, yes! Yes indeed; why should you volunteer?' pondered the doctor, tapping his walking stick against his chin. 'Well, first of all, the superintendent of this institution has promised to suspend indefinitely this terrible corporal punishment you are about to undergo. Secondly, at the end of the experiment, he says that you will be reinstated into the inmate population with your full privileges restored. There is also another factor here; your obvious instability, which I find most interesting. If you will meet me half-way I do believe that I can bring you peace of mind – no more inner conflict; no more fighting with the administration. It's all up to you.'

Head bowed in thought I struggled to come to a decision, torn between telling him to go to hell, and truly wanting to reach out for the peace of mind that he was offering me.

Harshly interrupting my thoughts and pushing his big belly further into the bullpen, Captain Nicholson barked out, 'Well, what is your choice going to be?'

Casting my mind's eye down into the Limbo Room deep in the catacombs of the prison, passing over the long leather paddles hanging on the whitewashed walls, lingering on the shackles and the restraining belts, I gave a visible shudder as fear gripped my heart. Raising my head and staring helplessly at Dr Bonin I nodded agreement with his proposal.

Removing the handcuffs, the Captain had the last word as he warned, 'Just you remember, Caron, the paddle has been only suspended; one wrong move while you are in this gentleman's care and it's going to be your hide. Understand?'

I understood only too well.

The new Psychiatric Unit was a show place and had only been in operation one month before I was recruited. Although it had a capacity for holding thirty patients and accepted patients from all the regional provincial institutions, there were only twelve of us on the ward. Dr Bonin wanted to keep the number down for the first few months so that we could get used to the staff, especially the female nurses, and vice versa. There would be only one uniformed guard on the ward and his job would be to unlock and lock barriers; and if he had a problem all he had to do was to press one of the many panic buttons to summon the goon squad. This was the only part of the prison that hired female staff, and that was quite a switch for guys like us to get used to, especially since most of the uniformed nurses were young and pretty – that is, except for the boss lady, Miss Carter, a regular old maid, hard as nails, whose favourite vocal utterance was an emphatic 'No!'

When the elevator door slid silently open, the Captain, Dr Bonin and I faced a long marble corridor that extended all the way to a sunlit dayroom in which a handful of patients decked out in grey pyjamas were playing cards and reading books. Solid doors branched off the corridor to the right and to the left, concealing a tiny mess hall (the grub was delivered from the main kitchen in a steam wagon). There were offices for Dr Bonin and his very sexy secretary, an examination room cluttered with electronic equipment, a lounge for the staff, laundry room, shower room, and a total of six private hospital rooms with barred windows. There was also a well stocked dispensary and four six-men dormitories.

A very friendly nurse with a lovely behind took charge of me and introduced herself as Jenny

'Talk about rescuing someone in the nick of time!' she was chatting as she led me down the corridor. 'It's just gruesome,' she shuddered. 'I'm so glad for you that Doctor Bonin was able to save you from that dreadful punishment. I have seen the Limbo Room you know. Oh well, let's not talk about that anymore. Come, let's meet your roommates.'

Of the dozen patients on the ward, only three of us were in our teens. First there was George, a clumsy, slightly overweight kid who had never done time before. He came from a rich family and was serving eighteen months on a manslaughter beef resulting from a car accident. A real momma's boy (she even bought him a new T-Bird). He didn't seem to have any mental hang-ups, and so we all assumed that his mother had arranged for his stay on the ward in order to keep him safely away from the regular population jungle where the buzzards would pick his bones clean. On the ward we had things pretty soft; we even had mattresses, a great luxury unavailable elsewhere in the institution. George took advantage of that – snoozing most of his time away.

My favourite person was seventeen-year-old Todd. A frail, pale complexioned, sandy-haired, moody and sensitive kid. Todd wore thick glasses and was serving an unusual indefinite sentence. His was a sensational crime that had been exploited in all the news media. They called him the 'phantom sniper' because one crazy night he climbed on the roof of a movie theatre and starting taking potshots at everything that moved below. When the law surrounded him and demanded his surrender, he chose instead to shoot himself. Later the doctors were able to save his life, but because they were unable to remove the bullet that was lodged close to his heart, Todd was left practically an invalid and couldn't even play sports or get overly excited.

There was also Charlie, a guy that I used to rap with a lot. He was a big gentle giant in his late twenties serving a twenty month sentence. Charlie's job on the ward was taking care of the small kitchen. When he wasn't doing that, he could always be found in a sunny corner of the dayroom painting with water colours: something he was good at, having been a commercial artist in the outside world. His downfall was the woman he married, who one day in a jealous rage slashed all his paintings. Charlie lost his cool and slashed her throat and then saved her life by rushing her to the hospital.

All the nurses were great, but Miss Jenny was the greatest! She never failed to boost my morale whenever she was on duty with her bubbling personality and deep concern for her patients. I was always observing her from a distance, and I guess I would have walked on fire if she had requested it. Although I wanted very much to talk to her, I shied away because she always left me tongue-tied and red-faced.

On one occasion, I was late getting out of my bunk for breakfast; everybody else was seated in the dining-room. That was when Miss Jenny came bouncing gaily into the dorm. Laughing happily, she proceeded to drag me out of bed, while in panic I clutched desperately at the blankets, turning crimson, and shouting that I was naked as a jaybird. Giggling, she pulled all the harder, amused at my acute embarrassment until I had only a pillow left to protect my manhood. Naturally just waking up I was aroused and spotting the results she let out a shriek and rushed out of the dorm in mock astonishment, joking, 'Oh dear, I've brought out the monster in him!'

I played the duck to her for the rest of the day. I also made sure after that scene that Todd got me on my feet early for breakfast. Nor did I ever tell any of my friends about that happening or other friendly gestures that Miss Jenny made towards me. I'm sure that she wasn't on the make, just having fun.

The guard on the day shift was quite a character and was very easy to like and talk to. I guess that's why he was given the regular turnkey shift on the ward. Old Man Jolly was originally from England; during the Second World War he'd been a belly gunner in a bomber. Later on when he came to Canada he worked for years as a traffic cop. Now, working as a guard, he was marking the bit of time he had left until retirement. Fat, gossipy, and prying, he wore thick police suspenders and smoked a corncob pipe, but more often than not he chewed tobacco.

All in all, he reminded me of my father. Whenever he overhead a group of us talking about the pros and cons of a criminal career, he would object emotionally by countering our view with statistics that crime didn't pay. Hooting.

we'd deride him for his stand and sometimes he would get so excited that he'd swallow his tobacco!!

After ten days on the ward, I was still not called upon to act as sacrificial patsy for Doctor Bonin's experimental gadget, and so with my defences slipping I was starting to feel really good about the bargain I'd struck. Very little was expected of me on a daily basis, except for submitting to a battery of personality tests, giving interpretations of what I saw in the ink blots, drawing sketches of what my father and mother looked like to me, putting puzzles in order, etc. All of which took about an hour a day.

Things changed drastically on the eleventh day. The main event was about to take place. Four of us were seated on a wooden bench just outside of a locked room waiting nervously to be called in one at a time. Everybody stared at their feet, much too tense to make small talk, imaginations running amok.

Suddenly the door swung open and Miss Carter's impersonal voice snapped us upright in our seats. She pointed an accusing finger at a balding little guy in his forties who had arrived a week earlier from a minimum security camp. His eyes were strange-looking and he blinked all the time.

'Come, the Doctor is waiting for you.' They disappeared into the room, the door opening in such a way that we couldn't see what was inside.

Just a few minutes later, our collective ears picked up the sound of strange moaning coming through the door, getting louder and more garbled by the second, until finally it became heartrending sobs, so profound, so raw, and so eerie, that I felt my hair standing on end. This went on for nearly ten minutes before it dribbled to a stop. The sound was so memorable that I can still hear it in the recesses of my mind. Meanwhile, those of us remaining on the bench exchanged pained expressions as we slipped back into our own little worlds.

Again the door swung open and this time Miss Carter beckoned to two nurses to enter the room. A moment later they emerged with this guy sagging between them and hustled him towards one of the private rooms where he could rest and regain his composure.

The boss lady then wiggled her fearful finger again. 'Garry, you're next; come inside please.'

Garry was also in his forties, but because he was all wrinkled he looked twice that old. He always referred to himself as a professional hobo and was serving six months for stealing and butchering some farmer's bull. All in all he was a lot of fun to talk to.

Then we heard him. He, too, did the strange, mumbling chant; later we heard him plainly, talking about constructing a log shack. During the last few minutes, he did a lot of wild cursing and then loud and clear he added, 'Yes sir, you are a horse's ass!'

When he emerged he did so on his own steam, but was obviously right out of the picture. His eyes were showing a lot of white as he was guided to his bunk in the dorm.

By now I was champing at the bit and very anxious to get it over and done with. That was my nature; if something or somebody was going to do me harm, I wanted to get it over and done with, and no fucking around!

Nevertheless, I was destined to be the last one to squirm in Doctor Bonin's mysterious temple. The third patient to step through the door was a purebred Indian from a reservation in Manitoba. Chippaway was serving a year for assaulting a cop while in a drunken rage. In his mid-twenties, Chip's one joy in life was playing his guitar.

Whatever the shrink did to Chip it sure put him in the mood to sing. After the drunken carols the joyous singing turned to wild, uninhibited laughter. It was the type of laughter that gives you a sore belly afterwards, only he ended with wracking sobs – really spooky!

When Chip was turned over to the nurses, they almost had to carry him to a recovery room: hair matted to his forehead and grey pyjamas blotched with perspiration.

By then I was really spooked, but when I was called into the room I tried not to show any emotion or curiosity. I sure as hell did a lot of looking all the same. It was a large windowless laboratory crammed with all sorts of electronic equipment, medical instruments, and an operating table under a powerful lamp. Strapped to the table was a canvas sack the full length of a man's body with a heavy-duty zipper running from head to foot. Standing at one end of the table was the doctor, fiddling around in a preoccupied manner with a rubber oxygen mask and some dials attached to two cylindrical tanks. His gorgeous secretary sat a few feet away from him on a high stool, poised with a note pad and pencil. Efficient Miss Carter stood at the door with a stethoscope around her neck. What chilled me the most were the six burly guards deployed around the bed flexing their fingers and staring fixedly at me.

'Remove your slippers Roger Caron, and climb up on the table,' said Miss Carter in a no-nonsense tone of voice. 'That's it, now slide down into the opening there, arms at your side. That's it. And now just relax.'

She then zippered the bag all the way up to my neck. I was in a straight jacket. At a nod from the shrink the uniformed guards then reached out and gripped firmly various parts of my body in such a way that I was unable to move. Completely immobilised and at the mercy of what I now believed to be a deranged head-shrinker, I started sweating and cursing at the choice I had made weeks earlier.

My eyes widened as the mask descended towards my face. Licking my parched lips, I tried to remain cool, still cursing myself for being so trusting. The mask clamped firmly over my mouth and nose and suddenly I found that I could not breathe!

Thinking that the Doctor goofed and that I was about to suffocate, I tried communicating my panic to Dr Bonin with my eyes, but his face remained impassive. Then I heard the ominous hissing of gas and still I couldn't breathe. Horror-stricken, I started thrashing about while the hands that were gripping me squeezed more tightly then ever. There was an eerie buzzing in my ears like an angry horde of wasps trying to chew their way into my brain. And I still couldn't breathe!

My struggle was now taking on a new tempo as a peculiar source of strength began coursing through me, making me feel as powerful as the Almighty Himself! The arteries in my neck were swelling to the point of bursting as I exerted even greater force than the hands that were holding me down until it felt like something was going to break. Even through the thick canvas, I could sense their awe and fear as I tossed them about like corks on a rough sea.

Now, the faces of the doctor and Miss Carter were getting all hairy and the room was spinning around in a maddening circle and I was being engulfed by a big wave as thick and dark as molasses, a wave that was carrying me off into a shadowy world full of lurking horrors, a universe of flashing lights and buzzing sounds, sounds that were getting louder and louder until I was being consumed!

The mask was off my face. Never had I felt such anger! It jumped, pounded, and raced through my arteries like a meteor; my eyes wanted to jump from their sockets and attack! I was strong, stronger than those who were holding me and they knew that! Their hands were slipping and I could hear the canvas tearing as I struggled mightier and mightier! Oh, God! Oh, God! Oh, God! – the vials of hate in my belly were eating me alive – Help me! Help me! Help me!

From very far away, I could hear someone calling out my name over and over again and with the greatest effort I tried to wind myself down so that I could make out Doctor Bonin's voice:

'Hey, hey, it's going to be all right, Roger, lie still. Stop screaming. Just take it easy and everything will be all right.'

Again, I renewed my screaming, so fierce, so unearthly, so profound, that it had to be primeval. Miss Carter crammed the end of a towel into my mouth while I struggled to break free from my captors, still unable to see or think clearly. Again the doctor talked soothingly to me and slowly I regained my senses so that the gag was removed and I was able to draw in great gulps of air, all the while observing that everybody was breathing and perspiring just as heavily as I was. Even Doctor Bonin's face was flushed and had an awed look.

Two guards, followed by Miss Carter, started to help me out of the room as the doctor reached for his secretary's notebook and mumbled, 'Don't worry, son. The next time will be more moderate.'

It never did get smoother. As a matter of fact, it got more and more turbulent, until finally, just a few days before

Christmas, they had to carry me into one of the private rooms after my seventh encounter in three weeks with the gas. I can't recall doing it, but apparently about twenty minutes later, Mr Jolly, the guard on the ward, heard the sounds of breaking glass. He rushed into the room to find me standing in front of broken windows, both my hands and the top of my head bleeding. By then I was in a state of complete shock and did not know where or who I was.

Functioning like a zombie, I was transferred to another room and kept under close observation. Dr Bonin was very distressed at the turn of events and in the next few days he had me checked out by a variety of experts. They even hooked me up to an electroencephalograph. Electrodes attached to wires were taped to parts of my scalp so that the electrical activity inside my brain could be charted on a machine that graphed a series of lines on moving paper.

Four days later, on a cold Christmas afternoon, I became aware of Miss Jenny covering me with an extra blanket. My head was hurting so much that I had to close my eyes for long seconds while the wind wailed outside my barred window and the snow spattered against the glass. Snuggling down deeper into the blankets, I again opened my eyes and observing the concerned look on her pretty face as she fussed around my bed, I whispered, 'Good afternoon, Miss Jenny.'

Startled, she let out a tiny squeal, then covering her mouth with her hands she stammered wide-eyed, 'Roger! Oh, it's so good to have you back.' Still flustered, she stooped down quickly and to my great astonishment kissed me fully on the lips! After adding a hasty 'Merry Christmas,' she fled from the room in search of Dr Bonin and Miss Carter.

By the time they showed up on the scene, my imagination had got the better of me and I was blustering angrily that nothing in the world was going to get me to go back into that chamber of horrors.

'I don't care if you whip me!' I shouted. 'I want off this goddamn bug ward!'

The doctor tried to calm me down by pointing out that his machine was being dismantled, never to be used again, and that I had nothing to worry about. But, by that stage, I was too sceptical to believe anything they told me and so they had to knock me out with a needle.

A little over a week later, around 9 o'clock in the evening I had put into action a desperate escape attempt. Outside my window a raging snowstorm all but obliterated the barbed wire fence and not even the powerful spotlights from the nearby guard shacks could penetrate the dense snowfall. I had sawed through two of the window bars and was in the process of lowering some knotted sheets to the frozen ground below when the door to my room crashed open and in rushed the goon squad with their clubs upraised! A lieutenant advanced on me with a pair of handcuffs.

Fighting and struggling like a man possessed I gave them a tough time so that they had to club me to the floor before they were able to overpower me. Even then I was beyond reasoning and so they had to carry me all the way down to the tower, whereupon they tossed me naked into the bull-pen.

Since there were no blankets or even a bed in the barred cell, I had to spend the night huddled beneath the heavily barred window, pressing up tightly to the old radiator that barely gave off any heat, shivering with cold and listening to the raging storm outside as it bore down on that reformatory with a terrible vengeance.

The storm within me was just as furious as I swore over and over again that I would escape, no matter how much they tortured me, I would find a way, somehow, someplace. With that resolution confirmed in my heart, I let my mind dwell on the horror that awaited me in the morning, that fuckin' Limbo Room.

CHAPTER SEVEN

January 1956: A few minutes after some guards deposited me in a cell in the segregated unit on D-3, Sergeant Tracy showed up at the front of the bars and with an unusual look of concern on his rugged features he said, 'That's a strange way for you to be walking, lad, let's see what they did to you?'

Standing in the centre of my cell and trembling visibly I dropped my pants and when the sergeant saw all that mangled flesh his face went livid with indignation and pounding his hamlike fist into the palm of his hand, he muttered, 'The goddamn simpletons! Do you know who did it to you that way?'

Unable to talk because of the cotton inside my gums and being extremely upset I just shook my head from side to side.

Giving me a penetrating look he added, 'All right then you just calm down and I'll go and get the nurse. As for working you spend the rest of the day in your cell and tomorrow too.' Still clenching his fist he stalked off.

Lying on my belly on my bunk I gritted my teeth as the male nurse applied iodine to all the lacerations on my buttocks, my lower stomach, and the back and inside of my thighs, where the sadist wielding the strap had purposely extended his swing so that the thick leather would encircle my hips to lash at those sensitive areas. It was a calculated effort on the part of the officials to try and break me down and make me beg for mercy so that the victory could be theirs.

I was only seventeen years old but even then I would have choked on my own blood before giving them that satisfaction. So it was that I received the maximum number of strokes and even the nurse who was accustomed to treating the after effects of corporal punishment was appalled by the grisly sight. Each stroke from the paddle had raised a welt one inch thick, four inches wide, and about fifteen inches long. Multiply that by twelve and you can picture the soggy mess, somewhat like second degree burns. (I learned later that Sergeant Tracy had stormed into the doctor's office and threatened to perform major surgery on his face for having stood by while I was flogged in this illegal manner.)

Later that Monday afternoon when my neighbours trooped in from work, those that were still on the Buller when I left stopped briefly in front of my cell to give me words of encouragement and, as was traditional, to ask to see the degree of punishment I had received at the hands of the enemy. In a way it was like a warrior's test, something to be proud of if you withstood the very real temptation to ask the enemy to stop, because then it could be said that they had failed to break your spirit.

On the other hand it was common knowledge that the first ones to break down and to beg for mercy were the loud-mouthed bullies. Always they would try to cover up by saying how brave and rebellious they were while getting their ass beaten, but the guards never failed to spread the real version in their contempt. They would tell how, after the first stroke, the guy never stopped screaming and begging for mercy and that they stopped after five strokes. I am not saying that I could blame anyone for breaking down under such torture. What is contemptible is for a coward to brag that he was extraordinarily brave. On the same subject, it was strongly rumoured that a certain individual high up on the administration totem pole got off his jollies each time he attended one of these bruised flesh matinees.

Later that night in cell-to-cell conversations I learned that the Buller's project for that winter was not the usual trek from the pit to the lake, but rather the stockpiling of large stones inside the pit, to be used somewhere in the spring to create a bridgeway on the prison property.

A few days slipped by and then it was Friday afternoon.

The temperature inside the pit was cold enough to freeze my blood but not frigid enough to deter my crazed determination to escape, even if it meant another visit to the Limbo Room or getting my melon blown off. It was one of the strangest compulsions ever to possess me and I just couldn't shake it off. My burning desire was to get far away from Guelph Reformatory.

In 1952 a prisoner by the name of Collins was probably experiencing the same emotions when suddenly he tossed his working tools down and ran blindly towards the picket blocking the entrance that led out of the pit. When Collins refused to stop his headlong flight the picket shot him in the belly with a slug from his revolver. The prisoner was so compelled by some mysterious drive, that he crawled on his belly with his guts trailing in the dust, right past the horror-stricken picket and beyond a hundred feet until he passed out. I always remembered that story and it spooked me because I had come to believe that some prisoners, like Collins and myself, were jinxed in some mysterious way.

Furiously I drove the pickaxe deep into the earth, again and again, trying to work the soreness out of my body as my eyes brimmed over with tears of pain which instantly formed into icicles. Each time I dislodged a large rock I would shout, 'Jug up!'

A rolling team consisting of two prisoners would run over and tumble the boulder clear from the face of the wall for a big guy wielding a heavy sledgehammer to smash into manageable pieces. These in turn would be lifted into a buggy and wheeled through the trampled snow to the centre of the pit where a huge mound of stones was rising higher and higher like some primitive temple for devil worshipping. Already it was so steep that the buggies had to be hauled up a wooden ramp with grappling hooks and ropes.

Standing at the top of the rockpile, like Napoleon observing his troops, was The Dick, as gloomy and stony-faced as ever. On the ground, overlooking the prisoners producing the stones, was Tomato Face, badmouthing and urging everybody on to a more concerted effort. The Corporal seemed to be getting more and more ornery. Probably his bleeding ulcers were making him act that way.

I had been labouring inside the pit for an hour when I stopped to brush away some icicles that had formed on my face. Glancing up along the rim which encircled the pit, I observed the pickets hunched down inside their brown greatcoats stamping their feet against the cold and I couldn't help thinking that they did not look very alert. But then again why should they? Nobody could possibly escape from the pit. There were eight shotgun pickets on guard duty to make certain that no one did. The one picket standing at the narrow entrance leading down into the pit could hold off the gang were they foolish enough to charge him head on. Besides, no prisoner had ever successfully escaped from the Buller.

About fifteen minutes later, I again paused in my work to clear some icicles from my face and to soothe some cuts made by flying pebbles given off by my pickaxe. I happened to notice a lone prisoner pushing a buggy laden with a milk can right past the entrance picket and down the slope. It was as if I was watching Coco, the runner, carry out his water-bearing duties for the very first time because I was now observing him form a different point of view. Good ol' Coco. Crazy ol' Coco! To us he was all of that and more. His one goal and passion in life was to date Elizabeth Taylor. He was serving six months for breaking into a theatre and damaging a movie projector in a wild effort to run an Elizabeth Taylor film for his own private midnight viewing. Once inside, he got banished from the general population for throwing ink on the man who was reformatory censor because he wouldn't let his letters through to Elizabeth Taylor. Coco, in his early forties, had no ears; his father had cut them off when he was eleven years old.

As runner on the gang, Coco made two trips a day to the cannery to fill the milk can full of drinking water. His other duties were to maintain the tools and spare parts for the buggies. In that capacity he often visited the old blacksmith shop to get a buggy axle welded or some such thing. Normally, Sergeant Tracy was supposed to give the entrance picket the high sign to allow Coco to pass through. However, for more years than anyone could remember no runner had ever tried to take advantage of his trusty status and jackrabbit. Besides only those with less than thirty days of their sentence remaining were considered for a trusty job. Therefore, little security attention was paid to a runner and Coco often passed in and out of the pit unnoticed.

With these facts tumbling into place I gradually became more and more excited as an extraordinary Go-Boy plan began to formulate in my mind. Finally the answer emerged and with a pounding heart I cried out silently to myself, 'That's it! Why run? Why not just walk off the gang? Well, why the hell not?'

A moderate snowfall was beginning to darken the skies overhead when The Dick blew his whistle for the mid-afternoon rest period. Grimly determined to go through with the play I dropped my pickaxe and hurried over to where Coco and Big Mongo were trying to roll cigarettes with frozen fingers. Quickly I outlined my plan and asked for their help.

'You must be ribbing us? You wanna get blown away?' exclaimed Coco in bewilderment.

'You gotta be out of your tree man! Nobody walks from the Buller, they run. They run like hell!' advised Big Mongo in a booming whisper.

'It ain't never been done, Roger. It's just plain crazy. You sure they didn't beat you on the head last time in the Limbo Room?' asked an Italian named Dino.

Irritated, I waved their comments off and countered with, 'That's why I'm going to make it. Because it's never been done before and so they won't be expecting it – especially in the wintertime. So, c'mon guys; quit trying to discourage me. I am going, and it's going to be today.'

'Okay, okay, kid. If you've got the balls, then the least we can do is back up your play,' agreed Mongo, and then turning to Coco he asked, 'You game?'

'What can I lose? I've only got sixteen days and a coffee left. Besides I just happen to have a letter here in my pocket for Miss Taylor.' Sliding the kite into the pocket of my jo-jo Coco added, 'Mail it for me on the way out, will ya?'

And so the plan was put in motion. Big flakes of snow were falling and that fit the scheme of things beautifully. I wouldn't have to worry about Tomato Face because where he stood post he couldn't see the entrance; however, The Dick could. So it was decided that someone would have to create a diversion to occupy Sergeant Tracy's attention while I pussyfooted out of the pit. Rocko, who had joined the conference, supplied the information that a guy on the gang called Gordon had bragged that morning that he wanted somebody to bust his leg with the sledge so that he could score the hospital.

'Call him over here,' Mongo told Coco; then turning to Rocko he asked with a sly smile, 'You'll help the gentleman out won't you?' Rocko gave him a wolfish grin.

It turned out that Gordon was all mouth and no longer wanted to exit from the gang on a stretcher. The fact that Rocko was feeling Gordon's leg like a horse trader didn't help. It was decided that Rocko and Mongo would see to it that somebody's buggy load of rocks would tumble accidentally over the edge of the mound of stones furthest away from the entrance to the pit – in a spot where The Dick would have to turn his back to my departure. Just before the whistle blew to resume work I asked Sergeant Tracy for permission to join the buggy line, giving him the excuse that I wanted to work the cramps out of my sore legs. A penetrating look and a curt nod was his way of saying, 'Yes.'

It didn't take long for the word to spread among the sixty prisoners on the gang and with it came an air of excitement as the odds-makers got into the act and bets were exchanged. I became a five to one underdog on the assumption that I'd either be pumped full of lead or punched out by The Dick. At least Mongo and Rocko were accepting the odds and that was a good sign. The main thing was for everybody to play their roles just right and not draw any heat on me. Then maybe, just maybe, I'd have a chance of escaping.

It was a little after 4 o'clock and I had just completed a dozen trips up one end of the rockpile and down the opposite end when I got the green light from Coco and saw him step inside the tiny tool shed to make himself scarce. Pulling off to one side of the rocks I exchanged my buggy for one loaded with spare parts and rejoined the buggy line. I was just turning into the ramp when Rocko, one pusher, and three buggies, went tumbling down over the edge of the

100

mound amid bloodcurdling screams and a great deal of pandemonium. With a roar of disapproval, The Dick pulled Mongo out of his way and glaring down over the edge he started shouting orders. Quickly I changed directions. Wheeling my buggy uphill towards the guarded entrance, I fervently started asking my protector Saint Joseph to look over my shoulder for me and to keep Sergeant Tracy off my back because hunched down inside my jo-jo and with the wind and snow blowing in my face I couldn't hear what was going on behind me. There were eight shotgun pickets either observing the foul-up back at the rock pile or else taking a bead on me and that thought made the flesh on my back crawl. Not daring to look up from under my peaked hat or to look over my shoulder, I strained to push the buggy uphill on a direct line with the picket blocking the entrance, while hoping with all my heart that he wouldn't challenge me because if he did he was going to have to shoot to stop me.

So far he was just standing there blocking the way with his shotgun cradled in the crook of his arm, his attention fixed rigidly on me. Not knowing if his suspicions were aroused I kept closing the gap between us until only ten yards separated us. Still he showed no sign of moving out of my way! I was now at a point where it was too late to back off and too far to attack him with the pickaxe handle that was lying in the buggy with the spare parts.

Suddenly he moved! His weapon swung up and around until it was pointing directly at my head! I stopped dead in my tracks while my heart leaped into my throat. My muscles tensed. I tried to gear my mind into some kind of action and then . . . I relaxed. What I had taken to be a hostile act on his part was simply his bungling feet slipping out from under him as he attempted to back up a slight incline to get out of my way.

Too close! Now I was hoping that he would be so rattled and preoccupied with pulling himself back together that he wouldn't pay close attention to my features as I moved past him, thinking that I was laughing up my sleeve. I trudged right on by, no more than ten feet from him, and he didn't challenge me!

But now that I had my back turned to him, my mind started playing tricks on me. Thinking that he only let me past so he could shoot me in the back, I was so intent on what might be shaping up behind me that it was moments before I realised that I was almost up to the cannery building and obviously free of any pursuit from the direction of the pit. My heart was beating with joy and I had to remind myself to stay alert because I was now in the centre of the enemy camp. To be precise, I was now within the industrial area without a pass!

If it hadn't been such a life and death matter I might have looked ludicrous to anyone observing me wheeling my buggy along the ploughed roadways, hemmed in by shop buildings, passing right by scores of guards and escorted prisoners, just as if I was a nosy tourist on an inspection tour of the joint.

Trying to look very sure of myself as if I had a definite goal in mind, I just kept moving along, down one street and up another, hoping to reach the opposite end of the camp. Just as I reached the busy intersection leading on to Migs Alley I had to pull up short to give the right of way to a tight formation of fish screws, about two dozen in all, marching past on their way to a row of white military barracks, with a noisy sergeant barking at their heels. Standing there boldly, as if I was waiting for traffic lights to change, I knew that I was daring them to do something, to challenge me, anything at all. Moving a leg I gasped in pain and realised for the first time that the area of my thighs, belly, and buttocks, was a searing mass of anguished flesh and that the blistered areas had ripped open and were now bleeding. Briefly my thoughts flashed to the Limbo Room and what I saw waiting for me there banished my feeling of power and sobered me up. Grimly I shook my head and buckled my thoughts down to the weary task that lay before me.

Five minutes later I parked my chariot beside a cow barn in the centre of a field. Anxious to get off the prison property before the alarm was sounded, I floundered through the snow until I reached the boundary fence. Scrambling over it, I jumped on to a narrow country road and hobbled along for a distance. Then I faded like a shadow into the dense bush.

CHAPTER EIGHT

January 1956: About six hours after entering the woods and floundering through endless miles of deep snow and heavy brush I was at my wit's end. My feet and legs were wet and frozen from breaking through ice and the areas of my flesh where I had been whipped were now the only part of my body that seemed alive.

Knowing that patrols would be hot on my trail, I had done my best to cover my tracks, travelling mostly along ice-covered creeks. On three occasions I heard the ominous baying of dog packs, but they never did get to close in on me. With all that manoeuvring I was now utterly lost and in grave danger of freezing to death. I dared not stop moving. My miraculous escape from the evil clutches of the reformatory filled me with such a rage to live that, even if my legs had failed me completely, I am positive that I would have found the will and strength to crawl out of the woods on my belly.

It must have been around 11 o'clock when it stopped snowing. A bright moon filled the sky above the trees. Stumbling and half-crawling up a high knoll I slumped breathlessly against a large boulder amid some tall trees, struggling to control my breathing. I was eating snow to put out the fire in my lungs as I prepared myself to climb a tree.

It took a lot of doing to reach the elevation that I wanted and now for the first time since entering the woods I could see a great distance. After five minutes my hopes were dashed when not even farm lights appeared over the tree tops and rolling hills. Fear crept into my heart. I was getting colder and colder. Not only was I lost and wet and exhausted, but I didn't even have a lighter to make a fire. I was just going to slide down the tree when suddenly I spotted a moving light off in the distance! I watched it awhile until I realised that it was a vehicle of some kind and it was about a mile away and gave the impression that it was moving straight through the woods, which of course I knew couldn't be so. Carefully I made very sure of the direction and slid down to the frozen earth and stumbled off once more.

It was about one hour later that I emerged from the bush on to a freshly ploughed country road and sank down to my knees. After regaining some of my strength, and my breathing had slowed down I staggered to my feet. I explored either direction with my eyes and saw nothing but an empty ribbon of road and endless forest. After a pause I picked a direction and stubbornly forged ahead, asking Saint Joseph not to lead me back to the reformatory.

I must have travelled about two miles when I came upon a little grey house squatting in the middle of the woods like a grotesque frog. The moon was shining brightly. Blowing gently through the trees, the wind eerily whipped up little clouds of snow against the front porch.

Now, I do not really believe in ghosts; nevertheless, the place had an unworldly quality. Sometimes I really believe that I am psychic and can detect evil vibes in spooky places or circumstances. This place had all the makings of an environment that should give me the creeps but strangely enough I felt at ease. Shivering violently and with my teeth rattling from the cold I decided that I would enter in search of some dry clothing. The driveway was about a hundred feet long and covered with almost a foot of snow and so it was a good bet that nobody was home, at least there were no footprints.

Underneath the new layer of snow was a hard crust and each step I took sounded alarmingly loud. Just maybe, there was somebody home. Breathing hard, I plastered myself up against the front of the house and tried peering into the window. The blind was down but there was no light inside. Moving around to the left I located a door that did not seem to be very secure and so I decided to batter it down.

104

My overall state of misery must have driven me to great indiscretion because I simply backed off a few paces and charged! There was a loud crash and the door flew in and so did I, as if I had hitched a ride on the tail end of a jet stream. Unable to stop my momentum, I hurdled through the black void straight across a heavy table piled high with dishes and nose dived to the floor on the far side with enough noise to wake up the dead! Good ol' Saint Joseph must have been riding right along with me because I didn't break my fool neck.

Struggling to my feet, I started blindly groping around in the dark and soon came to the disappointing conclusion that there was no such thing as electricity in this strange little house. It also seemed that the owners were either moving in or out because everything was in boxes or else orderly piles. I raised the blinds on two of the kitchen windows to let in the moonlight and started prowling around for a flashlight or a lamp. The bottom floor of the house consisted of only a kitchen and a small living-room. I finally came up with some matches and a handful of tiny birthday candles. Gripping about a dozen of them in my left hand I lit them up and started up a winding stairway with my shadow dancing mysteriously ahead of me on the grimy wallpapered stairwell.

At that very moment, if something had popped up in front of me, the guys back on D-3 would have heard my scream and I would have gone straight through the ceiling! Stepping into a small, cluttered bedroom with a slanted roof I did not bump into any ghost. The feeble glow from the candles displayed a pile of clothes on top of an unmade bed but my fingers were getting burned and I had to blow out the light. In the pitch-black darkness I discovered to my great displeasure that the dripping wax from the candles had sealed my fist shut. Extricating my fingers, I lit a few matches one after another until I had picked out a short jacket, a black turtle-neck sweater, and a pair of black slacks, but no footwear.

In the dark I removed my prison jeans; they were frozen so stiff that they stood upright by themselves. I also had to throw away my long underwear because it was caked with dried blood. By now I was in misery but this did not blunt my sense of humour when after five frustrating minutes of trying to get the zipper on the pants to stay in front where it should belong, I came to the shocking conclusion that what I was trying on was a pair of woman's pants! So were the sweater and jacket. As there were no men's clothing around I decided to keep them. While fumbling through another closet I came across a real gold mine in the form of a double-barrelled shotgun and a high powered rifle! There was also plenty of ammunition. I settled for the shotgun, a pocketful of shells, and a dagger. I was now anxious to move on; if a patrol came along and spotted those tracks in the driveway they'd be sure to check them out. Not knowing how far I was from the reformatory was a great disadvantage; for the past seven or eight hours I could very well have been running in circles.

Outside on the road I felt free and easy and brimming over with a fierce confidence. I thought to myself how unwise it would be for a patrol to try and recapture me, armed as I was. There was just no way they were going to get me back into the Limbo Room.

Feeling like a sassy wolf cub, I raised the shotgun skywards and fired off both barrels at the moon! There was an ear-splitting sound like twin thunderclaps followed by the solid recoil of the stock against my shoulder. Just then a red fox broke cover not ten feet away and hightailed it down the road, then stopped about fifty feet away to look back at me. Grimly I snapped the breech open, ejected the spent shells, rammed two more home, and with a knowing twist of my wrist I brought the hinged parts together and shouldered the weapon all in one swift movement. Suddenly I stopped my finger and said out loud, 'Go boy, go!'

About five miles down the road I was just rounding a sharp bend with trees and brush flanking both sides (including a deep gully, next to where I was walking) when the sound of a car motor caused me to look back over my shoulder. I spotted a flashing red light through the evergreens. A cruiser! A split second before I would have been captured in its headlights, I dived headfirst into the gaping chasm. I must have somersaulted for thirty feet through the black void

106

before making a landing in a deep soft snow drift and springy boughs. Still gripping the shotgun, I scrambled behind a big forked tree and breathing heavily I tried to regain my cool.

It was an OPP cruiser. The damned thing slid to a halt at almost the exact spot where I had bailed out. From my place of concealment I observed somone descend from the passenger side and brandishing a powerful hand spotlight he flashed it around, mostly to the left and right of me. Fortunately, I had landed in thick spruce and the branches had immediately sprung back into their natural state. The gully was heavily treed and after a few minutes he gave up. As the light went out I heard him say, 'Aw fuck; guess I was seeing things. Hang on just a minute, will you? I gotta have a leak.'

I'll be damned if he didn't do just that, I mean pissing in the same direction that I was hiding! By then I had the shotgun solidly positioned in the fork of the tree and aimed directly at his legs and I couldn't help thinking, 'If I was to squeeze the trigger right now, the dirty sonofabitch would need a straw to piss through from that moment afterwards.'

In a few minutes the cruiser drove away and I breathed a sigh of relief. It was only then that I realised that I had lost the dagger that I had tucked away in my belt. Luckily it didn't end up embedded in my guts.

Not long afterwards I came upon a single set of railroad tracks cutting through the woods which I decided to follow in the same general direction that the road was leading. Less than one mile along, I started encountering houses which were straddling a busy highway. A bit farther on I saw the highway sign which read, CITY OF GUELPH, pop 33,860. I stopped dead in my tracks and groaned and moaned for a full minute, as if I been stabbed in the back with a pitchfork. All those torturous miles – all the time I had been moving in a big circle.

After sitting there mulling over what to do I decided that maybe it was for the best. A darkened service station lay about five hundred yards farther on; parked in front were half a dozen cars. I figured it would be a good idea to bust into the place and get a key for one of those cars. Besides I was bushed and trembling so violently I just had to come up with some warmth and transportation; maybe a little money, too.

I entered through a rear window and muffled the sound by holding my jo-jo snugly against the pane of glass. This precaution was necessary because of the nearby houses. Inside, the place consisted of two compartments: a place for repairing automobiles and an office containing a large desk, a soft drink cooler, and a cigarette machine. I was disappointed to learn that the cash register was empty and that there were no cars inside. With the aid of some tools, I first attacked the Coke machine. Between it and the cigarette machine, I scored about thirty bucks. I drank two pints of chocolate milk then wandered into the office and eased myself gently into the stuffed chair behind the desk. Taking my rubbers off I plopped my frozen feet on top of the desk, right next to an electric heater that was warming up. With my shotgun across my lap I relaxed a little for the first time since I got out of my bunk some twenty-five hours earlier.

After I'd been sitting there awhile I began paying attention to the view seen through the large window. There, a few hundred yards down the highway in the direction of town were stately trees and behind them some kind of hospital or factory or something . . Holy Mother of God! It just couldn't be? It couldn't possibly be the joint? It had to be a nightmare! Both feet and shotgun were now on the floor and, leaning closer to the window, I gasped and blinked my eyes. Then I started to chuckle, which soon turned into sobbing laughter because the scene of lights that was causing me to come apart at the seams was the reformatory I had just escaped from!

I must not panic; I must make the best of it. I put my feet back up on the desk and just sat there studying the pinpoints of light, trying to figure out where D-3 was situated and visualising my friends tossing about in their sleep.

What had happened in the pit after I had made my hasty exit? When The Dick blew the whistle to line up for a head count before marching in for supper, it was probably then that I showed up as missing. A successful escape from the Buller! That must have sent everybody concerned into a tizzy. The thought of everybody running around in circles

108

warmed my heart. At my elbow was a telephone. I picked it up and dialled.

'Information?' answered a sweet voice.

'The number for the Ontario Reformatory please.' I scribbled with a pencil on the back of an envelope; hung up; then dialled again.

'Mr Revere, Duty Officer speaking.' It was the gruff voice of a captain I did not know.

Muffling my voice and making it sound mysterious, I whispered into the mouthpiece, 'You better hurry on home; your wife is balling the day shift.'

'Well just so long as she saves some for me,' replied the captain chuckling.

Angrily I roared, 'That wasn't supposed to be funny, you stupid jerk!' Dissatisfied, I hung up on him, not knowing why I had called in the first place.

Searching for the keys belonging to the cars parked on the lot out front I came across a four hundred pound safe inside a large cabinet. This was the first pete I had encountered. I couldn't imagine anyone owning a new one like that without stuffing it full of thousands of dollars. I was aware of the generalities of peeling open a pete, but as I was a novice it would call for a lot of noise and this wasn't the place. Besides I was keen to get away from this district. Excited and dismayed I was pondering what to do when suddenly the office became shockingly and totally illuminated by the bright headlights of a speeding car that came screeching in off the highway and straight for the front door of the garage! With a roar it skidded around the gas pumps on the wet snow, regained traction, leapt back on to the highway then disappeared in a pall of gasoline fumes. Groaning in pain and shaking like a leaf I came up from the floor behind the desk, gripping the shot gun with white knuckles. I was so shaken at being scared by some nutty car jockey that I just had to boot that desk about ten times.

I decided to get the hell out of there and with a handful of keys I let myself out the front door. Ten minutes later I was back inside and again dismayed, none of the cars had any batteries! I was now mad at the operator of the service station and I thought, 'OK if that's the way you wanna be, well I'll just go into town and get me a car and I'll drive back and kidnap your lousy pete! That's right . . . I'll take it to Toronto with me!'

Seated once more behind the desk I picked up the blower and called a taxi with a number from one of the calendars. I gave the dispatcher the address from an envelope on the desk, then hung up after being informed a cab would pick me up in ten minutes.

It was fifteen minutes before I spotted the cab and shivering from the cold I flagged it down and told the driver to drop me off downtown in front of a hotel. It was now almost two o'clock in the morning and the wide main street was surprisingly heavy with traffic, mostly revellers from the movie houses and local taverns. I paid off the driver with loot taken from the vending machine and stepped out into enemy territory just as cool as you please.

Angle-parked across the street was a row of cars. Reaching for the screwdriver I'd tucked inside my belt I walked straight up to a 1951 Ford, popped open a small vent window, unlocked the door and slid behind the wheel. Fiddling around with some tinfoil I soon pressed the starter and presto the car roared to life! After asking a cop standing near a traffic light for directions to the highway that led back to the service station I floored the accelerator and soon raced out of town.

Dousing the headlights, I quietly nosed off the road towards one of the two big overhead doors leading into the garage, praying that, if the owner lived in one of the nearby houses, he was fast asleep. I was not being very sneaky about the whole thing. Leaving the motor running, I hurried around to the rear of the building and once more crawled through the window. Moments later I had one of the overhead doors open and drove the jalopy inside. Then I pulled the door down again and locked it.

I tossed out the rear seat of the car in order to make room for the safe; then working like a man possessed, I started inching the unwieldly block of iron out of the office and over towards the car. The safe was grey in colour and about three feet square. Ten feet lay between it and the car. Heaving it

110

end over end, I had just reached the doorway leading into the garage section when it keeled over and pinched my left hand in the door jamb. Choking back the scream that welled up in my throat I struggled frantically to break loose while conjuring a mental picture of myself being arrested in the morning like a turkey in a snare.

With a great effort and an unknown reserve of strength, I finally extricated my hand. With relief I saw that none of my bones were busted. However, my middle finger was split wide open the full length, very deep. The pete had exerted so much pressure that it burst like an overly-ripe cucumber. It was dripping blood all over the place but still too numb to really give me a lot of pain. In my hurry, I did an incredible thing. Under my feet was an utterly filthy grease-stained rag, half buried in cinders. Scooping it up, I gave it a shake and tore off a small piece. Then as unconcerned as you please I wrapped it tightly around my mangled finger to stem the flow of blood.

It took the better part of one hour, but finally with the aid of a hydraulic jack I was able to boost the pete into the back of the car and immediately added more air to the rear tyres to compensate for the additional four hundred pounds. Not having any key to the trunk, I had to cram a variety of tools which I decided to take along, plus hundreds of packages of cigarettes, and even a spade, in and around the safe. All in all it was quite a load. The shovel was added in case I failed to locate anyone to bust open the pete for me. If so, I would bury it in a field for a rainy day. Labouring long and hard on a task I could be very stubborn concerning the results.

The early hours of Saturday morning saw me barrelling down a lonely, snow-swept highway in a hot car, all the booty in the rear, and my double-barrelled shotgun across my lap. I was feeling as happy as can be; physically I was a wreck.

Thirty-six hours later in Toronto (after I had slept around the clock in a cheap flophouse) I rounded up three under-world characters in a pool hall and drove out to the country-side with the safe. In a horse shed at the rear of an abandoned church we pried the door off and cried – the loot was twelve stinking dollars!

After that fiasco we sold the cigarettes and I sawed the barrel off the shotgun, only to lose both the weapon and the car to a traffic cop in a limited hours parking zone.

Father Hamill was the only legit person I knew in Toronto. I had met him through my Dad at my October trial. Desperation drove me to him to get my mangled finger attended. At first he began asking me a lot of questions but when I started to bolt for the door he cooled me off and settled for patching me up.

On my third and fourth day of stolen freedom I went on a one-man crime spree that terminated abruptly during a midnight high-speed chase. In a hair-raising attempt to circumvent a highway roadblock I tried to clear a culvert with the new Mercury I was driving and failed disastrously! The area soon became a bedlam of activity, wailing sirens, flashing lights, threatening voices, as shadowy forms crawled all over the vehicle which was now lying on its side wrapped around by a barbed wire fence.

A uniformed OPP officer poked a shotgun through a hole in the busted windshield and was yelling for everybody to keep their hands up where they could be seen from outside. Andy, my black partner, was watching with fearful eyes as the police snipped away at the wire on the passenger side.

Protesting hysterically from the back seat, a bearded old hobo in an army overcoat was pleading, 'Just hitch-hiking. I ain't no crook. Don't shoot!'

Scattered along the front seat were a pile of death certificates (I stole the car from a funeral parlour). Gritting my teeth, I just lay there, unhurt, but crumpled up just the same behind the wheel of the car, sulking at my lousy streak of bad luck. One more hour and we would have been operating in Detroit.

After we were extricated from the wreck, the OPP detachment from Chatham transferred us to their hillbilly lock-up for a fierce interrogation. We were to be kept on ice for the Toronto police since I had stolen the car in Toronto. Andy who was on parole from Guelph Reformatory was really shook up and scared about what was going to happen to him. Even though it was his fault that the law became suspicious of us and latched on to our tails I told him that I would get him off by making a deal with the Toronto cops and confessing to all my crimes over the past four days. Enough that I was in deadly serious trouble – Andy didn't have to suffer along with me.

We were kept in a dimly lit basement in separate wire cages each containing only a hard bunk. Adjacent to the station was an all-night restaurant and through a small window at ground level the sounds of girls laughing and the haunting of a melody floated down clearly to where I lay in the shadows, loneliness eating away at me. The music stirred old memories, some of which at the age of seventeen I would rather had never happened.

CHAPTER NINE

April 12, 1938: The man who had the greatest influence over my formative years was my iron-willed father, a French Canadian born on a farm in 1891 in northern Ontario. During the early years he owned a small bakery which he ran with the help of his first wife and their ten children. Dressed in a raccoon coat for protection against the bleak winters, he would make all his deliveries deep into the countryside in a horsedrawn rig. It was a rugged life but he had the constitution and build for it: barrel-chested, with a deeply-grooved face that was proud in bearing, topped by bushy black eyebrows and deep-set eyes that could spit fire or dance merrily with mischief.

Dad wasn't exactly worldly-wise, but he was god-fearing and I guess that counted for something in those days. Popular and also stubborn beyond belief he loved to sit around with his cronies, drinking beer, chewing tobacco, and swapping stories. And when he laughed he would laugh uproariously, rocking back and forth in his chair, and slapping

113

his knees with his big, calloused hands. But if he was in a fit of rage, he would bellow and beat his mighty chest with his fist like a wounded gorilla.

It was his ability as a storyteller that I remember most fondly. On those cold and blustery winter nights when my little sister and brother and I were supposed to be fast asleep, we huddled close together in an upstairs bedroom in our longjohns, peering down through the grate in the floor at the grown-ups gathered around the kitchen stove. We listened with bated breath as Dad spun one of his scary tales delivered in broken English with lots of hand gestures.

Like that time back in 1933 when he was whipping his horses along a snowy country road, muffled up against the cold, and taking little comfort from the ghostly light given off by a full moon. Suddenly, out of the forest growing thickly on either side, emerged what looked like a shaggy bear!

'Whoa! Whoa!' Dad cried, hauling back on the reins as both horses reared up on their hind legs, snorting in terror at the thing bobbing and weaving in front of them. Throwing off his bearskin rug, Dad snatched up the club at his feet and roared at whatever it was to clear the way! When it made human sounds and pointed to its mouth hungrily Dad recognised it must be the raving lunatic who had been living wild in the bush ever since his family was destroyed in a fire years before – a fire that he was accused of setting himself. The shaggy form continued gesturing in a threatening manner until Dad threw some bread into the trees. When the madman scrambled for it, my father whipped his horses into a furious gallop and raced off.

A few miles down the road he pulled into a farmyard where two old maids lived in a big house all alone; he warned them of the danger. This electrifying news sent the old girls into convulsions of fear as they repeated how in the past few weeks something had been prowling through their barn, eating their chickens raw, and lapping the cream off the top of the milk cans.

'Oh Donat, please!' They begged and clutched at him. 'You've got to sleep here with us tonight.'

After much coaxing my father did spend the night with them, and from that day forward never managed to live it

114

down. Actually Dad was a harmless wolf who loved to whistle at passing girls, but it never went beyond that.

His first wife was a saint of a woman and when she suddenly died my father was deeply grieved. Shortly after that he went bankrupt; that was a black day in his life because he had four boys and six girls to care for. With only thirty dollars in his pocket he loaded the kids into the old Chrysler sedan, piled the household goods high on the roof, and journeyed to Cornwall where a job was waiting for him, delivering bread by horse and wagon.

He rented a house beside a big black barn in the north end of town right next to the railroad tracks. The rent was twenty-five dollars a month. One time it had been a grand old house with two living-rooms, fancy chandeliers, and two front porches with separate entrances. When Dad moved in with his brood, the roof was leaking, the plumbing was failing, and the foundation was so eroded that each fall it had to be shored up with loads of black earth to keep out the winter chill. The two car garage at the end of the drive served more as windbreak than shelter, its windows all broken and the roof gaping with big holes. On the unpaved street where the house stood, there were many big trees, mostly maple, which kept the wood stove going year round for cooking and heating. There was also a big rear lot where Dad was able to coax a lush garden so that we at least had fresh vegetables to eat. What was left over was canned and preserved for the winter months.

At this point in time my mother came into the picture. Her name was Yvonne and she was a slim, attractive girl with high cheek bones and hair that was turning prematurely grey. Her ambition had been to become a schoolteacher in the country, but jobs were almost non-existent in Cornwall then so she ended up as a housekeeper for Dad. Coincidentally, she was born in the same farming community as Dad and also had a lot of brothers and sisters. It came to pass that they fell in love and got married, and in my eyes that makes Dad quite a guy, because all he could offer her were hardships and his undying love – and to top it off he was twenty years older.

I was born in that house April 12th, 1938, just as Hitler

was flexing his muscles and sending the world into a paroxysm of fear and paranoia. All in all, it wasn't the ideal time to be born of impoverished parents, and from an early age I had the feeling that I was unwelcome. As a matter of fact, I had to struggle to survive the first few weeks because of my breathing. Mom said that I couldn't keep down my food and that I was always gasping for breath; on occasion I had to be rushed to the local hospital. Even today after all these years I am very edgy about anything affecting my breathing; I can't even swim for that reason, or stick my head under a shower for very long. Mom says that I was a quiet and secretive child who preferred to play alone, hiding behind the chesterfield while she frantically searched everywhere for me. My favourite pastime was taking clocks apart.

By the time August 1939 rolled around I had a little sister, Suzanne; before my kid brother Gaston could make the scene in June 1944, most of my half-brothers and sisters were marching off to war. The big house become relatively quiet with just Noella, Jeannine, Theresa, Susie, Gaston, my parents, and myself.

The house with all its many rooms literally made a slave out of Mom who was compulsively clean; sometimes she would make herself sick with overwork. Her one pleasure in life seemed to be the awestruck look on the face of newcomers over the way the antique furniture shone and the amazing orderliness. Antiques were plentiful in the house, from a hand-cranked record player to a grandfather clock, but to us they were something to use and not to gawk at.

Even before I was old enough to know what the word ghost meant, I was spooked by things that happened to me in that old house. The vibrations given off each time a locomotive hurtled past didn't help – the beds would actually shift around at night and the dishes downstairs would rattle. Religious articles abounded, including lifelike statues and a mammoth sized catechism illustrated with macabre pictures of black-tailed devils leering as they fed little babies to the flames – just because they died before they could be baptised.

The cellar terrified me the most. Its winding passageway and low beamed ceiling was illuminated by a feeble bulb that cast eerie shadows near the coal bin; the fat grey furnace emitted strange sounds. Even my mother was scared when she went down there, but for her it was the rats. Whenever I was dispatched to fetch a pail of coal or a jar of preserves, I did so with the utmost speed! Once my Dad and older brothers locked the door when I went down there for something and then made strange scratching and booing sounds, but they never did that again because I threw a twister and broke a lot of things.

Until I was eight years old I was plagued with horrifying nightmares that always left me physically sick. I can still visualise the worst of them with gut-wrenching clarity. Just mentioning it now still disturbs me. They centred around the old-fashioned crib where I slept. It stood in the darkest corner of a large upstairs bedroom, a room in which two older half-brothers shared a brass bed. Here, late at night, the terror came. Sometimes it was as if shadowy apparitions were reaching through the bars of my crib and choking me. Other times it was as if huge waves were boiling over me. That was worse. They would clutch at me, cutting off my breath, drawing me into their murky depths. I'd wake up crying in terror, clawing wildly at my gate then have to pull it down to get out. In the bathroom I'd be violently sick in the toilet bowl. Afterwards, I would sit there on the floor bathed in the protection of the overhead light. Everybody in the house worked hard and nobody liked to be disturbed in the middle of the night by a child whom they were convinced was only looking for attention.

It was our parish priest who came to my rescue. I was eight years old and Father Lebrun looked enough like my Dad to be his brother; he had grown up on the farm next door to my mother. She said he had been a holy terror as a kid and a bit of a wolf. He became a fire and brimstone priest who would speak his mind and give his congregation hell if he deemed it appropriate. I told him about my nightmares, and explained how a few years earlier, while playing, I accidentally broke off the hand of one of the largest statues in the house, Saint Joseph's. I voiced my suspicion that Saint Joseph's vengeful spirit might be choking me in the night. Holding my hand he marched me right up to the altar where

117

there was a life-sized statue of the saint. Making me kneel down and pray for forgiveness because I was just a little boy who didn't know better, Father Lebrun said nice things about me. Then he hung a silver medallion around my neck. He told me Saint Joseph would be my protector from then on. My nightmares diminished after that.

Sunday mornings meant church-going for the whole family; my father and three oldest brothers were the official ushers. Big, good-looking and aggressive, they carried out their functions proud as peacocks, with a lot of heel clicking while passing out the collection plates. At home it seemed we were always kneeling down saying the rosary. On New Year's morning we always solemnly knelt down before Dad, one of us at a time, to ask his blessing for the coming year.

It was during the late war years when Dad had trouble feeding his family that he started bootlegging. At first it was on a small scale, but as the years slipped by the business grew until he had to rent parking space for his customers, and find stashes for his surplus booze. He became a target for the local police who raided the house gangbuster style. I got used to being wakened in the middle of the night with a flashlight in my eyes, as a big, uniformed cop looked under my mattress for contraband booze. After a while I quit being scared and would just turn over and go back to sleep.

One day a patrolman made Dad an offer. For twenty-five dollars a week he would warn him of all impending raids. It was a terrific bargain and Dad jumped at the deal, drastically cutting down his court appearances. The whole family was in on the big secret and often I would be the one to answer the phone when the cop called, asking me to pass the word on to Dad and his customers that the law was coming! Pandemonium would reign briefly, as everybody rushed out the nearest door to hide the tell-tale bottles in the field next door. By the time the cops made their dramatic entry the scene that greeted them would be domestic in the extreme! Mom would be sewing, we kids would be playing Monopoly and Dad playing bridge with his friends and drinking coffee. Empty-handed and frustrated the police would leave the house scratching their heads, while my father would chuckle once more at having outwitted the law. I sat

118

observing everything. What was right and what was wrong?

Dad prided himself on being an honest man who would rather starve than steal another man's money or property; yet he wouldn't hesitate to take a keg of nails home from the factory, or a fish out of season, or bootleg. As he saw it, the nails belonged to the millionaire who owned the factory, the wriggling bass would otherwise be caught by rich capitalists with their fancy boats and fishing equipment, and moreover by selling booze after the big hotels were closed, he was simply offering a service to his friends. And all this resulted in his being able to feed his family! So how could God hold that against him? Besides he turned over a portion of his earning to the church.

By the time I was eleven years old I was different from most kids my age; apart from being sulky and rebellious, I was a loner who could trust and love only my pets. I found I disliked my father's customers more and more especially when one of the drunken slobs killed Howie, my pet bantam rooster. He said it was a mistake when he stepped on him, but I flew into a rage and attacked him just the same. When my father beat the living daylights out of me, it kind of made me hate him too. It was like the time he gave away my dog Butch.

I must have only been eight years old but I can still remember that vividly. Dad and my two brothers were struggling to hold me down in the driveway as a man led Butch away at the end of a rope. I cried and screamed, 'Butch! Butch! Butch!' I can't remember now why the dog had to go, but I still feel betrayed.

All my anguish and torment at that early age didn't entirely stem from my nightmares or the beatings I received from Dad, or from being separated from my pets. Mom and Dad fought all the time. It was a rare day when there was peace and quiet in our home. Mostly it was only chest and table thumping but Dad was very jealous of Mom and one day he flipped out and punched her in the eye. Falling backwards she begged me in French to help her. I did nothing, and that fact still bugs me today.

It was around this time that my father had become an alcoholic, probably helped into that intolerable condition by

119

his steady customers who didn't want to drink alone. That became another reason why I hated them. My father was a strong-willed man and later when he saw what he was doing to himself and to his family he finally quit boozing. He and Mom were happier after that, but they still argued a lot. Everybody in our family liked to argue.

I didn't much like people in those days but I did have one friend whom I could trust. He was a wise old gentleman by the name of Mr Proulx. A dapper little man with white hair and moustache, he sported a big gold watch in his vest pocket. It was his job to control the traffic at the railroad crossing behind our house by raising and lowering the gates. The four massive levers that operated those gates were high up inside a red tower that overlooked the railroad station and miles of track. Since Mr Proulx was in his late fifties, climbing those winding stairs to the tower was a chore; that's where I came into the picture. In return for running errands for him, he would let me hang the oil lamps on the gates just before sundown. But my biggest thrill was when he let me help him lower the gates. We let them down one at a time, releasing the brake and pushing back on the lever; it required great strength. He used to laugh when I tried to do it by myself.

'The day that you can haul up both gates at once, that's the day you'll become a man, son.'

I keenly looked forward to that day.

But I was turning to bad seed. Lying, cheating and stealing, I felt a tremendous drive to do something shocking; the more people badmouthed me, the worse I got. Soon everybody was predicting my doom, saying that I was going to die at the end of a rope like a notorious neighbourhood bandit. Not wanting to let them know they were wounding me deeply, I'd just laugh recklessly and then run off and do something bad. Dad, with the help of my half-brothers, would whip me like you would whip a grown man, but that didn't help either. Sometimes I would punish myself, by beating my fist against the shed door until my knuckles bled. My fist still bears the scars.

Scars became a way of life. My first serious accident occurred when I was only five years old. It was as if the iron

120

monster that was our washing machine tried to swallow me whole. It had no safety release and when Mom came into the kitchen and saw me dangling there – with the rollers grinding away at my left shoulder – she threw it in reverse, and then fainted! I very nearly lost my arm at the elbow, the flesh there having been literally ripped apart from my upper arm. It took a lot of sewing to get it all back together and today I still carry the broad scars.

The second accident occurred right in front of the house – the street was our playground. A car smashed into me. I can still recall lying on the veranda, bleeding profusely from a head wound, as a policeman with a shiny badge peered down at me. From then on, the tempo increased, dogs biting me, a heavy horsedrawn sled running over me, more cars hitting me. Once I even got an arrow stuck between my eyes. Mostly the top of my head took the real beatings; often it hurt to comb my hair.

We north end guys were always at war with the east end gang and my problem was always forgetting to duck. I got the nickname Coon, short for racoon, because I was always sporting one or two black eyes.

There was no doubt about it, I was the truant officer's favourite fugitive and a prize catch on those rare occasions when he was lucky enough to corner me. My school was Saint John Bosco and most of our lessons were in French, taught by women teachers. If a man's help was needed, the old principal would press the panic button, to summon Father Lebrun from the Rectory next door. If it was me acting up, he'd box my ears, and then hold me while the principal beat my hands with a leather strap.

One day when I was about twelve years old I really made a big splash at school, one that elevated my prestige with my hard-nosed companions. The day before a gang of us had broken into a boxcar loaded with canned goods. When the law swooped down on us, I made a spectacular getaway by scuddling through a policeman's legs. Somebody ratted and a hulking motorcycle cop was standing in the centre of my classroom, gripping me tightly by my wrist and declaring loudly that I was under arrest. He was so big that I reached only slightly above his gunbelt. Stuffing me into his side-car we roared away as my pretty school teacher, Miss Lachine, and all the girls and boys leaned out the window waving good-bye. It made me feel like Dillinger. Since it was my first court appearance, the judge let me off with probation and a stern lecture.

My favourite companion in those days was my alley cat Tiger, who carried on more like a dog than a feline. We were inseparable from the time I found him starving near the tracks. I believed we could actually communicate through mental vibrations. Tiger had a built-in clock that would inform him exactly when I was coming home from school because he would meet me half-way and leap into my waiting arms. A real scrapper, there was no dog in the neighbourhood that cat would run from, not even the two hundred pound mutt next door who chewed off his ear.

His favourite game was ambushing me. The snaggletoothed little bugger would wait patiently until I was directly below his place of concealment, whether garage roof or tree, and then with a low growl and a blur of motion he would spring on my back, scratch and bite at me and then bound away with me in hot pursuit. He also had a yen for birds, especially starlings which were in great abundance in our tree-shaded neighbourhood. I was very handy with my slingshot, which I kept inside an old cupboard in the shed. Anytime he was hungry for a bird and caught me in the shed, he would go into his act, licking his goofy chops, meowing, and doing flip-flops in front of the cupboard. I'd watch him carrying on like a prize fool for a minute or so and then I'd walk away. Zoom . . . the little devil would be bouncing off my back in a tantrum, meowing like a kitten, and using every means of persuasion he could think of.

'Okay, okay, you big slob,' I'd say, reaching for my slingshot. 'Let's go and see how my aim is today.'

Old widow Atkins across the street was always complaining to my father about my killing birds and Tiger beating up her cats. Dad just laughed.

One summer day Tiger came along as usual when we all drove downtown. We left him in the car while we shopped. When we came back to the car he was gone! Heartbroken, I searched and searched, but my cat was nowhere to be found. I suspect some farmer stole him. I grieved for a long time.

Even Mom had liked Tiger and, as clean and fussy as she was, it's a wonder that she had let him sleep under the wood stove.

Although Mom worked very hard cooking and doing household chores, she was neverthless very young at heart; she was good company and popular. Church socials, bingo and gossiping on the telephone were her pastimes. She was always telling the fortunes of friends by reading their tea leaves, predicting the advent of tall, dark and handsome strangers in their lives. When she was in her late thirties Mom's hair had turned silver white. With her silver-rimmed glasses, she was a handsome woman. She also possessed a fiery temper when aroused.

Everybody in my family possessed volcanic tempers and were so opinionated that sometimes their arguments bordered on madness. Can you imagine a circle of big hairy gorillas all beating their chests sitting around the kitchen table at mealtimes? When they pounded the table Mom would get upset and yell at Dad and the boys to shove their stupid arguments. Then it would really begin to get hot and heavy.

Leonard was the oldest of the boys and the quietest. Light complexioned and blondish (the rest of us were dark) he was good-looking and average-sized but a brooder whose mercurial temper could flare into violence in the blink of an eye. Mom used him as the enforcer when Dad wasn't around, and I still resent the vicious beatings he gave me. My feelings about him are mixed but I've got to admit he had guts. Late one evening, for example, two boisterous drunks pounded on the front door, wakening everybody with demands that Dad sell them some booze. However, my father had a policy not to sell to drunks and he told them so. They refused to leave and sounded menacing. The lithe figure of Leonard suddenly materialised from among us and attacked with a fury! In less than a minute both toughs were lying in pools of their own blood as my father struggled to pull Leonard away from them. All this because they showed disrespect to our father. Sometimes Leonard in

123

his quiet way could be downright spooky. He died in 1953 of an unknown illness while holding tightly to my mother's hand.

To be accepted by the north-end gang of Saints and Sinners every so often you had to do something gutsy (or foolish, depending on your point of view). Raiding old widow Atkins' apple tree and risking (we believed) the danger of being boiled in a pot was one stunt which we all tried at one time or another when sleeping out in our back-yard tents. Playing chicken behind the slaughterhouse with abandoned electric street cars was another – or it was, until Slugger broke his back in a head-on collision.

Because I had more balls than good sense, the older boys were always getting me to crawl through narrow air-shafts to steal things. The neighbourhood bread company was a prime target for such forays! The top floor of the big grey building was stacked high with delicious pastries. Once inside, the goodies would be lowered to my friends below by means of a rope and basket.

In the early forties I used to accompany Dad on week-end fishing trips to catch food for the table. Later on, when Dad's bootlegging business boomed, the trips were done for the quiet pleasure of getting away. In those days the rivers and creeks near home were teeming with fish; with the ur-banisation and industrialisation after the war, we had to travel further and further to find a good fishing hole.

Right after church on Sunday mornings our driveway would be bustling as family, relatives, and friends tied down bamboo poles to the roofs of cars, stuffed old tyres to be used to feed the bonfires into the trunks, packed in the enor-mous lunches made up by the women folk and – the most precious items of all – tomato cans teeming with juicy worms, the night crawlers, picked from the lawns the night before by us kids.

By noon we would all be spread out along the grassy bank of our favourite river, a muddy channel leading to the St Lawrence some fifty miles away. Concealed from the gravel road by trees, we were just a stone's throw from an iron bridge leading to a cheese factory. Our basic prey was catfish or barbotte as my father called them in French; but of

124

course we would take anything we caught. It was needed on the table.

Some of the characters strung out along the bank were so colourful in appearance or action that even when the fish weren't biting, there was never a dull moment with lots of good-humoured talk, beer, and cigars. I liked it best when it got dark and the bonfires were set, their light illuminating all the bamboo poles resting on forked sticks, white corks bobbing gently in the breeze, and fat worms wrapped around barbed hooks – wriggling their tempting morsels at the lazy catfish or maybe a passing eel. When somebody did get a nibble and the float started to bob around teasingly, there would be a shout of joy and everybody turned their full attention to the feverish fisherman, until he either landed or lost his prey.

I can still recall vividly one dark, moonless night when, by the light of the crackling bonfire, I shouted to Dad in the squeaky voice of a twelve-year-old that something was nibbling at my hook. It was the first action in almost an hour and so everybody gathered excitedly around me as I slowly raised the pole in my trembling hands.

'Non, Roger!' exclaimed my father coaching me with lots of hand motions. 'Wait 'til floater go ziggy-zag in the water.'

Gripping the pole tighter I prepared to give it a sharp pull to sink the barbs deep.

'Ha, dat's no barbotte!' whispered Dad knowingly. 'It fool around wit de floater too much.'

With bated breath we all watched for long minutes as the fish teased with a series of feinting nibbles, followed by a long stillness, then one good jerk, more stillness, a few more feints, and then the cork went under.

'Ya! Ya! Now pull hard!'

What I pulled out of the water that night turned out to be the biggest and fattest black bass anybody in our family had ever seen! I was proud as a peacock when my father, clutching the squirming fish in his big hands, kept shouting, 'Sacré Bleu! What a big fish!'

There was only one thing wrong with our beautiful trophy – black bass were out of season and catching one carried a whopping fine.

'No sir,' said Dad, shaking his big shaggy head and beaming proudly at me. 'Him we keep, if not some rich son-of-a-gun catch him next moon in his big boat and put on wall. Ha! He go into kitchen pot.'

That fish must have had a built-in alarm because a few minutes later the game warden emerged from the trees, and while still at a distance shouted, 'Good evening, gentlemen. How are the fish biting tonight?' There was a flurry of movement as he strolled over to the fire and flashing his light into the gunny sack, he chuckled and said, 'Hope what's in there is in season, eh?'

'Heh, heh,' Dad giggled nervously from where he was sitting at the edge of the muddy bank. 'Yes sir, dat's all you're gonna find in there, just three good fish and two eels.' By then my father's left cheek and eye were twitching and blinking like crazy.

'Well, I've got to finish my rounds and so I'll let you boys get back to your fishing.' Walking away he added over his shoulder, 'Remember to put the fire out.'

As soon as he was out of sight my Dad came straight up off the ground, holding the seat of his pants like he's just been prodded by a spear. He started letting out a series of muffled whoops, circling the fire as if he was doing a war chant. All the time the game warden was there, he had been sitting on the fighting bass and, indignant at the ponderous weight, it kept sticking its barbs into Dad's backside! We laughed for a long time over that.

Sometimes we supplemented our lunches by cooking the fish over the fire. Often, added to that were free curds from the nearby cheese factory. Later on, after dark, we kids would arm ourselves with clubs and flashlights and spreading out along the marshy river banks we'd search for big fat bull frogs. Stealthily as Apaches, we would stalk closer and closer to the deep-throated croaking sounds, alarming the crickets as we passed through their territory. When we spotted our prey, we blinded him with the light and swung the stick all in one motion, 'THUD!' Later, back at the campfire we would proudly dump out our booty, anxious to see who caught the biggest and fattest. Frogs' legs made a fine snack.

Very late at night the men drove the long miles back

home, while we kids slept exhausted in the back seat, grimy and soot-covered from the bonfires. Next morning the neighbourhood kids would gather in our backyard to see all the fish swimming in the washtub where Dad cleaned them. These times are happy memories for me because it wasn't often that I was able to feel close to my father.

By the time I was fourteen I was becoming more and more of a loner and I had a hair-trigger temper that kept getting me into trouble. On the surface I was rather quiet and easy-going, especially in the presence of strangers; but in the environment of my home or school I was strictly trouble. I didn't know why, nor was there anyone around to explain my conduct or dark moods to me.

I hated school with such a passion that it was like entering a cell each time I dragged myself to a desk. In those days outside of school I hardly ever walked; I ran. So I kept skipping school to go fishing or hunting where I felt at peace with myself. By then I had acquired a rod and reel and a full tackle box, plus a secret fishing spot, which is where I went when I skipped school.

That spot held such an element of danger – of my breaking my fool neck or drowning – that I became deliciously intoxicated by it. The city powerhouse was situated on a spit of land between the canal that fronted the main street, and the St Lawrence River, that separated the town of Cornwall from the USA. To draw the energy it needed to turn the enormous turbines, the power station gulped in huge quantities of placid water from the canal then spewed it out violently into the St Lawrence River in torrents of rampaging water that smashed into a foamy spray against the jagged rocks and landscape below.

So eroded was the precipice leading down to the water's edge that no path existed. Since it was down there among the exposed rocks that I did my fishing, I had to lower myself and my gear by means of a stout rope. Just one slip would have been disastrous because I couldn't swim. Exhilaration was my overwhelming feeling each time I navigated the climb safely. Barefoot and with my faded jeans rolled up, I would skip along the wet rocks with a wall of water cascading down behind me, drenching me with angry spray as swirling water tugged at my feet. Standing on the furthest rock a good distance from the bank, I needed only to lower my lure into the rushing water, and in the blink of an eye, a hundred yards of nylon cord would hum off my reel sounding like a mad hornet. Lurking in those waters were beauties like Great Northern Pikes, huge sturgeons that fed on muskrats, and enormous eels as big around as a man's neck.

I got started hunting on the fishing trips with Dad when I was little. If the fish weren't biting I would wander into the bush with my slingshot to see what I could trap or shoot. It wasn't long before my backyard at home was looking like a miniature zoo with a variety of pets, including hawks and even a racoon. I was always showing up at school with some kind of animal tucked away inside my coat or maybe a groundhog on a leash. I felt I had a knack for training animals and, because I handled my pets with such ease, a lot of people thought they could do the same, not realising that a black squirrel can bite you nine times before you can say 'Ouch!' Having never forgotten or forgiven that drunk for killing my rooster I wouldn't protest when one of Dad's drunken customers reached for a pet squirrel only to find that it had sharp teeth.

Occasionally, I made some pocket money selling the pets I tamed, asking for a good price because taming them in the very beginning was rough on my hands. Even when I had to kill an animal it wasn't wasted either because I had a steady customer who would pay me for both pelt and meat. The man's name was Max and he operated a run-down shoe repair shop across the tracks in shantytown. He lived all alone and was also my fence for the things I stole around town. He relied heavily on the cheap meat I got for him. Squirrel stew was okay but not chipmunk; he said chipmunk had less juice than a dried prune.

When I was fifteen we moved into a house that Dad bought a block away from the old one. It included a restaurant, operated by my brother Jerry, and a small barber shop rented out to an alcoholic who took a swig of booze for every head of hair he cut. By this time father no longer had the protection of his early warning system and was taking some nasty falls; the judge told him that his next arrest would mean an automatic jail term. That was the day Dad quit bootlegging. Meanwhile nobody seemed to care much whether or not I attended school since I was rarely at home, but out running around wild. I had all kinds of jobs; jockeying cars around a big used-car lot; working as a helper in an autobody shop; delivering ice; working on a soft drink truck; and helping a legless gambler with his Crown & Anchor wheels at the local fairs and race tracks.

By now I also had an impressive arrest record. My last bust made such a big bang that it woke up the whole town! Two brothers and I stole the town's cache of Dominion Day fireworks, including three kegs of gunpowder. Too damned inexperienced to realise that we were toying with a sleeping dragon, we touched off the whole works late one night on the official lacrosse field. It was spectacular! The ground convulsed in ear-splitting booms as the kegs of gunpowder exploded. Rockets blasted off into the sky in every direction, blazing dazzling trails through the heavens that could be seen across the border. Rattling, popping, thumping sounds gave way to exploding stars showering the field with a kaleidoscope of brilliant colours, erupting again and again in glorious patterns. Amid the smoke and man-made hell on the ground were the fireworks that had fallen on their sides, zig-zagging through the lush grass, each one a lethal threat to me as I lay writhing and hugging the earth in terror, while acrid smoke spiralled up from the gaping hole in my right thigh. The fuse on the keg of gunpowder had been touched off by a spark before I had time to get clear; it had blown me thirty feet through the air!

By the time the police and fire truck got to the scene my friends had carried me home where my mother almost fainted at the sight of the smouldering crater in my leg, big enough to put a horseshoe through. The youngest kid had had all his hair burnt off; when he was taken to the hospital the police got into the act, and from Shucks they got my name.

Our fathers paid whopping fines and we three got off with suspended sentences. I was bedridden for six weeks and limped for almost a year. It was an omen that my time on the street was running out.

September 8, 1954: After tripping the alarm in a sporting goods store the police caught me in an alley, but only after I bumped my head on a beam and fell.

CHAPTER TEN

February 1956: There were eight of us prisoners chained and seated on one side of the clattering passenger car, while across the aisle sat our ever-watchful guardians tapping their fingers nervously on the knees of their black, creased trousers – seven sheriffs all anxious to get the four-hour train trip over and done with. I was uncomfortably aware of how out of place I must have appeared in this clutch of battered and worldly men with my boyish features and tinted cheeks. Sinking even deeper into my seat I turned my thoughts back to the courtroom and the reaction of the news media to my sentence – a total of twenty-five years for my three day crime spree.

They chastised the judge and decried a system of justice that had no better alternative for rehabilitating a youth of seventeen than to toss him into a concrete pit full of perverts, drug addicts, murderers, and hard core criminals, expecting him to come out reformed. One banner headline read, 'GRADUATED FROM THE REFORMATORY TO THE BIG HOUSE WITH HONOURS'. Names of several infamous Canadian criminals were churned up and they questioned whether the system was going to mutate me into a carbon copy of one of them. One tabloid ended its commentary on an ominous note, '. . . when the boy becomes a man and is released from the pen, who wants to be the cop to meet him in a dark alleyway with a gun in his hand?' However, the photograph that accompanied the articles showed the face of a boy, not a mad dog. Four days after I was sentenced the courtroom record was clarified to read that I was serving only five years, a total of twenty years running concurrently.

By mid-afternoon when the train pulled into the station, a severe snowstorm had cut visibility to about ten yards. The passengers gave a wide berth to the custodial circus as we slowly shambled along the aisle and descended to the wooden platform amid swirling snow and a handful of policemen. Hunched inside our overcoats and dragging our chains, we were herded towards three battered limousines and squeezed into the back seats for the three mile drive to the pen, a cruiser leading the way.

Kingston Penitentiary seen through a winter blizzard was enough to strike terror into the bravest heart. Nine acres of cement and steel perched on the very banks of Lake Ontario and buffeted by a bitter and howling wind blowing off the frozen lake. It had the appearance of a fortress: high, grey walls all around; and tall guard towers commanding each corner of the wall. Seated within, on high stools and cradling high-powered rifles, were the blue-uniformed sentinels with licence to kill and maim.

The oldest penitentiary in Canada, Kingston first opened its fearful gates as a place of confinement back in 1832. The old bulwark was slowly decaying, condemned to the wreckers' hammer but still used decade after decade. The high, cathedral-like structure inside the walls was the main cell house called the 'dome'. It was the heart and pulse of the institution holding more than six hundred cells under a cupola that soared to a dizzying height. The dome had no floors, other than the ground floor. Instead there were tiers of cells, four storeys high, two deep, back-to-back, in rows of twenty-one. Eight cell-blocks lettered A to H branched off from the circular dome like spokes of a wheel. Here fresh air was at a premium. Open the dirt-splattered windows on the cell-block walls and a damp, shivering, dungeon-like cold would envelop your body like a shroud. Close the windows and the air would become stiflingly difficult to breathe.

In many respects this human honey-combed beehive was like a small city: a mayor (the warden); city council (classification board); police force (guards in untold

131

numbers, above, below, and all around). It had a church, hospital, power house, clothing store, industries, movie house, recreation hall and athletic field, and finally a jail (solitary confinement). All the necessities. But no warmth and no love, just a permanent sickness of mind and stomach that never leaves a man.

There was a special kind of finality about the slam of that front gate and I could feel something inside me curling up and dying. Some part of me recoiled and shrank as I began to realise that I was different from others. Rejected by society, I was now something to be feared and shunned by decent people: a convict, a number, a robot to be manoeuvred by uniformed men, to be punished.

To enter the inside of the prison one passes through the North Gate, a sort of blockhouse with walls four feet thick. It's always dark and gloomy there, depressing as a tomb. Everybody who passes through those sinister gates feels the same ominous chill. So much suffering has begun in that small space. The prison armoury is also located there, behind an iron grill. Just four years earlier a guard had been shot to death there during a jailbreak. Later the prisoner responsible was executed in the county jail a few miles away.

From the North Gate we were paraded, under the watchful eyes of the guard towers, the distance of a city block along a snow-ploughed roadway to a small concrete building adjacent to the three-stories East Cell Block. Here was 'Reception and Discharge' and we were promptly mugged and fingerprinted and outfitted in ill-fitting grey denim with numbers stamped on every piece of clothing. My number was Y-3782 and the Y before my number stood for youth.

It also meant that the guards would watch me a little closer in an effort to keep the prison wolves away from my heels. I was to learn later that out of a population of one thousand men there were only four of us under the age of eighteen, which meant that I would have to guard my ass closely.

After being issued the meagre equipment necessary for the day-to-day survival, we were lined up and paraded off, this time to the dome where we would be assigned a cell. Minutes later we fish were gathered around the infamous brass bell on its pedestal in the centre of the dome listening to the keeper give us our welcome speech. Standing there, with my bedroll tucked under my arm, I hardly listened so engrossed was I at the sight of the shiny bell, having heard so many unkind stories about it in the county jail. To the guards, who were always grouped around it, the bell took on the proportions of a cherished symbol of authority. To the cons it was an object of repugnance and outrage, an unjustifiable punishment, a brass monster that we were convinced had been designed solely to shatter our nerves with its loud and strident ringing. Its grating sound controlled all our movements: woke us up, sent us off to work, to lunch, to supper, to secure the count, dictating when we must dummy up and when we must go to bed. Its clang reverberated throughout the cavernous dome one hundred and twenty-seven times a day! Multiply that by three hundred and sixty-five days a year and it is not hard to imagine how the damn thing could drive a man stir-crazy.

'Boy, I'm talking to you!' I nearly jumped out of my skin as the keeper jabbed me on the chest with a long key. 'You pay attention when I'm talking or I'll run you through that door over there.'

I followed the direction in which his eye was pointing, a closed door about twenty feet away. Stencilled above the doorway was the word DISSOCIATION.

'Okay, lad, just so you know.' His voice was now less gruff. He handed me a blue card which stated my religion, name, number, sentence and cell location, and told me to place it in the slot above my cell door. 'You'll be bedding down on 21-4-H. That's up top, last cell in the back.'

Lugging my bedroll and gear, I trudged wearily up the four flights of stairs and down a long, narrow tier that had a handrail along the outside to give a dubious feeling of security. At last I arrived before my cell – my home for the next five years.

The population was out to work. Come supper I would begin to meet the people who wore numbers. There was no mess hall, just a large kitchen where trays were shoved out to you through narrow slots as each con passed silently through the jug-up line. You had two choices: eat what was on the heavy metal tray or leave it. All meals were consumed alone in the cells; our utensils consisted of one large spoon. There was no butter and just a watery tea for dinner and lunch. The heavy steel mugs were used as much for battering in heads as they were for drinking.

Idly picking at the contents of my supper tray, I was lost in thought when a voice queried almost in my ear, 'Whatcha bring down kid?'

I whirled around on my wooden chair, stared through the bars at the grizzled old convict and answered cautiously, mindful of the tips I received concerning prison wolves. He was obviously one of my neighbours trooping in with his supper. I understood he wanted to know how much time I was doing, so I told him.

'A fin eh? I guess that can be a long haul for a boy of your age. Hey! You're the kid I read about in the paper, ain't you? The one who was driving around the country with pete and the big shotgun?'

I nodded.

'Aw, don't worry about a thing. You'll shake this bit off in no time, you'll see. Gotta go. Need anything, let me know. I sleep four doors up from you. Be seeing ya.'

My first lesson. Never ask a guy what crime he has committed. Ask him how much time he's doing, or how much he's brought with him, or how much the judge threw at him. If he wishes, he can tell you what he did, but never, never ask a guy directly. You can pretty well tell a guy's beef from the time he's shaking. The odd ones, like the diddlers, are fairly easy to spot because they seldom talk or carry themselves with any self-respect.

More and more guys paused before my cell door to say 'Hi' and to ask if I needed anything, and if I did, to remember that they bunked down on the same tier as I did. It was good to know that I was among people who wanted to do something for me other than crucify me. I was now living among grown men and it was up to me to start acting like one.

I wasn't dumb and I was acutely aware that a lot of these guys had been without a woman for a long, long time – long enough to want to make a pass at me if I showed that I was

134

interested. No convict in a Canadian penitentiary would ever take the chance of raping a kid, especially a straight kid, for fear of being killed by his own kind. It was part of the code.

I sensed the prison atmosphere slowly. It was one of constant restraint, of suspicion and bitterness and secrecy. Men let down their guard only in intimate conversation with other cons. They all wore a look that puzzled me for a while. I couldn't begin to guess the cause of the unseeing, lost-in-contemplation vagueness. Later I discovered it was the defensive expression of old-timers, choosing not to see the all-too-familiar surroundings and depressing faces around them. It was a look that grew with the years. One day I realised that I was wearing it too.

Sleep was one way a guy could escape the daily pressures of doing time and the deep hatred and gut-wrenching frustration. Even from the beginning the individual cells were okay by me, and I appreciated their approach to privacy more with each passing year. We could go to bed after the count whenever we felt the yawn to do so, turning out the light and trying to escape reality in sleep. Or we could read, pace the floor or listen to music over the headphones. A prisoner could also wish that he either hadn't done it or at least hadn't been caught.

Sleepless nights in prison made me a specialist on sleep-talking and screams. I didn't know that a grown man could scream like that. During the first night I was brought wide awake about two in the morning by the long, agonised scream of some poor bugger clawing his way out of a nightmare. Since then I've heard them all. I've heard terror in screams that left me shaking nervously for minutes afterwards. I don't know what caused their nightmares, but they really helped me in a way. They brought home the knowledge that I had no corner on grief and trouble and pain. I was growing up in a hurry.

The work board assigned me to the mailbag department. In every prison in Canada this division was the rebel shop and any fish who possessed a dubious conduct record ended up there. Your work and your conduct would be closely observed for three months and if you kept a low profile you

135

could again appear before the work board and request a better work location. However the chances were that you would get into some kind of trouble, either with a shop instructor or in a fight with another con. There were sixty guys in the shop – of all types. Supervising was a shop foreman and two floormen. In an elevated cage in a far corner was the armed guard. Our job was to make and repair mailbags by the hundreds of thousands and repair and paint mailboxes. There was a constant hum of heavy-duty sewing machines and conversations punctuated by the odd outburst. The smoke periods in the morning and in the afternoons were reserved for bull sessions, and the exchange of gossip and rumours humming over the grapevine.

Food was terrible and it was a rare night when we didn't go to bed hungry and a rare meal when we wouldn't have taken the joint apart if a leader were to yell out, 'Let's tear the kitchen apart!'

Many things plagued us, but our empty bellies bothered us most. We were not exactly starving – starvation makes men listless, makes them dread violence. We were just plain, everlastingly hungry, and this made us an angry bunch of convicts. Water took the place of food; cons are the greatest water drinkers on earth.

Six months later I got a transfer to the tailor shop. Working conditions were a little better, but I was still pushing a sewing machine. I also got a cell change into one of the older blocks inside the dome.

My cell was so narrow that even at seventeen I had no problem stretching out my arms and touching both walls. The only furniture was a narrow steel bunk fastened to the wall by a short chain. In order to eat at the small table the bunk had to be hooked up to the wall to make room beside the cold water tap, brass sink and hundred-year-old toilet. The chair was a simple, folding affair that caused backache. There was very little else in the cell apart from a couple of grey army blankets, one sheet, a lumpy pillow and a thin mattress. The only opening for light and air was the narrow, barred gate thirty inches wide set in a concrete arch three feet thick! The windows, which were beyond my second floor gallery and set into the outer corridor wall, towered

136

thirty feet high. Because of tight security all the windows could be opened only a few inches, which was not enough to let in sufficient air, but wide enough to let through a large variety of birds from pigeons to seagulls. Along about 5 o'clock each morning they would band together in one big, deafening chorus of shrill chirping, cooing and squawking, until a guy was ready to pull his hair out. The administration did not offer to put up screens.

A lot of the cons fixed up their cells with knick-knacks, primitive and crude by some standards, but of great value to us. I wasted no time getting my drum into shape. I painted the inside a new coat of regulation green and white. I polished the brass sink until it gleamed. I waxed the concrete floor, made shelves, scored some cabinets from the carpenter shop, made curtains from blue canvas air mail sacks and finally padded my chair with material smuggled out of the upholstery department. Like everyone else, I also pasted pin-ups on my wall – Sophia Loren being my all-time favourite – and stocked up with books from the library. To cut down on the painful glare from the bare, dangling light bulb I traded three bales of tobacco for a skilfully-designed Chinese lantern made from coloured cardboard. A guy had to be careful how he splurged his nine cents a day. A butt wouldn't finish rolling on the ground before it was scooped up and hoarded by some nicotine fiend.

In those days the first thing you did when you moved into a drum was to make a heavy cover for the lid-less toilet. The maze of sewers below was infested with bloated rats as big around as a groundhog and with big yellow teeth. If you forgot to cover your toilet you might suddenly wake up about 3 o'clock in the morning to find half your toe chewed away! When that happened the six hundred cons sleeping in the dome would be rudely awakened by a scream of rage or blind hysteria which would reverberate through the hollow confines until he either worked up the guts to kill the rat or was dragged out of the cell by the guard.

Going berserk was the wrong thing to do because it also sent the rat into a frenzy, so much so that it would forget how to get out and attack blindly, too fat to squeeze through the bars. With all that furniture breaking and

137

cursing and screaming you'd think it was a death battle between two rogue elephants.

Not only were rats running amok inside the network of underground tunnels, but there also were untamed cats. In the old days when the cattle barn was inside the walls, the cats were tame. But not the new breed, born and raised in the sewers! They were scarred from battling for territory with the rats. They would venture forth from their underground lairs only late at night. Often we could hear cats fighting among themselves for scraps from the garbage cans and it was very sad. But there was nothing anyone could do because it was impossible to capture one of the wild creatures without killing it or being attacked. It was believed there were tunnels deep underground where no human had trod for a hundred years. None of the guards wanted to go down there with just a net and a flashlight and so the cats kept the rat population from taking over the joint.

Everybody remembers the time that Shorty smuggled in a three foot snake from the quarry outside the walls and how after a week of having it for a pet the keeper caught him playing with it and ordered him to flush it down his toilet. One hour and ten cells away this blond, willowy drag-queen called Linda was busy painting her toenails when suddenly she got the eerie feeling that something was watching her from the back of her cell. Slowly turning her head around she was thunderstruck to see a beady-eyed snake slithering over the side of her toilet bowl and plopping on to the cell floor! Her terror was so great that she just flipped her wig right there and then and even after the guards wrestled her down to the hospital Linda didn't stop screaming. I guess she had a phobia about snakes.

The cells on each gallery could be locked or unlocked by spinning two spoked wheels outside the locked barrier at the end of the range. Hinged to the concrete arch enclosing our cell doors was a vertical locking bar with a protruding horizontal handle. The overhead travelling bar had a series of slots, so that when the needle indicator beside the wheel showed that an open slot was directly above the vertical locking bar, the cell doors could be opened by raising the protruding handle a few inches, at the same instant the prisoner within must push his gate outwards. However, if the action was to lock the doors the travelling bar would then be in a position so that there would be no open slots above the locking bar. It was a simple but ingenious device ironically contrived by a fellow convict a century ago.

Even when the doors were in the unlocked position the guy within the cell could not reach out through the bars to raise the handle because it was inaccessible and that's where the tappers would come into the picture. An inmate tapper was assigned to each floor level and his job at the sound of the bell and the spinning of the wheel was to race down the range raising each handle as speedily as possible and without missing a stroke. These guys were as nimble as mountain goats and had the sleight-of-hand dexterity of pickpockets. Snapping up the handles a few inches into a notch gave off a staccato Tap, tap, tap, sound for thirty-two successive ranges, each one followed at the sound of the bell. The tappers' movements were so finely timed that if by chance one of the handles was in a raised position there was a grave danger of a broken wrist. The tappers were also responsible for passing out hot water at night for the guys to shave. They were also an intricate part of the grapevine.

As I said no self-respecting con would risk his health and his reputation muscling a young prisoner to be his sweet kid, but then again there were other more subtle ways. The basic trick was to egg a kid into a game of chance, such as cards, get him hooked real heavy, and then offer to clean the slate for certain favours. If the kid refused, then the guy was justified in beating him up for welshing on a debt.

In prison a con looking for sexual outlet with a sweet kid is called a wolf. He needn't be a homosexual nor necessarily is the kid, who with his adolescent smile, his unsophisticated manners, soft skin and aesthetic proportions, embodies the female. However, for one reason or another, a marriage of convenience might take place. A wolf will protect his sweet kid with his life and an intimacy and friendship so loyal as to defy belief can spring up between the two whom society has rejected as losers. They feel that it's just the two of them against the prison jungle and thus they help each other to survive and share each other's loneliness and hopes for the

139

future. The kid's ol' man will make all sorts of sacrifices in order to provide the boy with little gifts and extra food. More than anything else he will make very certain that the kid stays out of trouble (because the lock-up in turn means separation). Because it has a steadying effect guards usually leave this type of relationship alone.

Any kid who comes to the pen and who does not possess a strong mind, and a really tough core, indeed feels very much alone and extremely vulnerable and insecure. Most kids there have come up the hard way through orphanages and training schools and are old hands when it comes to having sex with guys. Striving for attention, acceptability, security, and some sort of recognition, they accept the best offer that comes their way. The better looking and the more class a kid has the more likelihood that he will get hooked up with one of the tougher and more popular convicts inside the joint. One wolf cutting another wolf's turf is frowned upon in the inmate code and if he gets a shank though his heart, nobody will feel sorry for him.

The real homosexuals in prison are the drag-queens who have no place in their lives for women and don't hesitate to let the whole world know about it. They are real swingers and you would have to be blind not to be able to spot them around the cell-blocks and on the yards, swishing around gaily in their tailor-made clothes talking their fool heads off. Surprisingly their crimes are always for something other than sex and they have a reputation for being very solid. Thus they are completely accepted within the prison culture, even by the guards who will sometimes pat one on the fanny for a laugh. They all have stage names and work either in the tailor shop or the laundry. That way they can keep clean and well-dressed and also take care of their old man's duds. Because of their hunger for men and sex they are responsible for most fights and shivings.

In my case I was a super straight kid with a Puritan's outlook on sex and I wasn't giving anyone the opportunity to lug me. Until I came to jail I didn't even know that there was such a thing as a queer; that was a real eye-opener for me! I was plagued daily with offers of marriage, money and food, until my mind was reeling with the magnitude of it all.

140

Gradually the wolves came to realise that I did not go that route and that I was a confirmed loner and they started getting off my back and showing some respect. But by then I had already started my eerie withdrawal from the world of reality.

I didn't notice it at first but I was talking less and less and seeking privacy more and more. By the time I had served one year behind the walls of Kingston Penitentiary, I was a mass of inner hostility, a bubbling volcano full of bewildering emotions. I felt so crowded and surrounded and frustrated and so distrustful of everyone that I soon found myself withdrawing more and more, building walls around myself like a fortress so deep and mighty that none could penetrate.

I had no need for friendship because friendship caused pain. Sick at heart, shielded inside my armour, I lost myself in the mystical world of literature. I joined Sir Edmund Hillary on his historic climb up Mount Everest with his Sherpa guide Tenzing Norkay, conquered the North Pole with Commander Peary, explored caves, deep-sea dived for sunken treasure, visited lost tribes and lost continents, tracked man-eating tigers in India, and followed the abominable snowman high up in the Himalayas. I studied volcanos and earthquakes, psychic phenomena, reincarnation, ghosts, sorcery and hypnosis, and made long treks through the deserts with the French Foreign Legion. By the time March 1957 rolled around my retreat from the living world was complete. I felt scared to talk, thinking that if I remained silent I would be safe from the outside world. I stopped talking altogether and did not utter another word for two years!

The day I stopped speaking was the day that I started having migraine headaches so severe that during my waking hours my existence became a struggle not to throw myself over the railing from the fouth range as so many others had done before me. The dull throbbing would leave my head only late at night after I managed to fall asleep. When the wake-up bell sounded at 6 a.m. the following morning and my eyes popped open, the waves would engulf me once more. By 7 a.m. I would have washed in cold water, swept

141

my floor, hooked my bunk up against the wall, folded my one sheet and two blankets neatly from three pegs on the wall according to the rules, and would be waiting in the chill of a false dawn for the tapper to spring my door open for breakfast.

Stepping out of cell No. 7 I would join the silent ranks of grey denim shuffling down the tier to the circular dome with its maze of stairways, passing uniformed guards along the way and formations of prisoners returning to their drums with their jug-up. All around us would be the sounds of footfalls, ringing bells, tapping of door handles, but no voices because of the 'No Talking' rule. In single file we moved down a cell-block and turned right into a narrow passageway fronting the kitchen where a blank wall displayed three small wickets from which we were fed like robots. From the first slot emerged an iron tray containing a scoop of jam made in the joint cannery, one dry piece of toast with a small pat of margarine, three slices of home-made dummy, and a scoop of CNR strawberries. Next came a bowl of porridge and an iron mug full of steaming chicory coffee, the only one we would have that day. Blind to what was on our tray, we would stumble back to our drum and push the stuff through the hole in our faces while a guard carefully made his way down the tier making the first of numerous counts that day, prompting some sage to comment that they 'feed us like swine and count us like diamonds'.

Eight o'clock – the doors would again swing open, this time for work – single file and silence all the way. By 11.30 a.m. we would be back inside our cells with our dinner tray, sipping a watery tea and picking at lima beans with a spoon. Most of the cons would spend the following ninety minutes listening to music over their radio headsets. At one o'clock the doors would again swing open for work. Come 3 o'clock a whistle would blow in the shop and this time we would parade out to the yard for forty-five minutes of fresh air and recreation. By 4 p.m. we would again be in our drums with our supper tray – deadlocked until morning. You could read, listen to the radio, pace a few steps back and forth, exercise, dream, talk to yourself, watch your neighbours

142

through their reflections in the windows, crack up and smash your cell furniture, slash yourself with a razor blade to break the monotony, hang yourself or join in on range conversations until the silence bell sounded at 7 o'clock. One final ring at 9.45 let us know that the lights were going out in fifteen minutes. This would be followed by a gurgling of toilets, running taps, coughs and curses, and then a long silence until morning, interrupted at intervals with night-mares or outbursts as one prisoner warned another to come out swinging when the gates opened in the morning.

Two years passed. It had been one year since I'd stopped talking, even during visits with my folks. In the shops and on the yard and in the office of the shrink I was the subject of many conversations because of my seemingly inex-plicable behaviour. Fish arriving in the joint at first assumed that I was mute. Yet although I was so harshly withdrawn within myself, I always had a quick smile for anybody who addressed me kindly. But at night alone in my cave no smile would touch my face, often silent tears, but no smile. Loneli-ness sat heavily on my shoulders and my throbbing temples made sleep more and more difficult to attain. I tried stren-uous calisthenics until I exhausted myself.

I had no enemies in the prison and the toughest cons and guards would go out of their way to help me. There were four guys who had made themselves my friends. Skinny Billy was a hospital orderly who walked with a terrible limp, having stopped a Horseman's bullet during a bank robbery. Billy was a classic hood, an old-timer who possessed a staunch code of criminal ethics and was thus highly respected by other cons. Sitting down in the dusty yard against the prison wall he would tell me stories about what it was like in the old days, finding in me a willing and uninterrupting listener.

There was also another Bill from whom I learned a lot but this time from an academic point of view. Bill was a burly ex-schoolteacher serving a life term for a crime which he never volunteered to tell me about. His sharp intellect and gentleman's ways belied his pugnacious appearance. Quiet and peace-loving he now worked in the prison library and took it upon himself to talk to me about the ways of the world while we paced the yard. He chose books for me to read. He was a lonely man who kept his feelings to himself but his face would always light up and a smile crease his face at the sight of me.

'And how are things with you, o silent one? Cheerful?' 'Good boy!' he'd exclaim at my nod. 'Well, what's it going to be today? We were anatomising the splitting of atoms that last time we talked.' He would then string off a series of subjects until I nodded agreement. 'Okay then, let's blast off into the universe on a mind-expanding excursion.' I really liked Bill.

When I took up the sport of weight-lifting I spent most of my time with Chuck and Jake. Chuck was in his early thirties, over six feet tall, with narrow hips and massive shoulders and biceps, so impressive that they looked like they were chiselled from rock. Topping this threatening frame was a small savage-looking head with piercing, blue eyes that glared out at the world. Compulsively clean and tailored, Chuck was aloof. He did not like the average person and made no bones about it. He had to have respect for you as a man before he'd think of you as a friend. He had the intelligence to be a master criminal or whatever he wanted to be. Chuck belonged to an elite clique of convicts who understood the inner workings of a bank vault and how to bypass sophisticated alarms. They spent most of their time in jail gathered in a corner of the yard exchanging information that might one day open that lucky door to a perfect million dollar heist. Chuck was also a veteran of the Korean war and carried a gruesome scar across his back from a skirmish with an enemy machine-gun. His temper was his worst enemy; he was serving eight years for crippling a stranger in a bar-room brawl.

Jake, in his early twenties, was Jewish and good-looking, but plagued with acne. He had curly-blond hair, a tremendous physique, and loved fun. Jake was shaking six years for B & E and was always bragging about easy women and yellow convertibles and flexing his large biceps telling you to, 'Eat your heart out!' He was one of four barbers inside the joint who travelled from shop to shop cutting hair. It

144

was an ideal occupation for him because it gave him the chance to argue.

Weight-lifting brought the three of us together as friends. Situated in the centre of the big yard and separated from the baseball diamond by an iron railing was the weight pit. It was one of the most active spots inside the prison, come rain or snow. I started a few months after my arrival in KP and at a body weight of one hundred and fifty-five pounds and a height of five feet nine and one half inches I had a normal enough build.

What was not normal was the black rage within me and I desperately needed something to dispel it. I found the heavy barbells a perfect distraction and like a drowning man I threw myself at them with a fury and a vengeance. I also discovered to my great relief that the more I strained, the less my head would ache so lifting weights became a daily habit.

It soon became obvious that in a year or two I would not only possess awesome strength but I would also have the physique to go with it. However my basic reason for lifting had absolutely nothing to do with something as plastic as that, it was for the easing effect it had on my mind. Nevertheless on field day I won first prize in the middle-weight class for strength. Using just one hand I could jerk a barbell weighing 187 pounds over my head and hold it there for long seconds.

The best lifters worked out in close-knit groups of three or four. They had their own little spot. Working out with Chuck and Jake was the inmate weight-lifting instructor in charge of the pit. In his thirties, Lou was shaking a fifteen year bit for armed robbery and had one of the softest jobs in the joint, in so far as he was his own boss and spent every day lounging on the yard and shooting the breeze. Lou was a powerhouse and had a heavy muscular build, dark curly hair, and always sported a deep tan. He had an easy-going nature and was very popular with the guys. A health nut who would not eat meat, his job gave him the freedom to move around the prison and he could usually be found at the back door of the kitchen, mooching canned goods and fresh fruit.

145

The three of them, Chuck, Jake, and Lou, observed me working out on the weights alone day after day in a grimly dedicated fashion and their respect for me grew, especially in view of the fact that I was so quiet. So one day they called me over and asked me to join their group. Chuck had no use for queers, so that was the clincher; Nobody bothered making passes at me after that because I was Chuck's friend. The three of them watched me very closely, always fearful that I might do the dutch by plunging off the range. There were also times when my volcanic thoughts outweighed the company of my friends; at times like that I'd suddenly wander away from them to a far corner of the yard, lost inside the cobwebs of my own prison. My friends were accustomed to my sudden changes in personality and took it all in stride. Even now when I look back, in retrospect it seems eerie that I could spend so many hours a day with them, not utter a word, yet be completely and wholly a part of their conversations.

One day in the summer of 1957 Lou was paroled, after serving eight of his fifteen years. His going left the pit job up for grabs and everybody was reaching frantically. Jake wanted it but Chuck didn't because as head tailor he was indispensable. However the decision was up to Lou to recommend a successor for the job and to my great surprise and pleasure he chose me! I would now be in a position to lift until my muscles screamed for mercy. Lou left with a wave and a wide grin and we were glad and yet sad to see him go.

The Yard was situated in the south-east corner of the prison. Not a blade of grass could be seen there; just dusty earth. Here the guys let off steam for forty-five minutes during each workday, and mornings and afternoons during the week-ends. There was baseball, handball, weight-lifting, and horseshoes. You could also just sit around in the shade of the wall or pace back and forth in the walking area and participate in the biggest pastime of all, 'One thousand and one ways to better thieving.'

The groups were there all over the yard, under the watchful eyes of the gun towers, while the yard bulls cruising in pairs disbanded any large cliques forming among the milling crowds. The prisoners would be either sitting, walking or standing around in tight little circles, all discussing the pros and cons of crime. To the experienced eye it was obvious that each clique was from a different level of prison society and that's what made a walk on the yard so intriguing.

The only characters on the yard who did not discriminate were the bookies who floated to all levels with ease and gusto. Large sums of money would be wagered every weekend when our all-star baseball team competed against a civilian team. A large sign behind the backstop declared that this was the home of the Saints – and what a colourful team they were! The Sunday afternoon ball games were usually broadcast through a local radio station with the sounds of screaming convicts shouting, 'Murder the bum!' in the background.

A few boxing matches were also aired and I still wonder to this day what went on in the minds of Kingston citizens when they heard their popular sports announcer's voice rising to a fever pitch as he described an incredible scene: '. . . and the one they call The Monster is taking a frightful beating about the head and body by his skilful and wily opponent who is dancing circles around him and flicking punches at will. Ooooow . . . the Monster now has his opponent down on the canvas and he's chewing his nose! . . . Now he's on his feet . . . A right boot to the head, followed by another boot to the ribs . . .'

Monster lost the fight for his poor display of sportsmanship.

I was transferred to the sports gang the same day Lou walked out the front gate. (Seventeen years later a crime commission named Lou a kingpin in organised crime in Canada.) The sports gang is always the most sought after unit, mostly because of the leisure time it gives a guy to play sports. The convicts working on it are usually the best athletes, the most popular guys, or the toughest guys.

The sports gang is also the pulse beat of the convict grapevine. Their job is to issue and take care of sports equipment and to maintain the baseball field and the grounds in general. Time in between is spent drinking contraband coffee inside the old stone shed, which is officially the sports

147

equipment shack, on plotting and shooting the breeze, sunning on the bleachers, or just kicking a football around. In winter it's shovelling snow, hibernating inside the century-old shack and trying to scrounge up fuel for the old pot bellied stove.

Counting me, there were thirteen cons on the gang, the most varied conglomeration of characters in the entire institution. It was like an exclusive club of rebels and madmen where anything and everything did happen. Many were on the warden's Black List and he was always pointing his swagger stick at us from a distance and ordering the tower guards to watch our every move, on the assumption that we were potential saboteurs. This was probably the reason he removed most of us from the industrial shops. I guess he also figured that by giving the rebels a good job they would be less prone to rocking the boat.

A yard boss would be assigned to the sports gang for thirty days at a time. Guards usually accepted the assignment with the enthusiasm of a soldier ordered to clear a mine field. Sometimes they lasted through the month-long mission and sometimes they did not, depending on how nosey they were. The sports shack was our private clubhouse and there was no welcome mat at the door. About fifty feet square and about the same distance from the baseball field, it was built in the days when convicts wearing chains and dragging an iron ball used to bust big rocks into smaller rocks, then chisel them down into building blocks. Our shack had concrete walls three feet thick, which was one of the reasons it did not burn down in the million dollar riot a few years earlier. Although in an extreme state of decay, the guys loved it and they did their best to make the inside comfortable.

Two doors led into the inner sanctum, opening with ominous squeaks. The first led into a murky outer room where the bulky maintenance equipment was kept in a wild state of disarray. The scarred and battered second door had a sign reading: BEWARE! Stoolies, Diddlers, and Turkeys; Enter at your own risk!

All undesirables avoided the place as if it harboured the Black Plague; while those with a clear conscience clamoured for admission. The yard bull and patrols avoided stepping inside for look-and-see, although they had strict orders to do just that. Best to stay outside where they could be protected by the sentries, especially if the cons inside were guzzling home-made brew. Under the best of circumstances, most of the guys on the sports gang were unstable; but with a bellyful of rot-gut – watch out!

Inside, it looked like an opium den with wisps of smoke spiralling towards a large naked light bulb hanging from the rafters. It took a while for your eyes to adjust to the gloom, for the large, barred window had given up any pretence of passing light through the grimy panes. Lining the walls were huge wooden lockers containing a variety of sports equipment and profusely adorned with pin-ups of Hollywood stars. On the ceiling was a six-foot long, brightly painted, fire-breathing dragon – the work of an inmate artist. In the middle of the floor a pot bellied stove warmed a grimy coffee pot containing hickory grains that were usually rehashed three or four times. For furniture there were half a dozen broken-down chesterfields and stuffed armchairs, all rejects from the upholstery department.

Slouched in those seats sat wild characters right out of a rogues' gallery and twice as unpredictable. Crazy Dean was by far the toughest and the spinniest, a living legend in the joint for pulling off some of the most memorable and hilarious stunts ever. Blond, big, and clean-cut looking, he was about thirty years old and had worked his way up from the orphanages, training schools, reformatory, and finally arrived in the Big House. Along the way he had been strapped and placed in solitary and beaten up by guards so often that Dean just wasn't quite normal anymore. He was what they call 'a product of the penal system'. His body was a mass of scars and he had three bullet holes in his chest, the result of shooting it out with the police with a gun in each fist. Playing baseball, the athletic and very unpredictable Dean would manoeuvre his hard head like a soccer player and permit a high fly ball to bounce off his melon before catching it with his glove, to the merriment of the screaming fans sitting in the bleachers. With Crazy Dean around there were always thrills galore!

One of the best capers that he pulled off took place a few years before I arrived in the joint. The victim of his joke was a pompous little tyrant whom everybody called Hitler because of his slight resemblance and because of his attitude. In those days it was compulsory to do fifteen minutes of general calisthenics in the centre of the baseball field. The hated exercises were carried out under the command of Hitler who was acting as drill instructor. Decked out in a bulky sweater and running shoes and with a whistle dangling around his neck, Hitler would line up a hundred convicts, at a time, in front of him. Flapping around like an overgrown albatross, or grunting through a series of push-ups, he put the guys through their paces. Eventually dissatisfied with being on the same level as the prisoners he decided to have an elevated platform constructed to give himself more stature. He requisitioned the lumber, explained it to the sports gang how he wanted it constructed, and ordered them to put it together.

That of course was a mistake. I mean having Dean and the gang construct his elevation. His suspicions should have been aroused when he saw how enthusiastically these usually lackadaisical fellows tackled the project. The platform grew six feet high and seven feet square, a thing of beauty with gallowslike steps leading up to a podium. On three sides of it was painted a picture of the flag.

The big day came when Hitler, beaming with pride, approached his masterpiece and regally climbed the stairs. At the top he turned like the Almighty himself and faced his throng of sinners with arms spread wide and whistle clenched between his teeth in preparation for the first of the exercises. Eager, knowing, and vengeful eyes followed his every move with bated breath. Pleased with his situation, he blew on his whistle piercing the sweltering midday heat; flapping his legs and arms about he barked, 'C'mon. Let's move it out there! Hup one, hup two, hup three, hup ... Yeeoowww!'

A splintering of wood, a spine-chilling scream, and Hitler disappeared from sight! His act was so sensational and so spectacular that the crowd went nuts with delight. The tower guard got so spooked that he fired a warning shot into the air from his rifle. A minute later, Hitler, looking extremely dishevelled and convulsed with rage, climbed back through the hole, spotted Dean rolling around on the ground overcome with laughter, and screamed at the yard bulls to run Dean into the cooler before he shot him dead.

Another guy on the gang was the one the broadcaster called The Monster. You could always expect him to do something weird. He was big and homely and a street fighter, but he had a loyal and good-hearted side, except when he was put in a position where he'd lose his temper. There were a couple of little guys who were pushing fifty and there was Louis who looked like he was going to lose his pants because of his pot belly. Louis' favourite pastimes were arguing with the screws, making home brew, and shooting crap behind the baseball backstop. There was Benny who was thin and sickly with a leaky valve in his heart and too terrified of hospitals to get the much needed operation. He loved a good joke and was always egging other guys on to do something crazy. There was Indian Bill, tall and thin with a tremendous hawkish nose. It was generally conceded that he was crazy because he always walked and ran backwards as if he didn't have any forward gears. He had accidentally killed his friend in the tailor shop and that was why he was on the gang.

There were also a lot of straight guys on the gang or as straight as could be expected under the circumstances. They were the top athletes in the joint. One guy, Randy, was the best runner the place had ever seen; quiet too. He got released directly on to the street from the sports gang and killed a guy a few days later. The government had him hanged not long afterwards. We read in the paper where he went out like a real champ and for days afterwards all the guys on the gang had long faces.

Talking about dying. One cold winter day everybody was huddled inside the sports shack soaking up warmth from the stove and drinking a potent home brew made from split peas and feeling just plain happy not to be stuck out there in the snowstorm. A non-drinker, I was just sitting on a broken down sofa and trying vainly to massage away a headache. Sitting cross-legged across from me was an old convict with a rubbery face called Happy. He had got no teeth and he loved to make us laugh by making impossible and hilariously funny grimaces. Happy also suffered from serious seizures but on this day, with a belly full of rotgut, he was in a joking mood and had everybody laughing. However, this time he was really outdoing himself, screwing his face up until it just didn't look human anymore. Then to everybody's great surprise Happy keeled over dead! He had been in the grips of an epileptic fit and his faces were for real.

When it came to scrounging up food and fuel the sports gang were very efficient marauders who often skipped their boundaries to go on raiding parties. During the coldest winter months we were allotted only one buggy load of coal; not nearly enough. The shop foremen soon learned to keep their chairs, benches, and anything else that would burn, behind locked doors when we were on the prowl. Our biggest scoop came when the carpentry instructor built a horse trailer and then made the fatal mistake of leaving it parked outside in the snow during a holiday week-end. When he returned to work all that was left were the wheels and the metal frame! Unable to prove conclusively that we were the culprits, he had to settle for hissing at us every time we approached his shop.

We did our best to waylay supply trucks driving in through the back gate, especially those making deliveries to the kitchen. However, our most reliable source of food and coffee came from the cons who worked in the kitchen. Like the industrial shops they too visited the yard on a daily basis for fresh air. Rather than stand around outside in the cold they would invite themselves in the sports shack on the pretence of just bringing contraband to us. Strapped to their bodies would be everything from eggs to coffee and of course it was most welcome. The five-man inmate Grievance Committee whose elected function was to mediate with the administration on behalf of inmates did most of their plotting inside the sports shack.

Kingston Pen in those days did not have a gymnasium where the guys could go for recreation during the winter. The weekly movie was viewed inside the chapel. The only outdoor sports functions during the long, dreary months were soccer, weight-lifting and handball in the snow. No matter how cold it was, Chuck, Jake, and myself never missed a day's workout in the weight pit, which I had to keep clear of ice and snow. Bundled up in as many clothes as we could get out hands on, we sure had healthy lungs.

By the summer of 1958 I was still mute and terrified of uttering a single syllable for fear that my little world would come caving in. My visits with my dad, mother, and little sister and brother were strictly one-sided conversations. They marvelled at my physique, dark tan, and the way my hair was turning prematurely grey. They soothed me with words of encouragement telling me that I would be home soon.

On several occasions, the head psychiatrist invited my parents right inside the heart of the prison to his office and in turn tried to ease their minds about my peculiar behaviour. The shrink was believed to be a very influential man and he convinced my folks and me that he would have me out on parole by early 1958. He even arranged for me to see a very important psychiatrist once a week while on parole, free of charge. He contended that being forced to grow up too soon in a jungle atmosphere was causing my withdrawal. He reassured them that a few months in the normal world would set me back to normal again.

My parole never did materialise and everyone was dismayed. My friends on the sports gang were ready to grab a hostage and demand my release. The day-by-day waiting for the parole to arrive drove me even deeper into my shell and at night alone in my cell my head would hurt so much that I'd sit on the floor at the rear of my drum and holding my head and groaning I would rock myself all right.

Outside of my cell I kept busy all the time, lifting barbells, playing five hours of handball every day, throwing a football, playing horseshoes, batting flies and grounders for the Saints during practice sessions, sharing precious minutes with a friend, or sometimes just looking for a corner to hide in.

Crazy Dean never ceased to do something wild every once in a while and he had plenty of nuts to assist him. One summer he and The Monster were raking the baseball

153

diamond when somebody pointed out some civilians in the south-east tower pointing their movie cameras at us. In the blink of an eye the two rascals disappeared behind the backstop, emerging a moment later balls naked. They started running across the baseball field with The Monster swinging wildly at Dean with a baseball bat, shouting, 'Take my cherry will ya!'

The cameraman was so shocked and rattled that when the CBC director shouted at him to cover the action, the camera fell over on its side and he, in turn, tumbled over it. Only the metal railing prevented both from falling into the yard. Dean was again hustled off to the cooler, but this time with The Monster for company.

In the fall of 1958 Dean did something so crazy that it may still be talked about. The victim was again the infamous Hitler. Although eight years had passed since Dean sabotaged his platform, Hitler was still sulking and casting about for ways to get even not only with Dean but with the whole sports gang. When he took charge of the gang for a thirty day stint in October he thought he had at last found a way. A water main had erupted directly in the centre of the baseball diamond and already a large portion of the earth had collapsed. Since it was in the sports gang territory Hitler ordered us to dig a trench six feet deep and forty feet long. We argued that two-thirds of the digging was unnecessary because it was obvious where the exact location of the problem was.

Cracking his imaginary whip, Hitler shouted, 'You'll all dig that goddammit hole or goddammit you'll all end up in the goddammit cooler!' And so we dug and cursed and dug some more.

By the third day, Dean's devilish imagination rewarded him once more. It had rained the night before and by mid-afternoon we were a muddy mess, slipping and sliding down in the trench. Where Hitler sat in the bleachers, he couldn't see directly down into the hole, but he could count the shovel motions. If we slowed down he would bellow at us.

Suddenly Dean, in an excited voice full of anticipation said, 'Okay, let's get on with it!' Lying flat on his back in the mud he then poured red paint all over his shirt front, his

154

face, and his hands. Roy and Indian Bill completed the gory scene by lifting a huge rock gently on to his chest. Seconds later blood curdling screams burst from the trench; the prison seemed to recoil and then hold its breath.

Dropping his cigar Hitler rushed madly over to the embankment. Peering down, he suddenly bit his knuckles and gave a sharp cry of his own.

Grasping the rock and staring up at Hitler with tortured eyes Dean whispered, 'It's all your fault; I'm going to die . . . You murderer!'

'Oh my God. No, it's not true! Goddammit, I didn't want you to get hurt.'

'You're lying! Oh, oh, oh,' he groaned. 'I'm dying.'

'Goddammit men, get that rock off his chest. Don't just stand there!' yelled Hitler, scrambling down into the hole. In his frantic efforts to lift the boulder he tore the ass out of his pants. 'Oh, you poor fool; you poor, poor fool,' Hitler was crooning and to everyone's great surprise he had tears in his eyes. When the rock was rolled off Dean's chest he immediately scrambled to his feet, scurried up the side of the trench, and running towards the Dome he waved his arms in the air bellowing, 'Help! Help! Hitler wants to kill me.'

His eyes half-crazed with astonishment, Hitler also scrambled up with his underwear sticking through his pants and started running after him and shouting, 'Come back you fool! Goddammit Dean, I don't hate you!'

A few minutes later Dean was breathlessly pounding on the door to the cooler demanding to be admitted! He was convinced that Hitler would shoot him this time. For that little caper the warden sentenced Dean to twenty-one days on bread and water.

The biggest and strongest convict in the joint was a mountain of a man called Red who weighed in the neighbourhood of three hundred pounds. He had biceps that measured a full twenty-one inches around and an enormous chest so strong that his lifts were just a few pounds below world records. He was also a wrestler. A patch of carrot hair and thick spectacles made his appearance only a little less threatening. He was a voracious reader and consumed as many as three.

books a day. A quiet man, he did not mix with the others. Since his job was cleaner in the change room he was more or less his own boss with the privacy to read and even to lift weights. Chuck was his best friend and sometimes on weekends Red would stroll out to the yard and do a work-out with us, to the great satisfaction of the gathering crowds. Red was in a night club once, the story goes, when a pimp was beating up a girl so viciously that Red felt compelled to intervene. Afterwards in terror of the pimp she followed Red up to his room. Two hours later the pimp showed up with gun in hand to demand his woman or else. Angry words were exchanged and without warning the pimp started squeezing off shots from his revolver and five bullets slammed into Red's enormous chest. The pimp's look of savagery was suddenly transformed into a mask of horror as Red kept shuffling towards him, reaching out with his huge paws. As the sixth bullet went wild and blew a finger off Red's hand, his assailant backed out into the hallway and was turning to flee when those hands latched on to him! Like a wounded grizzly Red squeezed the pimp and just before passing out he picked the guy up and threw him down three flights of stairs. They both survived!

In the spring of 1959 I suddenly regained my voice and it was Red's ferocity that was indirectly responsible for jarring me out of my shell. The incident took place during our weekly shower at the 'car-wash' on the second floor of the new pre-release dormitory building. Everybody referred to the tiled room as the car-wash because the actual showering facilities were designed in the shape of a horseshoe. Stripping naked at a bench and stuffing our soiled clothing into a basket we would push the contents through a nearby window wicket – shouting our number so that the duds could be exchanged for fresh items. Amid billows of steam and completely naked, we would be fed slowly into the maze-like horseshoe that contained sixteen shower nozzles operated by two guards on a raised platform. Urged on by the screws and the long line of bodies behind us we would move sporadically from spray to spray, stopping only for short seconds, until finally we would pop out on the far side next to a window wicket where our basket of clean clothing

156

would be awaiting us. Moving to a bench, we would dry off and get dressed.

Either Chuck or Red usually joined me for my weekly shower to holler my number and to make me feel less ill-at-ease, for at seventeen I was acutely aware that hungry eyes were crawling over my back. Nobody ever made it obvious and so there was never anything I could do, except wish that I were somewhere else. On this day Red was behind me and Chuck was in front. Behind Red was a big muscular black man with skull-like features and ready fists. Fairly new to the joint he had beaten up a couple of guys and already it was obvious he was building himself a reputation and, being a boxer, he had the clout.

We had been standing there for a while, amid the yelling and wisecracking, glistening with perspiration when the black man made the deadly mistake of whispering in Red's ear, 'Man, o' man, how would you like to get into something like that, eh?' He was pointing to my ass when big Red pivoted around with surprising speed and caught the guy a bone-jarring backhand that sent him reeling backwards into the crowd. While the onlookers scrambled to get out of the way, the black man was wiping blood and shock from his face with a thick forearm. Red handed his thick glasses to Chuck as the guy raised his dukes in a boxer's stance and slowly shuffled forward. Closing in he made a feint with his left and was following through with a tremendous right when Red brushed the punch aside and latched on to him. With a hip throw Red flipped his opponent who then went cartwheeling through the steamy atmosphere and landed on his face. Dropping quickly to his knees Red immediately seized his dazed and winded prey and pinned his head between his thighs – face down. He then wrapped his powerful arms around the astonished con's torso and started to squeeze in an upside-down bear hug.

Coming to his senses too late, the guy started to struggle, flailing with his legs and pawing with his hands in a desperate attempt to break loose, but it was fast becoming too late! His struggles and gurgling sounds were subsiding and he was going under for sure when two platform guards pushed their way through the naked crowd and started shouting and tugging at Red to make him let the guy go. With a roar and a flex of his muscles he sent the two screws reeling into the crowd where satisfied that they had done their duty they ran off for reinforcements. Like a man possessed, Red now shifted his attack to the black man's throat. Fingers curled into talons, he buried them deep into the guy's windpipe and started twisting and gouging until blood gushed forth from the anguished mouth.

Bewildered, I stared wide-eyed at the two naked giants – one stark white, the other jet black – while all around us sweating convicts stared hungrily, fearful of missing the killing thrust. It was then that something convulsed deep inside me and I suddenly found myself grasping Red's arms and shouting, 'No, Red, don't. You'll hang!'

Chuck was now beside me and together we slowly broke Red's grip and hauled him over to the bench. He was just beginning to come back to his old self by the time the black man was hauled away on a stretcher. About a dozen guards then appeared at the exit door armed with clubs and the one that got along best with the convicts walked over and said: 'We're gonna have to take you to the hole Red, okay?'

'Gimme a minute to get dressed.'

'Sure Red, take your time,' said the guard walking away.

Warmth was flowing once more into his ruddy features when he turned to Chuck and myself and said: 'Me on short time and I almost blew it. Thanks guys.' Then ruffling my hair he added: 'Leastwise, we got Roger talking again.'

My face flushed crimson red; echoing through my mind were the words, 'Leastwise we got Roger talking again.'

Three months later the Queen of England visited Canada to inaugurate the opening of the Seaway and the resulting general amnesty was enough to terminate my sentence. To shake hands with my friends who wore numbers was painful because I was going home and they were staying behind.

CHAPTER ELEVEN

June 25, 1959: A tremendous feeling of exhilaration filled my whole being the moment that I stepped through that big front gate into a perfect summer day. I stood at the edge of the old road that led into the city as shivers of anxiety made my legs tremble and perspiration break out on my brow. For the first time in five years I was about to venture into the world and I wasn't sure if I could make the grade or stand the pressures.

I was free, or was I? What about the jailer within myself? Him I must satisfy or be confined more solidly than the strongest prison. For me freedom was an obsession, but one that always remained just beyond reach.

'Hey, you down there?' inquired a guard from the wall, jerking me out of my reverie. 'C'mon. Let's move it! No loitering.'

Grimacing at the bitter irony of being ordered to leave the prison I stepped out from the shadow of the wall, caught the guard's eye and made a sharp gesture with my right thumb. I then sauntered on down the road with my suit coat draped over my shoulder and my flight bag gripped in my hand.

One hour later I was sitting on a bench in a beautiful tree shaded park in Kingston. Like a taut spring I was slowly unwinding. Across the street was the General Hospital and all these people were passing by; my attention was especially centred on the nurses, some of whom were dressed in groovy skirts, hip-hugging slacks and, best of all, skimpy shorts.

My mind went spinning back through all those endless nights of dreaming and yearning and hugging my pillow and wanted to be loved in return. I was now twenty-one and I still hadn't got around to sleeping with a woman. Realising that I was now a man and that a profound change had occurred in me since leaving home five years earlier I braced myself for the changes I was sure to find in the people that I left behind.

Short range plans for the future were to find a job, a girl-friend, and try to fit in – in that order. All I had to show for my long absence was an impressive physique, a tangled mind, and thirty-five dollars. It wasn't much to go on but more than some guys had. My biggest edge was the fact that I had a loving family. Since my sister Susie was now married, that would leave just my kid brother Gaston and myself at home with my parents.

I was released from the prison at 9 o'clock and, according to her letter, Susie was to meet me with Dad in front of the hospital at 11 o'clock. She said that Dad had an appointment with a specialist at 11.30 a.m. Afterwards we would have lunch and then drive home, a distance of one hundred and thirty miles. I wondered what could be wrong with my father and I unconsciously rubbed my medallion at the thought that he might be suffering from heart trouble.

Along about 11 o'clock a red car pulled into a parking spot near the end of the street in front of the hospital. An older man in a sports shirt and tan slacks got slowly out from the passenger side, while on the driver's side a dark and pretty girl in a colourful dress bounced out energetically and immediately searched the area with her eyes. It was them!

Grabbing up my bag and coat I quickly crossed the street and hurried towards them. Radiant smiles creased our faces as we approached and stopped and stared.

It was Dad who broke the long silence by saying in French, 'Roger, it's time you came home to stay. Your mother has fixed up a nice room for you.'

I was still nodding and lost for words when Susie asked, 'Gee how do I get a reservation in that place? You've got a better tan than I have!'

Feigning displeasure, I retorted, 'Remember how I used to tie knots in your hair? Well I can still do it.'

Flanking Dad we entered the hospital still joking and as

160

usual when I spoke to my father it was in English and as always he replied in French.

Although he was jovial something was obviously wrong. I kept glancing at him and soon a chill was passing through me as I came to realise that this was no longer the same man who once pounded his massive chest with a ham-like fist to emphasise what he was saying. The rugged features were deeply creased and the flesh was loose and behind the horn-rimmed glasses the eyes were strangely hollow. Always over-weight, he now looked trim – much too trim. The pipe, the heavy suspenders, the pocket watch, and the worn-out brown fedora crushed down on his grey hair were still there, but the burning vitality was fading.

The doctor he came to see was called away on an emergency and so his appointment was postponed until 3 o'clock. We decided to have lunch in the hospital cafeteria which was on the top floor. In the elevator my thoughts turned to Susie. Three years prior to my release she married a boy-next-door type. Still childless, they were both working and saving to buy their own home. Susie had always been a natural leader, very sensitive to people's feelings in a vibrant way and so friends just naturally gravitated to her.

We got a table right next to a large picture window and from that lofty vantage point we were able to view the city, particularly the lake front, so I was able to distinguish the walled penitentiary in the distance. Thankfully, by simply turning my head I was able to make the bastard place disappear, but I could not turn away from my sister's chilling words: '... and so he spent three months right in this hospital and we dared not tell you for fear of worrying you. They gave him cobalt treatments but it's not killing the cancer cells.' Her face was twisted with grief but she wouldn't cry as tears were alien to our family. Seeing Dad coming back from the washroom, she leaned across the table and touching my hand which had curled into a fist she added in a whisper, 'But he's taking it so well, Roger!'

I was now sick at heart and the meal that I had looked forward to tasted like sawdust.

As we finished, Dad's face suddenly brightened up and he said, 'Voila! I know what we'll do, we'll go and visit my friends,' (meaning the patients and the nurses). 'Hurry. Eat!'

This was what my father enjoyed best – meeting, talking, making friends. As I expected, the patients all greeted him like a long lost brother and the nurses squealed with mock anger and skipped aside to avoid his pats. Dad cracked jokes in his fractured English and proudly introduced Susie and myself to all who came near.

Outside the hospital Susie pressed the car keys into my hand and said, 'What do you want to do for the next two hours?' Turning to my father I asked him if he still carried his fishing rod in the trunk of the car, his reply brought an excited glow to my face and I said happily, 'I know just the spot where we can kill time.'

The car was an automatic and just a few years old and I had no problem threading it through the noon hour traffic and on to the road that would lead me back towards Kingston Penitentiary.

Passing the walls of KP we continued downhill into the village of Portsmouth, along a dirt road winding in and around some old houses, warehouses, and boathouses, and then on to a long wooden pier that jutted straight out into a small horseshoe bay adjacent to the west wall of the penitentiary. Here at anchor were a wide assortment of boats including an RCMP cruiser and a few sailboats and even an ore carrier which was fastened securely to bollards at the prison wharf and was disgorging coal to fuel the powerhouse within the walls.

Slowly I drove the car straight out to the very end of the narrow pier while waves coming in from the lake splashed foaming water around the wheels. It was for me a dream come true. For years, from the vantage point of the canvas shop and the tailor shop windows, I had gazed out over the walls pining away at the sight of people swimming and fishing from the pier and powerboats and sailboats slipping out of the breakwater into the lake for a wonderful day of happiness. When the wind was right laughter and squeals of joy would sometimes drift all the way across the blue water, up and over the walls through the barred window where I sat gripping the bars in mute silence.

162

On days when I was especially depressed those sounds were more than just heart-rending, they became a cruel mockery to me for having so foolishly discarded my freedom. When the weather was turbulent, huge waves would crash over the pier while ominous, black clouds scudded warlike overhead. Boats, fighting against their anchorage, would rise like stallions. Scenes like that I appreciated most; not only did they match my usual mood, but sent shivers racing up and down my spine.

However, on this beautiful sunny afternoon the waves were mild and the water was dotted with pleasure craft and as usual a dozen or so kids were noisily diving and swimming in the water. There was a handful of people fishing. Dad was too tired to get out of the car and so I left both front doors open so that he could benefit from the breeze. With Susie I walked the last few feet to the end of the pier and together we stared in silence at the old decaying bulwark where I had lived for so long. I was free and yet a part of my soul still roamed the tiers and blocks and may continue to do so until my dying day. I knew from experience that Susie and I were being scanned by at least two, crude but effective telescopes made from discarded eyeglasses. With this thought in mind I waved towards the windows of the canvas and tailor shops hoping that I would be recognised and that word would be passed on to my friends with numbers. I fished for an hour or so and caught nothing but that didn't matter.

Dad slept all the way home. Later, I drove the car straight over to the paper mill's athletic field; Susie's husband was pitching a company baseball game. Seeing us he waved and went on to pitch the last inning and then jogged over to the car where we shook hands warmly. I had met him earlier and liked him; he was the type who took life and responsibilities seriously. Rather shy and sensitive he was very protective of Susie. He suggested that we drive over to his place for refreshments and he could change clothes.

Susie told me that she wanted to throw a party for me when I got home, but I vetoed the idea. I knew that when I got out of prison I would feel tainted. I was also acutely aware that homecomings were for soldiers and not for ex-cons. My parents were still living in their double tenement house and since Dad was too weak to work and not bootlegging anymore, he was hard pressed to keep up the mortgages. So for the first time in their long marriage Mom had to work to make ends meet and for a proud man like Dad it must have been more painful than the cancer that was eating him alive or the knowledge that in a year or so he would be dead.

A few minutes before 9 o'clock the four of us left to pick up my mother after work; she and my half sister Rolly worked for a cleaning company. As we parked across the street in the twilight I was told that Rolly's added responsibility was driving the van and that she was a real daredevil. Just then we heard a loud squeal of tyres and a white van came careening around the corner almost on two wheels when it stopped, the door on the side slid open and out bailed half a dozen squealing and laughing females, including Mom, all accusing Rolly of trying to kill them. Unseen I snuck up behind Mom, grabbed her around the waist, and then swung her in a wide circle saying, 'Hey! Have you been into the spaghetti again? You're heavy!'

Squealing with delight, she kept crying out, 'Oh! Mon Dieu! Mon Dieu! C'est Roger!'

Laughing happily I gave her another twirl and said, 'Yes, it's me Mom and I hope you saved me some raspberry pie.'

Seeing me in civilian clothes for the first time in five years my Mom was proudly introducing me to the girls she worked with. I felt both pleased that she could feel so much pride in me after all the terrible crimes I had committed and also profoundly thankful that I was able to camouflage the bitterness that lurked in the shadow of my subconscious. My sister Rolly also greeted me warmly but our relationship was more like cousins, especially since she was so much older than I was. Rolly was married and the mother of a large brood.

She followed us home where I dug into a large slab of pie while everybody else got into the booze. Soon relatives and old friends, hearing the news that I was home, began dropping in to say hello and willy-nilly a party was in progress. Living next door in the double tenement was a sex bomb named Jean who was married and the mother of two small boys.

Hearing the music and laughter she popped her head through the kitchen doorway saying to my mother, 'Yvonne! Shame on you! A handsome man and all that booze and you didn't think to call me. Where is the gin?'

When she stepped into the house I gasped and knocked over my glass of milk! Her body was gorgeous and all she was wearing was tiny white shorts and a skimpy halter. All activity suddenly stopped and everybody's eyes shifted from me to her; they all burst out laughing as my face flushed a crimson red.

'Oh you poor dear,' said Jean as she swished over to where I was sitting and kissed me on the cheek!

By one o'clock in the morning everybody had cleared out of the house to go home to sleep as they had to get up for work in the morning. That left just my parents and my kid brother who was then fifteen. The family were very proud of Gaston who was a tall, dark and handsome boy. He had a wonderful personality and was extremely popular at high school where he played a saxophone in a band he had grouped together. He was the type of fun-loving kid who wasn't about to take life seriously and it was impossible to get mad at him. I was very fond of him.

Mom still kept the house painfully clean and attractive; the bedroom that Gaston and I shared faced the street and had twin beds. It was only when I sat on the edge of my bed to remove my shoes that I began to realise the effort it would take to undo all my old habits and instincts, but it must be done if I was to fit into this new and strange environment. When I was downstairs I had felt uncomfortable, not only because of the females around me, but especially because of the low ceiling and the wooden floor. In the pen the ceilings are all unnaturally high and the floors everywhere are concrete. Now in the bedroom I was finding the bed and the pillows ridiculously soft, much too soft. So I knew that I wouldn't get much sleep that night, especially if Gaston didn't soon dummy up and go to sleep. The kid was plying me with a thousand questions. In the inky darkness I just lay there with my eyes wide open listening to the traffic passing by outside and the loud ticking of the clock. Fascinated by the liberty to turn the light on and off I kept pulling down on the lamp cord. By 2.30 it seemed to me that all the clocks in the house were conspiring to drive me nuts 'tick-tock, tick-tock, tick ...'

I was slipping quietly down the carpeted stairway when my Mother stirred and said in alarm, 'Roger, is that you?'

'Yes, Mom.'

'My God! Where are you going at this hour?'

'For a walk, Mom; just for a little walk.'

'At this hour? The police will stop you.'

'I've got to get some fresh air.'

Dad told her to hush, that I knew what I was doing. Surprised and touched by his understanding of what I was going through I was further convinced of the vast change in his personality.

It was a beautiful summer night as I headed slowly towards the old neighbourhood. Although I was prepared for the sight, I still startled to see a bowling alley where my old home once stood. Even the big black barn had undergone change and was now the property of a company that sold farm implements. The sight depressed me. I drifted uptown to the canal and walked along the banks where I used to fish as a kid. Shivering in the morning chill I watched the huge lake boats drifting slowly past like ghosts in the night and I thought how much bigger they were. Then I realised they were large because of the Seaway – the canals were now much deeper. It was nearly daylight when I entered an all-night restaurant; nursing coffee and doughnuts I fed coins into the juke box. I was listening to some of the new songs when Dinah Washington sang 'What a Difference a Day Makes'. That I felt summed up nicely my first day of freedom.

On my third night I got to sleep with the aid of pills that Dad got from our family doctor. By then I was a bundle of nerves and my hands shook constantly. The first week I just tried to relax and spent most of my days at the beach. I still didn't talk all that much and was very moody. However, I loved to be around kids and Jean next door had two wonderful little boys that I took with me everywhere. On the

166

week-ends I would join my folks for picnics and we always had a wonderful time. All the boys were athletic and we never failed to get a football or baseball game underway with some of the girls joining in. Those were the good times and I still cherish the memories. I was always wearing faded jeans and a T-shirt and because of my physique people stared at me a lot and sometimes it angered me. I guess my folks thought me strange sometimes because seemingly for no reason I'd go from laughing and horsing around to sulking and walking away.

On my tenth day of freedom I finally landed a job. The Seaway project was ending and many were out of work. Yet this time not even my criminal record hindered me, for the only criterion was lots of muscle.

Hungry and eager faces watched intently as a well-dressed man approached the bench where two dozen of us were seated waiting for opportunity to knock. When the man spoke we were all ears, 'Boys, if you're interested I've got a job for every able-bodied man here – starting tomorrow morning.'

A suspicious voice piped in, 'What kind of work are you offering mister?'

'A chance to work for the CPR. I've got a railroad line some fifty mile outside of town that has to be replaced in thirty days. That's why I need all the help I can get and I'm warning you boys right now that the work is going to be tough. From sunrise to sunset, six days a week. You'll be eating and sleeping right on the site. Arrangements will be made to bring you boys into town for Saturday night and Sunday. Any questions?'

Another one piped up and this time voiced suspicion, 'Seems like you're having trouble filling those positions. Why is that?'

'Well, it's not a get-rich job and the hours are long, but it also means that there's a lot of overtime involved. Don't forget boys, jobs are hard to come by these days.'

'How much mister? How much an hour?'

'Ninety cents an hour boys, best I can do.'

'Shit!' exclaimed someone.

'Shove it!' muttered another.

Five o'clock the following morning in a foggy, drizzling rain eight of us signed up inside the small antiquated railroad station for a month at ninety cents an hour. A flatcar was hooked up behind a tiny locomotive with a high smoke stack and as soon as we jumped aboard with our gear there was a sickening lurch, a spinning of wheels, and slowly the locomotive pulled out of the station and headed for the countryside. While we did our best to hunch down out of the rain the train pumped out huge billows of black smoke, covering us with soot. Soon we were rolling along at a tremendous clattering clip down the single set of tracks. Hemming us in on both sides was dense bush and with the heavy mist the engineers couldn't see far ahead so they kept pulling down on the steam whistle cord, in case a deer or a moose was using the track to sharpen its antlers. Bouncing around behind on the flatcar and shivering in the morning chill I kept repeating over and over to myself: 'At least I am free.' Chugging along at dawn aboard a locomotive that belonged to the Jesse James era I almost expected a horde of Indians to come riding out of the trees whooping and hollering and slinging off arrows.

On a siding in the middle of nowhere were three old bunk cars with peeling paint and boarded up windows. Inside everything was gloomy, dirty, and a powerful stench permeated the rows of double tiered bunks. Clothes lay everywhere and it was hard to distinguish which bunks were empty and which were occupied. Two of the guys that signed on with me were big, clean-cut boys working their way through university. The others were older men, homeless and probably not ambitious.

Raining or not we soon joined the rest of the section hands who were already at work. Almost to the last man they were immigrants struggling to make a buck and able to speak only in their native language. The burly foreman could barely speak English himself and had all the likeable qualities of a toad. He drove those poor slobs as if they were human mules and they felt too insecure to complain. The university kids also got a rough time, probably because they reminded him of his ignorance. I gave him no cause to bug me because I was doing more than my share of work with a twenty-pound crowbar. All I asked was to be left alone.

When I returned to work after lunch I knew only too well that he was now aware that I was an ex-con because he gave me a job normally done by two men. He dropped little nasty hints about what should be done with jailbirds. It was my job to pry up old imbedded railroad spikes with a bar so that an electric machine following behind could find traction and pull the spikes all the way out. A tobacco-chewing friend of the foreman rode on top of that yellow machine and instead of just keeping pace, the bastard kept crowding me. I should have just up and quit but I figured the big monkey would climb off my back when he saw that I was truly a worker.

It turned out that he hated me even more for carrying the load that was busting my guts. Telling myself that I was a 'free man', no longer soothed me. Knowing my temperament I knew only too well that I would brood just so long and then I would explode.

On the fourth day we were tearing up tracks at a railroad crossing which intersected a gravel road in the middle of the bush when a shiny red convertible pulled up in a cloud of dust. The top was down and the radio blared rock 'n' roll. A guy and two chicks sat in the front seat. They just sat there for about fifteen minutes laughing and watching us work like slaves. Bone tired, sweaty, and thirsty, I was still doing the work of two men.

We had just about patched up the crossing when I gave a yell and leapt aside! The creep astride the machine had crowded me so close that he almost crushed my foot! I felt a searing flash of anger as I raised the bar over my head and he excitedly threw his machine into reverse and backed off at full speed. The foreman started towards us and then stopped when he saw me breathing hard and looking a little crazy. Totally disgusted I threw down the crowbar and my gloves and stalked away towards the bunk cars.

'Hey Roger!' said Jeff, the tallest of the two students. 'Where are you off to?'

'Home, pal. I just resigned from this rat race.'

There was a moment of silence and then he shouted, 'Well wait for us! We're leaving too!'

169

It was a long hike back to civilization. It was about 7 o'clock in the evening when I walked up to the house and I can still see my father sitting on the veranda in a rocking chair, watching me approach. I didn't know it then but this was going to be the last time that I saw him alive. My bag was in one hand and my jacket in the other and on my face was a look of shame. My first job and I botched it and now my father was sure to call me a bum. But I kept forgetting how changed he was. So when I sat on the railing and told him that I had quit my job, he quietly asked me why. I explained briefly, adding that the wages were only ninety cents an hour.

Incensed, he growled, 'You should have quit and come home the first day. Ninety cents an hour! Sacré Bleu I'm going to call the Manpower office and have that contractor blacklisted. Paying a man wages like that! Why he's nothing but a blood-sucker.' Calming down and wiping his brow with a handkerchief he added, 'Don't worry, Roger, you're a strong boy, there will be other jobs. Go in and have your Mother cook you a good supper.'

Soaking up water in the bathtub I felt a profound love for my father for the first time in my life, but also anger and sorrow that such a proud man could not die in peace. At the end of each month he became sick with worry that he might not be able to meet his mortgage payments. He might have sold some of his properties rather than pay mortgages, but for him that would be admitting defeat. The hospital bills were also weighing heavily on his mind.

With some definite plans in mind, I drove to the north-end poolhall where I had loafed around the better part of my childhood. I needed a partner to help me bust open a large safe that I knew for sure was crammed with money. I had been free less than two weeks.

CHAPTER TWELVE

July, 1959: I thought I got lucky in finding an experienced partner to help me bust open the safe in the general store, a pete that was known to contain a fortune in savings. However, things went sour and the place was surrounded by the law. The next thing we knew we were locked up in the Cornwall police station. Eight o'clock the following morning the Ontario Provincial Police transferred us to their headquarters a few blocks away. Keeping my cool even while going nuts with the bitter thought of returning to the penitentiary I broke away from my escorts, and with my manacled hands thrust before me, I dived headlong through a screened second floor window! It was a blind and foolish act because directly below the window was a paved parking lot, but in tumbling head over heels down the side of the wooden building and rolling with the impact I was able to limp away with only minor cuts and bruises. Before the dragnet could get into high gear I was beyond the roadblocks and fast approaching the city of Montreal.

The police raided my parents' home and after that close surveillance of the house was maintained on the chance that I might return. But I never did return, because I had a stricken conscience for once again bringing grief to my parents. I eased my mind a bit by keeping frequent contact with them through late night telephone calls. Mom would tell me of all the trips she was making to the parish church to pray for my safety, asking me time and time again to surrender before I was killed. Poor Dad, he just sat in the darkened living-room in the chair that the family bought for him, hollow eyes, bony hands gripping his cold pipe, and softly relaying

171

messages through Mom. To me it was strange that he never asked me to surrender to the law, all he asked was that I didn't steal for a living.

Keeping my father's wishes in mind during the following weeks I made my way as far as Fredericton N.B. A wonderfully scenic little town with tree-lined streets, parks, a massive steel bridge, and a colourful river flowing through the centre of the business district. Here I planned to save up some money for a boat passage to the city of Sidi-Bel-Abbes in Algeria where I would join the French Foreign Legion. I worked for a carnival that was in town and when it left I worked harvesting a farmer's hay. The farmer turned out to be a miserable little tyrant and after quitting in a fit of frustration I went a little bit crazy, stole an expensive car with a racing engine, and then drove seven hundred miles to Montreal at suicidal speeds.

The day after arriving in Montreal the city police picked up my tail and the pursuit was on! Dozens of police cars were involved in the wild chase, which then proceeded on foot through a maze of cluttered alleyways, until once again I was cornered by a dead end. I ignored warnings to raise my hands in surrender, and crazed with rage and frustration, I went berserk: smashing my fist into the boarded fence with a fury, stomping garbage cans with my feet, and then pounding my fist to my head. All the while the police just stood there watching me with drawn revolvers. When I quietened down, they cuffed me and led me away.

At headquarters I gave the police a bogus name and denied that I had a criminal record. Their search of my person failed to uncover two pieces of hacksaw blades with which I planned to cut my way to freedom. But before I could do this I was returned to Fredericton to face a charge of car theft.

The Fredericton county jail is situated on a quiet tree-lined street not far from the heart of town. Painted white and constructed of wood, it was two storeys high. The first floor contained offices, kitchen, and gallows; the second floor had three large cells facing the back; and the side facing the street housed the sheriff and his family. During the day the sheriff's kids could be heard running up and

172

down the corridor laughing and yelling. The rear of the prison lacked the conventional brick wall, just a run-down board fence, chest high, and a weedy backyard. Beyond the fence was an open market that bustled with Saturday activity. Running the jail was a dapper little moustachioed sheriff with a tough-guy attitude, whom everybody called Joe. His deputy was Otto, a huge hulk in his early forties, with hairy arms, who spoke with a heavy accent.

The first cell upstairs was reserved for female prisoners, the second for those condemned to hang, while the third was for those serving short terms and awaiting trial. It was more like a small dorm with three double-tiered bunks, a heavy oak table to eat and play cards on, a toilet and sink in a corner, and a large barred window with a ledge to sit on. At this window most visits were conducted with the visitors talking over the fence and the prisoner shouting back through the bars.

It was a warm summer night. Lying there on my top bunk wearing only my jeans, while my cellmates dozed all around, I was savouring the satisfaction of having sawed through the first bar on the window the evening before. My hands were trembling with suppressed excitement as my eyes roved slowly around the dirty cell and rested on the ponderous steel door with the peep hole. Everything was deathly quiet. If I didn't soon cut through that second bar before my fingerprints were identified, all hell would break loose. At that moment the sheriff had finished his last security check and retired to his quarters across the way and old man Buckley still hadn't started his riotous snoring, a sound I needed to cover up my sawing.

Leaning over the edge of my bunk I saw Buckley sleeping on his side, which was probably the reason he wasn't snoring. I reached down and gave his pillow a sharp tug, just enough to make him snort and turn over on his back. Immediately the cell was filled with harsh snoring, the grunting and growling pandemonium that caused everybody to turn over in their sleep into a deeper valley. Slipping off the bunk I padded over to the window ledge and in a few minutes I was slowly cutting into the second bar which was square shaped. Working cautiously I measured my strokes to the variations in the old man's snores, pausing whenever he did. The iron was soft, not like cheese, but surprisingly soft just the same.

My nerves were on red alert and I know I didn't do anything stupid, but along about 3 a.m. the lights suddenly came on and the heavy oak door slammed open with a force that brought everybody sitting upright in their bunks. Joe, Otto, and two uniformed cops rushed into the cell and caught me cold turkey with half a hacksaw blade still clutched in my fist and a dumbfounded look on my face. They quickly herded me out into the hallway and relocked the cell door.

'All right strip!' growled Joe in his most menacing voice.

'Where is the remainder of this saw?' inquired a burly cop holding the blade under my nose.

Clamping down on my emotions I reminded myself that as far as they knew I was just a kid picked up for joy-riding who had never done time before. 'That's all there is – honest! I found it crammed behind a loose board on the window sill.'

'Bullshit!' snarled the sheriff, grabbing my jeans and running his fingers expertly along the seams. 'My jail is clean of that stuff. You brought that saw in with you.'

'No, honest sheriff, I didn't! I found it and I panicked. Look, I'm sorry, I've never been in jail before.'

One of the cops turned to Joe and said, 'Say sheriff didn't you shake him down when he was delivered into your custody?'

'You know damn well I did,' retorted Joe, then realising the implication of what he said he added in a meeker tone of voice, 'Well I guess it's possible he's telling the truth; jail's been here long before my time; besides the saw does look old.'

With soaring confidence I pulled my clothes back on and walked half a dozen paces with the missing piece of blade taped to the sole of my left foot, and into the open door of the Death Cell. 'We'll get back to you later,' threatened the sheriff slamming the big door shut and locking it.

My elation at retaining the saw soon turned sour when I walked up to the cell window and focused my attention on

174

the solid plate of steel that was welded to the outside bars and covered the entire window! I'd need all the time in the world and a hundred saws to cut through that bitch. Dejected, I moved off to a corner of the cell and flopped down on a dirty mattress. Apart from the thin mattress and two blankets the drum was completely bare, except for a toilet in another corner and a light bulb screwed into a recessed socket high up by the ceiling. I never did get any sleep that night and kept alternating between lying down and prowling my cage searching every inch for any conceivable way out with my limited means. By sunrise I was in a state of despair, there just didn't seem to be any way out of that cell. They would not even open my door to feed me, instead they just pushed my food through a slot. By midafternoon the security measures got even tighter as a heavy hammering commenced outside my door and I realised that they were adding several additional locks. This could only mean that they were now aware of my true identity and the magnitude of my desperation. Alone with my thoughts inside that dark and gloomy cage I couldn't help feeling more panicky about the outstanding charges waiting for me in my home town.

It was early evening and somebody was tapping on the wall in the cell to my right. I realised suddenly that there was a girl serving a six-month sentence there for forgery. The guys told me that she was an Indian chick and stacked like an Amazon! The tapping had a pattern to it in so far as it started from the rear and led to a corner at the front of the cell. Probing where it ended, I soon discovered a small hole that was plugged with wet paper and quickly dug it out. Peering in all I could see was a pretty eyeball. Gesturing with my forefinger for her to back off I was soon able to see what my neighbour looked like. She had short black hair and large sad eyes in a pleasing face and wore a red blouse and checkered slacks. The twin mounds thrusting boldly against the material of her blouse caused my heart to give an appreciative thump, even though I was in a state of despair. She said that her name was Ninny and that she had already served half of her six months sentence. By her demeanour it was obvious that this young Indian girl was bored to death. Ninny had a very soothing voice and softly we

175

conversed through two feet of brick wall, pausing only when somebody came around to check the doors.

By midnight we were fast friends and things got informal to the point where she would strip down to her bra and panties and roll around teasingly on her bunk, which was directly across from the hole in the wall. The thought that I would be returning to the penitentiary still a virgin troubled me very much and that thought inflamed the passion and need in me for a girl. Ninny was well built and obviously enjoyed teasing me, but no matter how much I implored her to removed her brassiere she would not. Her body was almost a golden brown and when she smiled wickedly and arched her back I'd claw at the plaster and break out in a sweat.

'If you want me Roger,' she'd murmur silkily, 'why don't you find a way to come over and visit me?'

For the next three days I laboured like a man possessed. My hands were blistered and bleeding and wrapped in soiled rags from constantly pounding them on the hilt of the butter knife that Ninny supplied me with. The task of tunnelling through the wall that separated us was turning out to be much more difficult than I had imagined. Naïvely I earlier assumed that once I gouged through the thick plaster and dug out the first brick the remaining bricks would dislodge at a tug. Not so. Not with a butter knife! While I worked Ninny gave me 'six' by plastering her ear to the door and listening for activity out in the hallway. Ironically the sheriff in his panic to secure my door with extra locks and issuing orders that my cell was not to be opened under any circumstances, played directly in my favour. The cell was so large that the corner where I was working could not be seen through the peep hole. So to observe me tunnelling they would have had to enter my cell, which they were not prepared to do. From Ninny's side the men could enter her cell only when the matron was on duty; the matron left at 5 o'clock in the afternoon. I became so obsessed with my project that I had very little inclination for small talk and Ninny was beginning to pout. To keep her spirits up I would fill her mind with happy thoughts about what we would do together after we escaped but first I had to get through her wall in order to saw through her bars. I guess at first she was truly sincere about breaking out of jail with me, that is until the excitement started wearing thin and the dire consequences dawned dark and threatening.

It was about 3 o'clock Sunday afternoon when my luck gave out. I was busy working amid the rubble of bricks and mortar and feeling triumphant and happy in the knowledge that I was within a few hours of breaking through when I heard Ninny's door open. Freezing all my movements I cocked my ear to try and make out what the excited murmuring was all about.

Loud and clear I heard Ninny exclaim in a tearful voice, '. . . and he has a hacksaw blade too!'

With a groan of despair I staggered to the centre of my cell shaking my head from side to side like I couldn't believe what I just overheard. Out in the corridor there was a wild stampede of confused activity and hysterical yelling as the sheriff, Otto, and a powerful trusty, started fumbling with the locks and a heartbeat later my cell door crashed open! In rushed the sheriff while his two goons guarded the entrance only to be met by a bloodcurdling scream of rage on my part. Both my hands grasping his shirt front I propelled him straight back through the doorway with such brute force that all four of us fell into a tangle of limbs and flailing fists. My assault was so fierce and unexpected that I momentarily had the edge as I struggled to my feet with the trusty hanging on to my neck. With another scream of rage and a sudden hump the fink was sent sprawling on top of the sheriff and the deputy. I plunged towards the stairs, staggering down the first flight, tumbling head first down the final flight, and then rolled out into a long corridor.

Scrambling to my feet on the main floor I searched about feverishly, trying to decide on a course of action that would furnish me with a quick exit. Standing ajar a few feet away was an office door; hearing shouts and footsteps behind me, I plunged blindly inside. On a raised dais behind a desk was an open window with curtains flapping in the breeze. I leaped up on the desk and ignoring the venetian blinds I plunged through just as somebody burst into the office behind me. The main floor to the grass below was higher

177

than I expected but with the venetian blinds wrapped around me slowing my fall I landed with only a twisted right ankle. Shoeless, I staggered to my feet and hobbled on to the sidewalk and down the street by the time the sheriff had poked his head out the window, shouting obcenities in my direction.

The main street was three blocks away. A hundred yards beyond that was the river. I headed there hoping to find a boat because it would have been foolhardy to grab a car – much too easy for the police to set up roadblocks.

Prowling along the river bank I found myself behind a new hotel about seven storeys high and I decided that it would be a good place to hide. I slipped through a service entrance and made my way into the underground section, planning to hide until dark. What a spacious place! I am sure I could have stayed hidden down there for a month without anyone discovering my presence. Moving cautiously down one of the many corridors in my stocking feet I kept opening doors and looking around inside for a place to conceal myself. I saw boutiques and souvenir shops and decided to stay clear of that area because it was sure to be patrolled. I finally picked a large and dimly-lit banquet room, with row upon row of ghostly tables draped with white linen that reached all the way down to the floor. From a nearby laundry cart I scooped up a handful of towels and crawled under one of the tables to make myself a comfortable nest.

Along about 9.30 that evening I crawled out and discovered to my dismay that my right ankle was so swollen and sore that I had to walk with a limp. From the employee's locker room I grabbed a pair of loafers and a navy blue jacket and only then did I step out into the night air. Moonless with no stars there was the smell of rain in the chilly air. By now there would be a province-wide alert for my arrest as a fugitive and I figured that my only chance was to take to the back roads and keep right on walking until I was safe. Hitch-hiking was out of the question, anybody with a car radio would know who I was and would report me. I followed the river bank until I reached the massive steel bridge and scrambled up the embankment.

It was now near midnight and I was limping painfully along a narrow gravel road through dense bush, maybe ten miles west of town. For the past thirty minutes great peals of grumbling thunder had been breaking all around me followed by dazzling bolts of lightning that momentarily illuminated the shadows. Shivering inside the thin jacket I reminded myself once more that I had to find shelter soon before the heavens opened up and drenched me. Up to then I had avoided all vehicles, including the RCMP cruisers, by fading into the bush every time headlights flashed in either direction. The most intense search would likely come from the Mounties who had a large headquarters in town.

And then the rain came down faster and faster until I couldn't hear or see and there wasn't any shelter, not even a large tree to stand under, only a rain-filled ditch and the almost impenetrable bush. It was getting spookier and my superstitious nature started acting up as I tried to take comfort from my St Joseph medallion.

Limping into the rain and wind with my head down and mumbling something about at least being free, I did not hear the car come up behind and almost jumped out of my skin when it slid to a stop right beside me! I was just winding up to leap across the ditch and run into the thicket when a young girl's voice, filled with compassion, arrested my movements.

'Good Lord, Daddy. It's a young man! Poor wretch looks soaked through and through.'

The dome light came on and I found myself staring into the face of a healthy and wholesome-looking teenage girl about fifteen years old. Seated beside her was another demure-looking young lady in her late teens. Obviously they were sisters. Behind the wheel was a big-boned man with a look of openness and understanding about him.

Leaning across to the open window he said, 'For God's sake, son, get into the car and out of the rain before you drown!'

Clutching my coat to my throat, as raindrops battered my face, I replied through chattering teeth, 'Thanks just the same, mister, but I'll be all right.' I turned and limped away into the glare of headlights aware that I was being observed

179

closely. It's strange but I was filled with consuming shame at my ragged appearance and empty pockets and wet clothes. I was also deathly fearful of the radio antenna on the car fender.

Again the car pulled even with me and stopped. I turned to face the gentleman once more, 'Son,' he pleaded through the open window, 'my daughters are threatening to disown me if I let you stay out any longer in this rain. Tell me how far are you going?'

'Montreal,' I stammered.

'Well, then that does it.' It was the voice of a man who has just made a serious decision. 'Get in the back, please. We can't let you go any farther tonight, you'll spend the night in our home.'

'Please get in,' said the brown haired girl in the middle. 'In the morning my father and I drive into town to work. We cross the river on the ferry and we will drop you off on the main highway where you'll find it much easier to catch a ride.'

I tried vainly to find an excuse that sounded logical for remaining in the rain without making them suspicious. I could think of no sane reason and so I nodded my head numbly and climbed into the rear of the car, relieved that at least the radio wasn't playing. All my instincts were screaming at me that what I was doing was wrong and dangerous. But I was feeling so miserable and my ankle was hurting me so.

I soon found out that they were a family returning from a church social in town. They lived just a few miles down the road in a little country house that was far from any neighbours. Cautiously they plied me with questions that revealed only concern for my present situation. The youngest daughter, Judy, wanted to know why I was limping and why my hands were battered. I concocted a story about my having been robbed and thrown out of a speeding car without my luggage and that I was now headed for home. They accepted my lies at face value.

They had a wooden house at the intersection of two secondary roads. On the front lawn was a brand new tent which I was told belonged to the eldest son who was attending

180

university. I was supposed to spend the night in the tent. They parked the car beside a smaller one and when I saw that the rain was letting up a bit, I tried to leave but they were adamant that I stay the night.

Rather than arouse their suspicions, I agreed to stay and they ushered me into the house to meet the wife and mother. I was becoming paranoid now, thinking that as soon as the woman saw me she would recall the radio bulletins and scream or something like that. To my very great relief there was no blaring radio to greet me when I entered the cosy and cluttered little house. I was introduced to the grandmother in a rocking chair who was reading a Bible, and to the mother, a woman who was quietly knitting.

What a wonderful and harmonious family and so full of kindness; I was profoundly moved by their combined goodness. Although I was hungry, I adamantly refused anything to eat or drink, pleading that I only be permitted to retreat to my tent. Sensing my acute embarrassment and shyness they finally gave up trying to domesticate me and led me out to the tent, or I should say as far as the front porch because it was still raining quite heavily. I dashed across the lawn, unzippered the front of the tent, and scurried inside.

It turned out to be really great! Especially for a tired traveller. There was a canvas floor, a fur-lined sleeping bag, and a small lantern. I was so exhausted I could hardly keep my eyes open and although I felt very insecure there, I decided that I would rest for two hours. after that I would strike out into the night. Just then I heard a shout from the front door. They wanted to know if I was undressed and comfortably inside the sleeping bag. When I assured them that this was the case, a moment later the father was handing me a paper sack and demanding my wet clothes. Instinctively I handed them to him. Rushing back to the house he shouted over his shoulder that they would be dry and ready for me in the morning. Only then did I realise that I was left naked as a jaybird and much more helpless if it came to fleeing. Like it or not I was stuck inside that tent until morning. Resignedly, I opened the paper bag and was delighted to find a Thermos filled with delicious coffee and warm egg sandwiches. Sheer luxury!

181

At 6.30 a.m. the sound of someone touching the tent flap brought me instantly awake. It was my dry clothes. With them came an invitation to join the man and his daughter for breakfast. Stepping outside I found it to be very cold with a mist clinging close to the earth. Inside the kitchen I washed and shaved and took the opportunity to patch up my hands. By the time I sat myself down at the table, I was so ravenous that I was embarrassed. The pretty girl seemed to take pleasure shoving mounds of food on to my plate; even while I protested, I ate everything including a full quart of milk! All the while I kept eyeing the radio and was greatly relieved that no one made a move to turn it on.

As we were getting ready to leave they gave me a beautiful woollen sweater that belonged to their son. It was a very thick and luxurious sweater and when they flatly refused to take it back, I reluctantly accepted, choking with emotion. They were so kind and generous to me that it was making me feel very uneasy, in the sense that I couldn't figure out what their angle was. I was also feeling guilty about having to represent myself as something other than what I really was.

We left the house shortly after 7 o'clock in the girls' small car, with me seated in the back. My thoughts kept drifting from the conversation to the silent radio on the dashboard and I wondered how long my secret would remain intact. I did not want to cross the St John River to the main highway because I knew that the manhunt for me would be centred in places like that. However the family argued that I would never get a ride to Montreal from the secondary road and so I had to give in, rather than risk their suspicion.

The heavy rainfall had caused the river to become bloated, irritable and murky looking. As for the ferry crossing, some enterprising farmer had the good business sense to gouge a dirt landing from some heavy brush along the river, built a flat barge, and then string two stout ropes across five hundred yards of fast-flowing river. The barge held only one car at a time. Mobility was achieved by two men pulling on ropes!

After a tough crossing, they deposited me on a scenic highway with the river on one side and towering forest on

182

the other. A man could step into those stately trees and walk in a straight line for hundreds of miles and never encounter anything but four legged animals. I thanked them profusely for all they had done for me and they asked me to write to them and I said that I would.

'Here take this,' said the father, handing me a paper bag through the window of the car. 'Judy wouldn't go to bed last night until she made this lunch for you. Good-bye and good luck.'

Bundled up inside the sweater and holding the sack I stood watching as the small car faded over a distant hill. Filled with an aching sadness I vowed that I would never forget their kindness and the warmth they had brought to my bitter shell.

(Within minutes after leaving me they turned on their radio and heard a bulletin describing me as a fugitive, dangerous, and probably armed. Realising that they had harboured a desperate criminal they immediately drove to the RCMP headquarters and told their story. This did not change my warm feelings for them; they did what they had to do.)

Of course I didn't know this then, but I did know that standing there on the highway was foolhardy: if a cruiser passed I would be a target in the opening. I made a deal with myself; I would try to thumb a ride from the first five vehicles that passed. If none stopped, I would then run into the forest and keep right on running until I fell exhausted.

This time lady luck was smiling down on me because the very first car that I wiggled my thumb at stopped and picked me up. It was a small foreign car and behind the wheel was a scholarly-looking gentleman who informed me that he was travelling only another five miles up the road. From there he would switch to a secondary road and drive another thirty miles to a small hamlet. 'From there it's only six miles to the US border. Will this help you?'

Trembling with relief, I couldn't believe my good fortune. We were now off the main highway and zipping along a narrow asphalt road with towering trees filtering out the morning sunlight. It was beautiful country for hunting and fishing and cluttered with gaudy tourist tents. The

183

bespectacled gentleman turned out to be a bank manager returning from a holiday. Again the radio was silent. It was a few minutes before 8 o'clock when we drove into this tiny hamlet that consisted of a general store, a garage, and a new bank in front of which we parked. Thanking the manager for the lift I soon left the place behind, heading in the direction of the border. After half a mile of painful limping I picked out a large tree by the road for concealment. From there I would observe the traffic coming in both directions and would emerge to thumb a ride only when I was positive that the vehicle did not contain the police. It took almost an hour before I got a ride. An antique 1933 Chrysler belching black smoke and huffing and puffing like it was about to fall apart stopped. Inside were three gangling teenagers whooping it up.

'Going as far as McNamee,' said a boy wearing a straw hat. 'That's if this old heap will make it.'

'Where is McNamee?' I inquired.

'A village just a mile from the border crossing,' added a kid in the back seat, wearing an old army jacket.

'That will be just great!' I shouted over the noise of the motor while scrambling into the back seat.

All three were home grown boys and very open and talkative. The driver was given the car by his grandfather and they decided to break it in by driving to Halifax – some 300 miles away. Along the way the car started losing power until finally the speed was reduced to 35 mph.

'That's why we had to turn back,' said the driver in disgust. 'Too many fuckin hills.'

Unable to fathom his reasoning I said: 'How's that?'

'Observe, hitch-hiker. Observe,' said the driver in mock despair. Turning to his companions he shouted: 'Hill ahead, bail out!'

Slowly the old car started chugging up this hill while gradually losing momentum, until eventually it started coughing and sputtering near the crest.

The driver, having seen my limp, pulled out the choke, then shouted, 'Grab the wheel friend or we'll roll all the way down again!'

While they pushed mightily, I steered from the back seat.

By then the jalopy had slowed down to barely a crawl and it didn't look like we would make it over the hill. With a concerted shout and a heave, the old heap crested the summit and started rolling down the other side. Laughing and shouting the boys ran along until they were able to leap on to the running board and then, to my great relief, the driver took control of the wheel.

From them I gleaned a valuable piece of information: I heard of an alternate route for crossing the border, illegally, and without being seen by the border patrol. They let me out in the village that contained a Provincial Police Headquarters; from there I hiked to the outskirts.

Straight ahead down the road I could make out the customs buildings on either side of the steel bridge. I then left the road and quickly faded into the bush to the left of the border. After floundering through dense brush for nearly a mile I came upon a single set of railroad tracks. They were set in a deep gully bordered by grassy slopes. I followed the tracks for another mile until I reached a sturdy railroad bridge spanning a turbulent river. This was the border separating both countries. Nestled in the sunshine, on the far bank was a quaint little village called Vanceboro. Everywhere on both sides of the river and the hilly terrain were small herds of cattle feeding on lush green grass; birds flew overhead. It was all so peaceful that I decided to climb a knoll to rest for a while under an apple tree and nibble at the lunch which had been packed so lovingly.

Along about noon a fierce looking bull came on the scene, snorting and pawing at the earth and so I discreetly moved camp down the river's edge. I sat on a large rock beneath the steel girders of the bridge; I could just barely make out the US customs building around a bend in the river.

By rights, I knew I should wait until dark to cross over, but I was too impatient for that. I soaked my ankle in the cold fast-flowing water until it went numb. Then I put my shoe back on and crossed the bridge as stealthily and quickly as possible.

Half a mile beyond Vanceboro, I found myself on a narrow road which snaked its way along the very edge of a huge lake for as far as the eye could see. To the left were cliff-like formations, some of them towering almost perpendicular for a thousand feet. Small trees grew outwards at impossible angles. Thus the road afforded no quick exits for me if I was suddenly jumped. In any case, I wasn't far from my vanishing point because the Maine turnpike was less than forty miles straight ahead. From there it was a straight run into Boston. My plans were still to reach Algeria to join the French Foreign Legion.

Certainly the Americans were not keen on picking up hitch-hikers. In addition to that, the traffic was very light and the cars that did flash by were usually overloaded with passengers. As usual I did my best to stay concealed whenever I was unsure of any approaching vehicle. However there were so many sharp bends in the narrow asphalt road that sometimes cars were upon me before I knew it. It was now early evening and just two hours to sundown; in all that time I managed to score but two short rides, the drivers turning off the road to go to their cottages. Even so I was less than five miles from the turnpike and was now concentrating on walking the distance.

Being tired and in a lot of pain from my ankle my caution became dulled and so it was that I didn't hear the vehicle come up behind me around a sharp curve. The brakes were applied and the squeal of burning tyres almost made me jump out of my skin!

'All right boy!' bellowed an authoritative voice. 'Just you freeze right where you are or I'll blow a hole in you.'

I was standing on the side of the road and half turned in the direction of the voice. A muscular-looking highway patrolman was levelling his revolver at me through the car window.

'Just raise your hands high and don't try anything.' He talked with a lazy drawl and wore a white cowboy hat.

Once again I was going through the agony of arrest and since he was looking right down his sights at me, there wasn't a thing I could do to free myself. While we stood there on the road, about ten feet apart, his radio came to life and I was astounded to hear my name and description come over the air.

'... the roadblocks are set up and the RCMP advises us

that the fugitive is considered dangerous and probably armed and should be approached with extreme caution . . .'

The big cowboy-looking cop picked up his mike with his free hand and with a satisfied grin and a sharp eye on me he started talking, 'Yup, sure enough he's my prisoner. Got the jump on him I did. You tell the captain it's me that arrested him.'

By the time the first cruisers slid to a grinding halt, the area was dotted with gawking tourists snapping pictures of me still standing there with my hands upraised. The police who piled out of the arriving cruisers were also dressed like cowboys; one even carried a telescopic rifle.

They shook me down and then chained me up with a restraining belt and pushed me into the back seat of a cruiser. Convinced that I had had a gun and ditched it, they spent some time searching the immediate area.

The Highway Patrol was soon joined by the Border Patrol, the McNamee and the Vanceboro police, and shortly after them came the Canadian Mounties. The air in the immediate vicinity crackled with the sounds of dispatchers on separate frequencies, each seemingly vying for attention – with me the patsy.

As I sat sullenly in the back seat of a cruiser, the police stood around outside in the twilight debating heatedly over who was going to win legal custody of me. Immigration seemed bound and determined to prosecute for illegal entry. The Highway Patrol wanted their pound of flesh for having spent so much manpower on roadblocks. Besides, they said, the governor of the state had sent down word to beef up the arrests because more and more prisoners were needed to work on the road gangs.

Soon it got dark. A frigid wind blowing off the lake was enough to break up their roadside conference and so they all decided to drive back to the customs offices at the border, where they could continue the debate. As for the cowboy cop who first arrested me, all that concerned him was that everyone spelled his name correctly in the reports and that he got the credit for busting me.

It was almost midnight before the two Mounties succeeded in convincing the Americans to drop the charges against me, explaining to them that I had enough charges facing me on the Canadian side of the border. Before turning me over to the Horsemen, the immigration authorities finger-printed and mugged me for future reference.

On the ride back to RCMP headquarters in Fredericton, the sergeant and the corporal finally explained who had fingered me to the Highway Patrol, a quirk of fate that could happen only to me. Sheriff Joe from the Fredericton county jail which I had escaped from had left for his annual holiday with his family, just about the time that I was crossing the railroad bridge into the State of Maine. The first leg of his journey was by way of Boston and sadly for me his car was one I had tried to thumb a ride from. Recognising me on the side of the road he raced off madly with his family to the Maine turnpike to seek out the Highway Patrol and set the hounds after me.

I spent a restless night in a holding cell at the RCMP headquarters, then appeared in a Fredericton court the following morning to plead guilty to car theft and jailbreak. The judge sentenced me to two and a half years in the Maritime penitentiary with the understanding that upon termination of my sentence, I would be transferred to the Cornwall county jail to await trial on charges of B & E, safe cracking, and escaping custody.

That very afternoon I was removed from the police cells, handcuffed and shackled. In the custody of a local sheriff and a uniformed Mountie we drove 150 miles to Dorchester Penitentiary. Quiet and withdrawn I was dimly aware that something new, something strange was taking shape within me, something impulsive and uncontrollable, something fierce . . .

CHAPTER THIRTEEN

August, 1959: Dorchester Penitentiary is isolated on a high knoll like a grotesque gargoyle overlooking a barren highway. It's a sprawling mass of grey masonry surrounded by high stone walls and watchtowers which are the bulbous eyes of the monster. Enclosed on three sides by dense forest it is infested with clouds of blood-sucking mosquitoes and flesh-eating black flies. To the front of the institution and down a steep slope of new mown grass stand the residences of the warden and the deputy warden. Lining each side of the highway are rows of ugly white houses constructed during the war, all identical and all occupied by the guards and their families. Beyond, on flat barren land runs the main railroad line linking east and west. The sound of its powerful and sleek locomotives late at night invades the prisoners' reveries and causes their hearts to beat faster. Half a mile farther out from the railroad lies a narrow, marshy inlet that is actually a part of the Bay of Fundy. During ebb tides it looks like a muddy creek; twice a day tidal bores rush in with a wall of water.

The unmarked car with the sheriff at the wheel threaded its way carefully up the winding driveway and came to a halt in a small parking lot that faced the prison. We had travelled almost two hundred miles and the handcuffs and leg-irons left me feeling cramped and sore. While the Mountie held the door open, I climbed out awkwardly directly under a watchtower, stretched, took a last gulp of fresh air, then shuffled bitterly towards the front entrance.

That very first Sunday inside the joint I had the first of many fist fights. For years to come my fists would act like demented playmates with a mind and temper of their own. It

189

was as if all the hate and frustration of being a born loser had seeped down into my fists; sick at heart from being pushed around I lashed out viciously at anything that was cruel to me. Afterwards I would be filled with deep remorse for having regressed to jungle law. Always and without exception the guys I struck out at were bigger than myself and were known to be cruel. I would soon discover how well-suited I was for fighting man-to-man.

My first encounter was with a heavyset and self-made hard rock called Buck. He was a few years older than I and very loud and aggressive. It was raining outside and so all recreation was taking place inside the main cellblock on the bottom ranges. Four of us were engaged in a game of cards. Buck turned out to be a sore loser and began cheating. Catching him in the act, I quietly told him to lay off. At this he got all big in the chest and red in the face. He obviously mistook my gentle geniality and quiet attitude for that of a pacifist.

Kicking back his chair he reached for me shouting, 'Listen, sucker ...' Before he could complete his move I tagged him with a flurry of hard blows that surprised even myself. His eyes turned over in their sockets and came up snow white as he sagged to his knees in front of me, bleeding profusely from his nose and mouth. I stood poised over him with my fist cocked as a crowd of curious prisoners immediately formed a circle and started egging us into combat.

'C'mon man, put the leather to him,' growled one blood-thirsty con.

'Get up Buck and get it on!' shouted another.

Buck started to keel over sideways just as some alert con yelled 'Six!' Throwing myself into the milling crowd I soon got lost in the shuffle before the guards could catch my number.

Later that evening from my cell on the fourth tier I soon learned from a water boy who stopped in front of my drum to gleefully feed me the latest from the grapevine that I was now a target. It turned out that Buck belonged to the toughest clique in the joint and that he was the right-hand friend and flunky of the most dangerous con in the institution. Joe was the leader and organiser in Dorchester Pen at that time and with his brother and cronies backing him up guys knuckled down or else. Joe had been born in Halifax and was practically raised on the docks. He was considered by many to be the toughest brawler on the east coast.

When drunk he had the reputation of being the meanest. At two hundred and ten pounds he had the physique of a Mr America with bulging biceps as big around as a man's thigh. His skin was stretched tight across a bony face and he had sparse brown hair and his body was scarred from a hundred brawls. His rock-like stomach was torn and ripped and sewn together in a lumpy mass (a splintered whisky bottle had once been shoved deep into his guts.) He was a boxer and a weightlifter and so awesomely strong that with just the use of one hand he could hoist a two hundred and forty pound barbell straight over his head, drop it, then catch it in the crook of both arms! He and his brother George who operated the weightlifting pit were also main attractions several times a year when the inmates put on a variety show for the civilian population in nearby towns. Joe would start his stage performance by walking stiff legged across the platform, from rack to rack, with an eight hundred pound barbell slung across his massive shoulders. Next he would have one of his buddies break a wine bottle across his skull. This would be followed by one-handed lifts and tricks performed by him and his brother who tipped the scales at two hundred and thirty pounds. Finally George would jump feet first from a ten foot ladder on to Joe's stomach and bounce off! They would finish their act with George breaking rock across Joe's chest with a sledgehammer.

Leaning closer to the bars the grizzled old con whispered hoarsely, 'Says he's going to jump you tomorrow and set the record straight. They all wanted to mob you but Joe said "no", he wanted to do it himself.' Picking up his hot water pail he added in a raspy voice: 'You're gonna need a bazooka, pal.'

I just sat there on by bunk, ice cold with the thought that tomorrow I was going to have my face rearranged or maybe even end up a basket case. Even worse I wouldn't know when it was coming or from where. At first I was scared and then I started to get mad.

191

I didn't get much sleep that night and by morning I had worked myself into a barely controllable rage. I was grimly determined that nobody was going to crowd me anymore, not without a fight. Better to have every bone in my body busted, better dead even.

After breakfast range by range filed out from the Dome; still more came from the direction of the B-7 cell block — blue denim prisoners all headed for their respective shops. The wall pickets and those in gun cages in the buildings inspected everything that moved. Stiffly like a walking bomb I moved away from the main crowd and cut across the gravel yard towards the sports shack, towards the nest of scorpions, the gang that vowed to get me, alone and a stranger. I spotted them when I was about fifty yards away, banded together for strength, eight in all, waiting for the man to show up and unlock the door to the shack. Joe was standing there with George and the rest of the wolf pack: every last one of them big and rough. It was the perfect way for me to commit suicide, but never have I been so grimly determined to carry out a plan.

A big guy with tattoos spotted me cutting across to them and whispered; soon they were all watching my approach, thinking perhaps that I was coming over to worm my way out of a tight spot. When I was about ten yards away Joe started badmouthing me but my ears were closed to his words, all my attention was riveted on his jaw where I planned to land at least one good punch before being set up by the pack. Two feet were separating us when Joe stepped towards me in a threatening manner, and I tagged him!

It was a lopping right to his rocklike jaw. The sound could be heard clean across the yard. The blow spun him completely around in a circle until he was again facing me in a dazed manner. Desperately I leaped at him to try and finish him off before he could come to his senses and while the pack was still stunned. Ring-wise Joe threw his bearlike arms around me and clinched me tightly to him until he could shake off the cobwebs from his numbed brain. Just then there was the sound of a whistle followed by an ear-splitting 'Crack!'

The warning shot fired from a gun cage was still reverberating when Joe shoved me backwards yelling, 'Beat it!'

Breathing hard I rushed into a crowd of cons who had stopped to watch the fight and they swept me along towards the shops before the guards could get my number (being a fish had its advantages). From a population of more than four hundred prisoners at least a hundred had witnessed the fight and the rest soon heard about it over the grapevine. Pleased and excited to see a heavy like Joe humiliated, they nevertheless gave me very little chance to survive in a second encounter, for there could be very little doubt that my demise was being venomously plotted that very minute.

I spent the morning working at my button machine in the tailor shop mulling over the fact that I was now more a target than ever, that this time the gang would probably strike in unison and probably murder me too! I must have been possessed by the devil or some kind of spirit because I really wasn't very scared, just worried about the condition of my hand. The punch had almost shattered my right hand and it was swelling so rapidly that I had difficulty making a fist.

It was lunch time and with other members from my shop I filed into the jug-up line in the Dome, picked up my tray from a wicket, walked across the concrete floor of the circular dome to a metal staircase, and climbed three flights to the fourth floor – aware that everybody was sneaking glances at me and pointing me out. Hero for a day. Shit!

I was half-way down my tier on 4-C when Joe popped out of somebody's drum where he had been hiding and – with only the back of my skull as a target – he let go with a lopping right and popped five big knuckles off my melon. He hit me with such force that my tray went one way and I went another on wobbly legs. Voluntarily I added the distance of another five cells in a desperate effort to clear my mind of what sounded like a ruptured water main. All the while I was aware that if I passed out Joe would toss me over the railing to my death far below. Shaking off the waves of darkness that threatened to engulf me, I halted my momentum and spinning around I met his rush head on with a crash of blows.

Punching one another on the narrow gallery neither one

of us wasted any of our energy on words or curses. Suddenly Joe shifted his tactics to grabbing and with one hand he grasped me around the throat and with his other he pinned my right arm to my side with awesome strength. Slowly and inexorably with fingers of steel he bent me backwards over the railing while I struggled to arrest the movement with a strength of my own. All the while we stared insanely into each other's inflamed eyes. With my free arm I lashed out with short left hooks at his unprotected face, trying to weaken his grip with awkward pummelling blows. Although I prided myself on powerful neck muscles, Joe's grip was too deadly and already I could feel the tiny vein at the back of my eyes rupturing and Joe's face becoming but a blur. Fear gave me additional strength and I punched harder and more frenzied than ever and abruptly Joe gave a cry and fell backwards into the cell bars and I was free!

Drawing in lungfuls of oxygen and with my shirt in shreds I staggered away from the railing. Gasping and holding my fist ready I stood in the centre of the tier. Wiping the blood from his face a few steps away from me was Joe, also gasping for breath. Eyeing one another fiercely we started to close in once more when suddenly there was the sound of running footsteps and bounding on to the tier came two of Joe's friends who had been busy decoying the guards.

'Pack it in!' one of them whispered hoarsely. 'The screws are coming!' And with that they pointed excitedly over their shoulders.

Still crouching Joe gave me an icy stare and in a controlled voice he said: 'I'll be fucking seeing you later.' With that threat hanging in the air he squeezed past me and some of my neighbours and raced to the end of the tier and around behind. From there he scrambled hand over hand down to the main floor and made his get-away to his own drum. Slipping into my cell I hurriedly pulled on another shirt just as the goon squad trotted on to the range to nose around, not really expecting to catch any cons fighting.

Not having a food tray and having lost my appetite anyhow I spent the noon hour nursing my wounds. There were welts under both eyes, my cheekbones were severely bruised and my throat muscles felt crushed, so much so that

194

it hurt to swallow water. I was like a man with an acute case of laryngitis whenever I tried to vocalise. Worst of all for my survival was the condition of my hand which was swelling grotesquely. The middle knuckle was obviously cracked making it impossible for me to make a fist.

I spent the lunch hour flat on my back staring up at the ceiling and wondering how I would manage with a wounded wing when this bass voice croaked almost in my ear, 'Wanna talk to you!'

I twisted out of my bunk to find myself staring at Joe standing outside my cell bars! Like a big gorilla wearing sunglasses he stood there glaring at me with a kisser that looked like it had just been dive-bombed by a swarm of angry hornets.

'Okay, I'm listening Joe,' I replied cordially.

'You shouldn'a done what you did today, kid. You made me look bad in front of my friends and now I've got to square things.' His lips were so swollen that he lisped when he talked. 'Yeah, I've got to do you in,' he said nodding to himself. 'No choice; my reputation calls for it.'

Bridling at the way he was coming on, I shot back: 'Okay, but just remember – it's a two-way street.'

His big ham-like hands grasped the bars and squeezing he hissed, 'Later today, a dead-end street is gonna be your funeral.'

Biting back a nasty reply of my own, I came right to the point instead, 'Joe, just say what you came to say and let's get this over with.'

Reigning in his emotions, he nodded and then slowly and carefully mapped out where and how the third round would take place without worrying about the screws showing up. Next to the south-west corner of the institution was an ancient horse barn made out of rough stones. It had a deep and cavernous cellar with dusty horse stalls and could be entered through a boarded-up window. Dark and damp and cluttered with cobwebs, it didn't take much for me to envision horrible things happening to me down there when they all ganged up on me.

'I'll be waiting in the barn for you when you get out of

your shop for your exercise period. There will be a baseball bat waiting for you just inside the window.'

With the blood flooding into my face and turning it a crimson red I replied very softly, 'Are you going to be alone?'

'Nobody is going to gang you, is that what you mean?'

'Okay, I'll be there then.'

His eyes did a double take when he heard my reply which made me suspect that he thought I was going to chicken out. That's when he noticed my swollen hand wrapped in a wet towel, and changing the subject he asked what happened to it.

Unwrapping the towel I held up my swollen hand for him to see, replying that I damaged it on his jaw.

'Lord Thundering Jesus!' he exclaimed in disbelief. 'Now how do you expect to battle with just one wing?'

We got to talking in a reasonable tone for a while and then he piped up and said. 'Fuck it, this has gone far enough. Let's shake hands and be friends, okay with you?'

With relief flooding through me, I nodded and when I saw he didn't trust me enough to shove his big paw through the bars, I ended up doing the honours. He was still leery of me.

Now that I was settled into the routine of doing time I finally started writing home once again. I explained that there was a way of ridding myself of the Cornwall offences by having the charges transferred to the jurisdiction of the New Brunswick courts and disposed of by a circuit judge. This was done and I received four additional months. Now that I knew I wasn't going to be saddled with a lot of time to serve I told my folks that I no longer wanted to escape. My biggest worry was the lingering death my Dad was undergoing as the cancer cells ate into him.

The best way to kill time in prison is to keep busy. That's what I did with a fury, involving myself in all kinds of sports. During one furious game of soccer I became embroiled in a fist fight with Dallas, the captain of the Shamrocks, who I thought was coming on too strong against some of the smaller guys on my team. By the time the players separated us he was staggering and bleeding from the nose. Tall and freckled with a shock of sandy hair,

Dallas was the best all-around athlete in the joint, including the middle-weight boxing champion. As a result of his embarrassment on the soccer field, he challenged me to duplicate the feat on the next boxing card. I had no choice but to accept. We were both the same age and roughly the same build and since the boxing matches would be taking place on New Year's Day, that gave me a scant ten weeks to learn the art.

In the meantime I swung a work change to the kitchen, a much sought after job in so far as there was plenty of opportunity to fend off hunger and, if you were a drinking man, to indulge in home-made brew until it came out of your ears. Around this time I also got a bed change to a three-man cell when a vacancy cropped up with two popular friends of mine, a Mutt and Jeff pair.

Thirty-three years old, Babe was the shorter of the two by more than a foot, tough as nails and stubborn beyond belief. He had a round baby face, a little protruding belly and was always getting into fights with big guys for the craziest reasons.

Stretch, in his late twenties lived up to his name by towering over six and a half feet. With his jutting jaw, short brush cut and exotic tattoos, he had a fierce look about him. Big bony knuckles and deeply calloused hands were reminders of all the years he spent toiling in the Cape Breton mines to feed his mother and five younger sisters. His favourite pastime was playing his harmonica and arguing with Babe about baseball.

When I moved into the cell it became immediately clear that one of my duties would be refereeing fights between these two lugs. A second would be to pilfer as much grub from the kitchen as I could get my hands on to appease their crocodile appetites. The one thing that did bring a bit of harmony to the cell was the fact that both Babe and I were scheduled to box on the next fight card. We made Stretch happy by nominating him to be our coach and manager, a role that he threw himself into with gusto. What he didn't like was when we strapped pillows to his big frame and used him for a punching bag! Babe was slated to fight an eighteen-year-old kid six inches taller than he was, while I was taking a shot at Dallas for the middle-weight championship.

Dorchester Penitentiary had the best boxing layout of any prison in Canada, and had some of the best fighters. Two were rated in official boxing magazines. The boxing shed was inside an old building near the huge powerhouse and had two barnlike doors. Inside were heavy punching bags, speed bags, bulky medicine balls, skipping ropes, jock straps, fight posters, and a boxing ring. Stale sweat and rubbing lotions permeated the area. A light heavy-weight black guy called Rudy, and a short stocky white guy called Red were the inmate trainers.

Boxing is a standup, stand away way to fight and I was just a brawler with a hard jaw and foolish courage – a candidate for slaughter against a crafty ring-wise boxer. I had to learn a whole new kind of co-ordination – moving with fluid motions, blocking and slipping punches, feinting, leading, countering, jabbing, and using crosses, hooks, uppercuts, etc. It was like learning to walk all over again acquiring the hundreds of combinations necessary to turn yourself 'off and on' with a cold and deadly efficiency.

Nothing brought home this message more forcefully than my first sparring match against a skilful light heavy-weight, who made me think that I climbed into the ring against a bobbing, weaving, hissing, cobra, as he slipped inside and away from my blows. By the third round my heavy boxing gloves felt like two garbage lids. Then he landed a terrific counter-punch with such force that it broke my nose! A fountain of blood gushed as I rushed him in blind rage until I crumpled to the canvas, choking and unable to breathe.

The joint hospital patched me up as well as they could, warning me to stay away from the ring for sixty days. A week later when the swelling went down I donned head gear and went on with my sparring, being most careful not to get punched on the nose again. It was a serious fracture and made eating difficult because I couldn't breathe through my nose, and for a while I did a lot of snoring, to the consternation of my cell-mates who threw things at me in the night. But I learned from that costly mistake.

Along about this time I became the institutional disc jockey three nights a week from 7 to 11 p.m. It was a very popular programme called 'Murder in the Night' and was piped from the small radio room situated in the dome to all the cells. In those days we were locked inside our cells eighteen out of twenty-four hours, and so the guys were starved for a little bit of entertainment and laughs. The radio room was stuffed with electronic equipment and we had thousands of records donated by local radio stations. The guards would lock me in an hour earlier to give me time to sort through the stacks of record requests. By the time seven o'clock rolled around I'd be settled in a comfortable chair in front of a microphone with a mug of hot coffee close at hand.

'Good evening, this is Roger with another session of "Murder in the Night".' That got the show on the road. Most of the written requests were bizarre in so far as each prisoner vied to be the biggest laugh-getter.

'The first request goes out to Big Sal from his sugar daddy Mouse who wants to know if we got the record "Two Ton Sally"!'

Even from the control room I could hear the thunderous laughter and catcalls, followed by the enraged voice of three hundred pound Sal, as he spewed out heinous threats to his miniature friend. During the evening I could count on receiving rebuttal wisecracks from the screws making the rounds of the tiers and notes from the victims badmouthing their tormentors. Before signing off I could never resist throwing a few curves at Babe and Stretch by playing the corniest record on hand, and declaring over the air that my two friends had requested that I play it. Needless to say mayhem awaited me by the time I returned to our cell.

New Year's Day dawned over the penitentiary gymnasium cold and crisp. By early afternoon the rafters echoed with the noise of four hundred convicts and a smaller number of outside visitors in the warden's section. Through the spiralling smoke of tobacco, the boxing ring shimmered ominously under the powerful glare of overhead lights. There were seven scheduled matches, two of them title bouts. A gambling fever ran rampant throughout the crowd as weed and cash changed hands. I think even the guards got into the act. The winner of each bout would receive a five dollar bag of food and tailor-made cigarettes, while the loser settled for band-aids and aspirins.

Sitting anxiously in the fighters' section at ring-side with my hands taped and my purple robe over my shoulders, I found myself champing at the bit, anguishing at the possibility of losing, and trying to ignore the fact that I was a three to one underdog. Watching Babe's match dispelled a lot of tension; the fight turned out to be a one-sided comedy in so far as the cocky kid had more mouth than guts. An angry Babe had to pursue the jerk all around the ring in a vain attempt to corner his opponent. What a contrast Babe was with the superbly conditioned youth and funny too, with his little fat belly and sagging drawers. In any event Babe won the match hands down.

By the time I climbed through the ropes and into the ring my primeval instinct was to conquer and survive. Sitting on the stool under the hungry stares of the crowd I was so anxious for combat that I almost had to sit on my gloved hands. Dallas, sitting in the opposite corner, looked in great shape and very much the boxer that everybody claimed he was. I looked out at the crowd that was expecting me to be sliced to pieces, the crowd that was saying that my only chance of winning was to land a lucky knock-out punch. 'We'll see,' I thought, 'we'll see.'

Rudy, Stretch and Babe were in my corner rubbing my shoulder muscles and whispering in my ear. I just kept nodding, all the time staring hungrily in the direction of Dallas. The MC introduced us giving our body weights at 163 and 165 pounds respectively. After receiving our instructions at the centre of the boxing ring we touched gloves and returned to our corners to await the bell.

At the sound of the bell, I sprang from my corner and began hammering away at Dallas, even before he fully cleared his corner. My heavy blows and the fury of my attack almost got the best of him and he staggered back into his corner.

'Don't take him into the ropes or he'll murder you!' shouted Rudy.

Too late! Dallas stunned momentarily soon regained his wits, and with a trick worthy of a magician he used my

200

momentum to spin me around, jamming me into the corner he had just vacated! With a flurry of blows he pummelled my face in an attempt to re-break my nose. Bleeding from my mouth I maintained my cool and countering with hooks and jabs I drove him back, back, back, while occasionally taking a counter-punch in return. Now Dallas was bleeding from his nose and from a cut above his eyes and the crowd reacted by screaming themselves hoarse. At the bell we both returned to our corners smeared with gore.

I sat on the stool while Rudy shouted excitedly in my ear, 'Shit man, now that's what I call laying on leather!'

'Lord thundering Jesus, boy!' exclaimed Babe, washing away the blood with a wet sponge.

Grasping my shoulders, Stretch was saying, 'That's one round that belongs to you, ol' partner.'

The adrenalin was flowing so thickly through my arteries that I was still in my own little warring world, itching to get on with the next round.

The bell rang for Round Two and again I rushed across the ring to clash with my opponent while the crowd roared its approval. For long seconds we stood toe-to-toe exchanging a combination of blows, then he started retreating once more while flicking out jabs, in the hope of keeping me at arm's length. Again I forced him into the ropes and again he spun me around tying me once more into the ropes, while rocking my head with tremendous right and left hooks until blood welled up in my throat. Furiously I struck back with uppercuts and body blows until I had him backed up into the centre of the ring, gasping for breath. Choking on my own blood I spit out the mouthpiece just as my battered opponent gambled on a knockout, by resorting to one of his ring stunts. Dancing and backtracking faster than ever he lured me after him into the ropes, intending to rebound with great force and use the momentum to catch me with a devastating punch. That was his mistake! Alert, I sidestepped the blow, his face rushed into view, and with all my strength I smashed my gloved fist into his jaw.

Half an hour later Dallas and I, side-by-side in the shower room, were washing away the traces of blood, not talking very much, yet aware of a bond between us. I was drained of

201

emotion and I did not feel the least bit victorious. Dallas had been unconscious for almost five minutes and now when I looked at his face I grimaced with shame, not that I looked much better myself. I also decided that I didn't like boxing, didn't like what it did to me. I shared my prize with Dallas. After we dressed, we decided that we didn't want to see the remaining fights and instead we wandered out into the now empty yard. It was snowing lightly and very cold; we ambled over to the hockey rink, an area where only the guards in the snow-capped gun towers could observe us, and stick-handled the puck around to stay warm. It was good to have the rink to ourselves, especially at this moment. The high snow banks blotted out the bulky outline of the auditorium, but not the roar of the crowd lusting for blood.

The following day I spoke to the chief keeper and re-quested a cell change back to the single cells, explaining that I wanted to be alone.

Summer was coming when I got myself into a serious jackpot. An argument started in the jug-up line as I was passing through the kitchen passageway to pick up my meal tray, having just trooped in from work. The con in front of me was a big shaggy-looking ex-coal miner from Cape Breton with the blunt name of Hammer. He was bone-headed, stubborn and aggressive. Hammer was always blow-ing in the wind about his ability to grab horses around the neck and wrestle them to the ground. By the time we got up to our fourth tier I was reasoning with him to please not bounce his handball off my wall during lunch hour when I was trying to doze.

'Are you threatening me?' he said.

'No, that ain't my bag, but you just don't bounce a ball off a neighbour's wall is what I'm trying to tell you.'

'Fuck you!' he says and spinning around he fired his dinner tray at me. Ducking I lunged at him and hit him hard in the belly, doubling him up, and then intending to explode a punch off his jaw, I came up with a short uppercut that missed its mark and smashed into his forehead, a blow that busted my knuckles! With one hand paralysed I had the choice of running or coming up with a miracle if I didn't want to be thrown over the range. Stepping quickly behind

Hammer while he was struggling to catch his wind I threw a half-nelson around his neck and started squeezing with all my might. Keeping the pressure on I slowly dragged him backwards to keep him off balance, causing everybody to scramble to get out of our way. In panic Hammer settled for trying to break my grip with overhead punches and although he was hurting me I wasn't about to let go. After squeezing the oxygen out of him for several minutes his tongue started protruding like a slab of liver and his struggles became more and more feeble. Just then two guards came charging down the tier and they were bellowing for me to release Hammer, but I went on squeezing.

'Let him go!' yelled a screw in my ear. 'You wanna kill him?'

By then I was leaning back against the railing with my left hand gripping my right wrist and still squeezing his bull neck against my chest muscles. 'Just a few more seconds,' I replied.

'No!' bellowed the guard. By then there were a whole bunch of screws trying to break my grip, tearing my shirt to shreds in the process. Eventually Hammer dropped at my feet and he wasn't even twitching. I was given the bum's rush towards the Dome. With my busted hand dangling at my side, I went silently to the hole. For this fight the warden levelled me with twenty-one days of diet and hard bed.

After I completed the bread and water session I was removed to the segregation unit where I was to stay for an indefinite period. Here were nineteen coffinlike cells with absolutely no plumbing and very little light. Completely cut off from the inmate population we spent 23 and one half hours a day entombed in our steel cocoons; the other half hour was spent walking silently around a tight circle in an enclosed yard. The date was June 14, 1960.

The segregation block was constantly in an uproar, an ugly place where violent and bloody confrontations were everyday occurrences, and where anything and everything did happen. Those of us who couldn't stand the pressures had the choice of banging our heads on our cell walls, or else we could rattle our bars like apes do in a zoo when frustrated with their keepers.

Being locked up all the time makes a prisoner do crazy and unexplainable things, sometimes to just break the gut-eating monotony. Even self-mutilation can bring about a strange relief. I did that once – carved myself up with a rusty razor blade. Removal to the joint hospital for an hour was a relief. They had to call in The Croaker from his home in the outside world and that made everbody mad, but I didn't care. Like a scarecrow I sat silently in the operating room surrounded by screws and people in white coats while the Doc sewed me up like a rag doll. As punishment, they drove a bayonet-like needle in my hip to put me to sleep and make me scream with pain, but I didn't care.

One year after being segregated I was removed from Rebel Block in bad shape, and admitted to the Psychiatric Ward to regain my wits and prepare myself for a journey.

The warden had decided that it was time to wash his hands of me. A few weeks later I was suddenly snatched from the bug ward in handcuffs and in the custody of two guards I was flown by commercial flight from an airport near Dorchester Pen, all the way to Montreal. It was late at night when I was deposited inside a walled fortress called Saint Vincent de Paul, the maximum security penitentiary for Quebec.

The biggest, meanest, dirtiest and oldest institution in the system, it was a hopeless quagmire of hate and despair that initiated twenty-seven suicides and murders in a period of two years, more than all the prisons in Canada put together. By the time I arrived with six months left to serve, I was stir bugs and with raging fists I blended into the atmosphere perfectly. Here I learned that my father had died. I went berserk!

After I had smashed my cell into a million pieces it took fifty-six stitches to sew up my forearm, and another thirteen to sew up my knuckles. I no longer had any intentions of going straight upon my release.

CHAPTER FOURTEEN

January 9, 1962: One week after my release from Saint Vincent de Paul I was sitting on a stool in the kitchen of an old flat in the heart of Montreal, bare to the waist, and my right arm oozing blood into a stack of towels from nine deep lacerations patterned like claw marks.

Clamping the lips of the wounds together was a swarthy middle-aged Frenchman with big hairy forearms. He was known throughout the underworld as Patch because of his mending abilities. His curly-haired mistress performed the duties of a sympathetic nurse. Without the benefit of anaesthetics, a clucking tongue did help a bit. By the time Patch completed the operation more than one-hundred and fifty metal sutures had been used to close the cuts.

Two members of our six-man gang were waiting for me in the living-room, guzzling down beer.

'Sacré Bleu!' exclaimed Lionel. 'Is that old fool a doctor or a sculptor?'

'Very funny,' I grimaced. 'Meanwhile it hurts like hell.'

'Well have a beer then,' offered Blackie by way of sympathy.

'No thanks.' Sliding into a coat that belonged to the Patch I added, 'What really hurts is shelling out half a bill for this rag.'

Snorting, Blackie replied, 'Just pick your exits more carefully the next time and your coats will last longer.'

He was right. Things could have been worse if I had hesitated to plunge through a large plate glass window. The city at this time was known as the bank robbery capital of the world. There was such a demand that you ran the danger

205

of arriving at a bank while another gang was making its getaway! With that kind of heavy traffic the law was out in full force setting up powerful ambushes around high-risk banks. The law had deliberately let word seep down through the ranks of the underworld that anybody caught in the act of an armed robbery would face severe consequences. That meant that they would shoot first and ask questions later. These ominous threats did scare some gangs off but in the long run it only made the bandits a little quicker on the trigger. With each bank a potential ambush you never knew when you were rushing to your death. The jug patrols were so well organised that it was suicide to remain inside a bank for longer than ninety seconds. With a countdown restriction on each heist, the take was small (whatever was in the tellers' cages) and so the ambition of the gang I joined up with was to hit that one big score.

Looking down on my two friends I thought to myself that I was lucky to have been accepted into their professional ranks so quickly.

I had met the gang through Blackie, who had been sprung from the pen the same day as me. A full-blooded Huron Indian in his late thirties, he had just wrapped up a ten-year bit for manslaughter and now wanted to make up for all that lost time. Short and slight, Blackie was very dangerous when drinking and armed with a weapon. Just two weeks before his sentence was up he had got into a drunken argument in the jug-up line and stabbed another con in the chest. Apart from all that he was far from being dumb or impracticable.

Lionel, one of those real nice guys you meet every once in a while, was the planner. Stocky, bespectacled, and good-looking in a swarthy way, he was in his late twenties and did everything slow and easy. Not physically aggressive, Lionel certainly wasn't a thief by temperament, yet he was so lazy and thrifty that stealing was an unavoidable route for him to take. Like Blackie, his weakness was fast ladies and booze, especially if someone else was paying the tab.

Talk about being a Scrooge! Just three days before being injured the two of us were in a business section of the city casing a score. It was a cold crisp day with snow piled deep, especially at the kerb where we had our car parked next to a

206

grocery store. Lionel was late and I had just bought myself an apple and was leaning against the fender of the Chrysler munching when I spied a bunch of school kids. They were on the opposite side of the street on their way to lunch and obviously having a lot of fun along the way. Impulsively I started pitching snowballs in their direction and in less than a heartbeat my challenge was answered!

By the time Lionel showed up on the scene, I had lost my hat and the car was pockmarked with snowball craters. Not having any sense of humour when he was on a job, he really got on my case about being irresponsible and all that sort of talk. Like everybody else on the gang I had learned that the quickest way to get over an argument with him was to let him run off at the lip.

However about a mile away from the snowball fight I came down with an acute case of embarrassment because of something I had suddenly realised. 'Turn back!'

'Why? So you can build a snowman with them brats?' shouted my friend, still angry.

Lowering my stare and mumbling like a greenhorn who had just been bucked, I said flatly, 'I lost my gun.'

This time Lionel didn't say a word, just kept giving me that smug look that was more damaging than his most damning tirades.

Half an hour after recovering the big automatic in a snowbank, I managed to get the last laugh. A bulletin came over the car radio explaining that a little nine-year-old boy had just been horribly burned in a house fire, and that my type of blood was urgently needed at the Red Cross headquarters on Dorchester Street.

'Let's go, Lionel,' I begged him. 'It won't take long.'

'No way, we've got to check out the alternate get-aways.'

'What are you griping about? I'm the one that's going to bleed.' I tried to reason with him.

'Don't care! If you want to give your life blood away to some stranger, you go ahead, but do it on your own time.'

I finally overcame his objections by pointing out that while he was waiting for me at the Red Cross, he could treat himself to free coffee and doughnuts.

'All right, but don't expect me to give blood.'

After locking our weapons into the glove compartment, I dragged him into the building, still protesting.

With two pretty nurses hovering around me, I had been bleeding for about five minutes when I heard a loud commotion at the entrance to the large room. It was Lionel in the custody of a huge amazon who was grimly steering him to the empty cot next to mine!

'Where you taking me?' he spluttered, clutching his coffee and doughnuts. 'My friend is here to give blood, not me, dammit!'

Gripping his arm, the head nurse propelled him forward paying no heed to his cries.

Before he knew it, he was bedded and bleeding into a bottle right next to me, all the while sending poisonous looks in my direction as if I had betrayed him.

Lionel had a very lovely sister in her late twenties who worked as a cocktail waitress. Tall, dark, and sensuous with beautiful long legs, she was generous to a fault. I was first introduced to Denise shortly after one of our partners got busted on a bank score trying to run a police roadblock. His name was Claude and since he was my best friend it was decided that I would visit him in jail with bogus ID. Denise was to accompany me as my wife to make it look legit.

Claude was a little younger than my twenty-three years, but mature beyond his years. An extraordinarily loyal guy and unusually brave, he was destined to become infamous in Quebec, with death riding high on his shoulders every inch of the way. Handsome and curly headed Claude had hitched a ride on the same vicious merry-go-round as me and neither one of us knew how to climb off. Now he was facing a penitentiary sentence.

When we did talk our way into the grim old Bordeaux jail (with prisoners whistling at Denise through their cell windows) we had to wait long minutes for Claude to be escorted up from solitary. As expected, he had got into a fight with the guards.

After a lot of small talk I gave him his choice. If he wanted to we would try to bust him free when he was escorted to court, or else he could sit tight and we would try and grease the way for a light sentence. After much agon-

208

ising he opted for the latter. After leaving him canteen money we said an emotional good-bye. It was a haunting feeling to walk out free while leaving Claude behind.

The following weeks were hectic and sometimes chilling. Moreover we almost lost another partner to the police. Babear was a super sharp rounder who moved through the underworld like a jungle cat, so cunning that in his mid-twenties he hadn't yet done time. A natural athlete, he was slim, sandy haired, and had hollow cheekbones. His passion was fast cars and guns, both of which he could handle like a pro. When I met Babear he had just been cut loose on a twenty-five thousand dollar property bail for his alleged part in a jewel heist. His two alleged crime partners, who had lengthy records, were unable to make bail and were sitting in the slammer awaiting trial. The only witness against them was an underworld fence who had gone into hiding until the trial convened. In late January, this stool pigeon was found slumped behind the wheel of his Lincoln with six slugs in his melon. The newspaper headlines called it a 'GANGLAND KILLING'.

Naturally Babear was a prime suspect in the murder and after days of intense grilling by the police his alibi checked and he was released.

To get away from these problems, I drove home for a long awaited reunion with my family and some good home cooking. My dad was dead and so there was just my mother and kid brother living in the house. My mother's favourite pastime was still talking over the phone, visiting friends in the hospital, and attending her weekly bingo games. My sister Susie and her husband Ronnie now owned their own beautiful house but they were still childless and that saddened them a lot.

My pride and joy was my handsome kid brother who was still going to high school and who had oodles of girlfriends. Studying to become an architect, he had trouble staying with one subject for long because he was so impulsive and energetic. My favourite memory involving the two of us on that trip home was the night we decided to jog from a bowling alley on the outskirts of town to a café in the town, two or three miles away. It was a stretch of highway glowing under a myriad of coloured lights from all the motels and restaurants lining it, but that Sunday midnight was very quiet.

Labouring to control our breathing we ran straight down the centre of the road, emitting huge clouds of vapour as our foot-falls crunched through the crust of snow. A bright moon illuminated the way for us. It was going to be a gruelling test for the two of us but it was also very important to me that we both finish what we started out together. At one point we found ourselves running parallel to a barren graveyard bordered by high snowbanks and a spiked fence. Resting deeply within the frozen earth and among the ageless tombstones was our father.

The remaining mile was straight down the centre of the main drag. By this time we were both staggering and gasping wildly for breath. My little brother's features were wracked with pain but he was a gutsy kid and grimly determined to push on.

'Don't conk out on me now, hotshot! We're almost there!' I gasped, urging him to dig deep within his youthful energy for that extra burst of speed before his legs gave out on him.

Totally exhausted, our eyes burning with sweat, we collapsed in a heap right in the centre of the street in front of the café, struggling to gulp down lungsful of oxygen. Staring out at us with big eyes through the café window was the Chinese owner and two waitresses – obviously convinced that we were drunk.

It took twenty-three years to finally lose my virginity and when it did happen it was as wonderful and fulfilling as the literature on the subject had prepared me to experience.

It all started out innocently enough with a phone call from Lionel's sister who had just moved into a new apartment. For many years Denise had been the mistress of a big shot who operated his own electrical company, but she had just severed her relationship with him forever and was now living alone with her eight-year-old daughter. She was asking me in a sultry voice if I would drive over to her place and rearrange some heavy furniture. Apart from her accompanying me to Bordeaux jail to visit Claude, I had seen her at the club where she worked when our gang was nightclubbing. As usual my partners never failed to jest about my still being a cherry in front of their girls, and Denise was not oblivious to these cracks, which now made me edgy whenever I was in her presence.

It was near midnight and the stereo was playing soft music as I slid one of her trunks into a large closet. I stepped back in surprise, gawking in amazement at her vast wardrobe, dozens of stylish dresses and whole racks of high-heeled shoes. There was enough there to furnish a small boutique and I told her so.

'Oh, that reminds me, Roger,' she said, laying down a stack of records. 'I promised my sister she can have the dresses I no longer want to wear but oh my, how do I choose?' Brushing up against me she pouted and rolled those big innocent eyes of hers as she stroked her silky gown. 'Oh I know! You will choose them for me!' Placing a palm of her hand flat against my chest, she pulled a dress free and murmured coyly, 'I mean I'll model them and you tell me the ones you think I should give away. OK?'

Feeling very uneasy I could only nod my head.

'All right, you sit there on the couch and I'll change behind this door . . .'

One hour later I was still seated, gripping an empty bottle of Coke so tightly that the veins in my hand were threatening to burst; my face was moist with perspiration. Across the carpeted living-room floor, Denise was standing in the doorway of the closet in her white panties and bra, her tawny skin glowing in the light of the table lamp, giving up all pretence of concealment while changing her clothes. Slipping into a black skin-tight dress, she seductively paraded before me, letting her hands run down the contours of her body asking demurely, 'I got this one in New York City three years ago. That is a very long time, so do you think I should keep it?'

Unable to speak I nodded my head vigorously.

'But Roger!' she exclaimed in mock anger. 'If you keep saying yes I won't have any dresses to give to my poor sister.'

I just couldn't help being awed by her manner, so ladylike, so tall and graceful, just like Sophia Loren.

Just then a knock on the door cooled the situation and donning a blue negligée, Denise went to see who it was, all the while smiling at me like I was a piece of cake.

Pleased at the distraction I took the opportunity to splash some cold water on my face and regain my wits. I also cursed my bumbling ineptness for not having the courage to make an advance to her. She certainly did things to me but I was scared!

The knock turned out to be a member of the city snow removal crew who requested that our vehicles be moved. Throwing on my coat I hurried outside and was appalled at the weather conditions. A storm had struck while I had been distracted by Denise. So much snow had fallen that it was obvious that the only way I'd get back to my apartment that night was by walking, but even that was dubious.

Reporting my problem to Denise she immediately insisted that I remain overnight, pointing out that I could sleep on the couch. This time her smile was really wide.

I thought at first that it was the storm that had awakened me because I could hear it raging outside the darkened curtained window. I knew I had only been sleeping minutes. Suddenly I heard the sound again, Denise's voice purring like a kitten, sending an electric current pulsating through my drowsiness.

'Roger dear are you awake?'

'I guess so.'

'Will you come here, please?'

Sliding my naked body into my pants, I padded slowly into her bedroom, feeling the night chill on my upper torso, and stopped just inside the doorway. The bedlamp was on and Denise was propped up on fluffy pillows, showing a lot of cleavage and crying!

Alarmed, I moved quickly to her side and asked nervously what was wrong?

'I'm hurting,' she said, pouting like a small child.

Bewildered I inquired, 'Where?'

'Here,' she sobbed taking my hand and placing it on her breast. 'It's my heart – I think you broke it.'

Sniffling back her tears, she smiled up at me as my fingers tenderly squeezed the soft mound of flesh. Never have I felt so confused while feeling so much pleasure. Brushing her tears away with my free hand I brought my lips close to hers and then we became as one as the tempo of the storm engulfed us ...

In the morning I awoke to the rays of sunlight and to the sweet smell of a woman's perfume. Nestling in my arms and telling me that she was in love with me was Denise, my lady, my love.

Later that same day I moved in with all my belongings, accepting the responsibility of caring for and loving both her and her daughter Diane, who was at boarding school.

I was living in bliss with her for almost two weeks when our gang was offered that one big score we all dreamed of. An ex-con in the city of Saint John in New Brunswick said he had a score that was worth almost a quarter of a million dollars and wanted to know if we were interested. Lionel and Babear immediately set out by plane to check it out personally. If everything looked as good as the parolee said then Blackie, myself, and a big guy called Marcel, would fly down with the weapons and knock it off. My dream at the time was to make just enough bread to invest in a healthy gym, thus joining the lunch bucket brigade, and maybe even marrying Denise to complete the picture.

Knowing that I had a big job ahead of me, one that had a big risk factor, and remembering all the near scrapes I had struggled through in the past seven weeks since my release from prison, I was kind of volatile, needing only a spark to make me explode in violence.

My partner Blackie provided the spark. Not long after getting sprung, he had become involved with an exotic dancer and had moved in with her. Ulla was a big bosomy girl in the style of Mae West and had just broken up with her gangster friend, Simon, who had used her mostly as a punching bag. This jerk now wanted her back and made his point with continuous threatening phone calls. Such phone calls often put a damper on parties at her place and for this reason the members of our gang tried to flush him out into the open, but the coward always remained well concealed.

It all came to a head one Sunday morning around 3 o'clock just when I was having my first real sleep in days.

Denise was shaking me awake while holding the telephone receiver in her hand, telling me that the call was urgent. With a great deal of difficulty I clawed my way back to consciousness to hear Ulla's tearful voice in my ear.

'Roger, please help us! Two of Simon's friends followed us home from the club and are threatening to break our legs!'

'Ulla, calm down,' I ordered her. 'Where are they now.'

'In the living-room with Blackie!' she cried out in a hoarse whisper. 'They are demanding money.'

A rage built up inside me. 'Stall them until I get there.' I hung up.

The streets were empty and bare of snow as I raced through them behind the wheel of my car, outwardly calm but a bubbling volcano inside that wanted to smash outwards until the ache in me was appeased. I didn't know if they had any guns, nor did I have a piece in the apartment, but right then it just didn't matter.

No more than ten minutes had elapsed from the time I hung up the phone until the moment I slid my car to a halt before Ulla's apartment building. In seconds I was descending the short flight of stairs to her basement apartment and trying the door which I found unlocked. Stepping into the vestibule I immediately observed Ulla cringeing on the couch with her baby doll pyjamas torn at the shoulder. Facing two young toughs about my age was Blackie with blood trickling from the corner of his mouth. He might have been deadly with a weapon but obviously without one he rather was inoffensive.

The two punks looked like they had just stepped from a gangster movie. Tall and well built with cruel pasty features, they were both handsome in a deadpan manner and looked enough alike to be twins. They wore grey overcoats and snap-brim hats pulled low over squinted eyes. Cigarettes dangled from their thin lips. They both had their hands shoved deep into their coat pockets.

Dream-like, no one uttered a word or made a move as all eyes watched me calmly remove my gloves, topcoat, and sports jacket, draping them carefully over the back of a chair. Quickly I crossed the room and, turning my back on

214

the toughs, I faced Blackie and asked one question of him.

'Do they have pieces?'

Not waiting for an answer, I suddenly pivoted and caught the first tough flush on the mouth with a looping right that splintered his teeth and sent him sprawling backwards on to the bathroom floor. His buddy was trying to withdraw his hands from his overcoat pockets. Quick as a wink, I caught him with hard rights and lefts, each short blow driving him backwards towards the kitchen where he crashed against the refrigerator and slid down into a sitting position.

Glancing over my shoulder I saw that the first guy was still on his back in the washroom while Blackie and Ulla were still rooted in their original positions.

Blood was streaming down the face of the guy at my feet and I was going to ease up on him when I caught him reaching into his coat pocket! I kicked him on the side of the temple and the concussion caused one of his eyes to pop out of the socket and dangle on his cheek! In an uncontrollable rage I grabbed him by his hair and hauled him screaming to his feet while reaching with my other hand for a gin bottle to clobber him with. Seeing what I was about to do he gave a yell, wrenched free and ran for the apartment door. Catching up to him I grabbed him around the neck from behind and started choking him.

Suddenly Blackie and Ulla came to life and started pleading with me not to kill the jerk in their apartment. Coming to my senses I released him – letting him fall to his knees gasping for breath – his face a grotesque mask of gore with his eye still dangling on his cheek. Just then the other tough, holding a hand to his bloody mouth, squeezed past me in a big hurry but before he could reach the stairs my right shoe arched into the seat of his pants with such force that he was propelled half-way up the staircase! Latching on to the one with the eye problem I gave him the bum's rush up the stairs and out of the apartment, releasing him with a boot, whereupon he hightailed it down the street about a hundred yards behind his buddy.

Back inside I found Blackie and Ulla in a frenzy of excitement, wiping up the blood from the floors and walls before it dried.

'I've never seen anything like that before. Not in the club and not even in the movies!' exclaimed Ulla in rapid French.

Blackie, who had witnessed some of my fistic capers inside the pen, including the time I broke the jaw of a jailhouse thief, was not so surprised as he thanked me profusely for coming to their rescue.

Talking very little I stayed only long enough for Ulla to bandage my lacerated knuckles.

Sick at heart I raced madly through the black empty streets purposely gripping the steering wheel until blood welled up through the bandages. I wanted to punish myself, confused within, hating the thing that was pushing me into a collision with myself. Denise lying warm in bed would listen and perhaps even understand why I did certain things . . .

CHAPTER FIFTEEN

February 27, 1962: The airliner lifted off into the dark snowy skies over Montreal. Far below my senses told me that Denise was still gazing skyward wrapped in her fur coat and with the tears still in her eyes, probably wondering fearfully if we had just kissed and hugged for the very last time.

Inside the first class section of the plane, seated with Blackie and Marcel and lost in thought, I couldn't help feeling an impending doom settling over the involved plans that necessitated knocking off both a bank and a Brink's armoured truck within a span of half an hour. The heist was scheduled for the first day of March on a Thursday payday and it was now late Tuesday evening. Waiting for us eight hundred miles away in Saint John, New Brunswick would be Lionel and Babear.

After landing, we instinctively headed for the warmth of the lunch counter. We were half-way through our lunch and coffee when Babear walked through the airport restaurant nonchalantly dressed like a longshoreman in jeans, checkered jacket and black tuque. By contrast we looked every bit like Montreal hoods with our dark overcoats and fedoras. It was clear that if we wanted to go unnoticed we'd need a quick change of costumes. Picking up our luggage, including a suitcase containing a small arsenal of weapons, we exited into a nearby parking lot where Lionel was waiting for us in a rented car.

It was a miserably cold night with a howling wind and blinding snow pelting the windshield of the car as it bulldozed along a narrow winding road.

Babear, as usual, drove recklessly and fishtailed dangerously in the centre of a steel bridge, regained control with a satisfied grin, and a moment later roared into the city; driving more sensibly as the big car plunged into a district of antiquated houses from the distant past. Not long afterwards we bounced slowly along a dimly lit street and came to a halt before a large wooden dwelling, once elegant, but now crippled with age.

Carrying our luggage we paraded behind Lionel who began unlocking one door after another until eventually we entered a furnished flat, one that had been rented for us.

Seated in an old stuffed chair and obviously waiting for us to show up was our contact man, Louis, quietly sipping hard stuff from a tall glass. We three latecomers were introduced. It was immediately apparent that he was a real friendly guy who could be trusted. He was about twenty-eight years old, with pleasant features, freckles and red hair. Released from the pen a few years earlier and determined to go straight he swung a job as a bellhop at the largest hotel in the city. A tireless worker who displayed a keen mind and a flair for leadership, he soon won a position as junior manager. Louis had lived alone and made no waves; then one rainy night he gave shelter to this bedraggled chick as one would a stray kitten. He became increasingly responsible for her well being, even after he learned that she was pregnant. As a matter of fact, he found himself promising to marry her when his parole was terminated, and raising the child as his very own. It was this decision that lured him back into crime, one last stab at obtaining a bankroll in order to provide for his wife-to-be and the child.

'There's just no way out of this city without running into roadblocks. I'm telling you, you guys have just got to sit tight until the heat blows.' Louis was telling us as we gathered around a map on the kitchen table.

'How long do you think we'll have to hold tight?' Blackie wanted to know, patience not being one of his virtues.

Slapping Blackie on the shoulder Babear exclaimed, 'Don't sweat, ol' buddy. Ulla knows you'll be bringing home the bread and she ain't dumb enough to mess things up by screwing around on you. Just ease up, okay?'

'My ol' lady has already picked out a new house for us to move into,' cracked Marcel. 'Even gave away her old wardrobe.'

To Louis in particular I said, 'Lionel says you're going to explain how the loot will leave town while we stay behind.'

Looking real smug about his devilish scheme, he went into his spiel, 'After everybody leaves the second getaway car, leaving the loot and the pieces behind, the wheelman drives straight to the Admiral Hotel, parks the car out front, then walks away. I'll be standing on point. I'll go out and drive the car around back of the hotel, carrying the bags into the check room and tag them. Then I'll take the car to a carwash, leave the windows cracked so that the steam will wash away any prints that may have been left behind, inside and outside. Then along about 3.15 I'll personally load the bags on to the hotel limousine, including some passengers, and drive off for the airport in time for the bags and the hotel guests to catch the 4 o'clock flight for Montreal.'

Looking straight at me Lionel added, 'Roger, we've decided to send the claim tickets to Denise by Special Delivery, and when she has them she can take custody of the bags until we all show up in Montreal for the split.'

Alarmed I snapped, 'Why Denise!'

Looking peeved Babear held his palms out and cracked, 'You prefer Ulla to pick up the bags? Even Blackie wouldn't be in favour of that.'

'I think having Denise hold the stuff for us is a good idea,' added Blackie.

'Your girl doesn't know what you're doing down there?' asked Louis.

'No, but she knows it's not a vacation,' I answered.

'All right then,' Louis said with a friendly grin, 'She doesn't have to know what she's holding in trust. Besides she's Lionel's sister and your girl. What better choice have we got?'

'Okay,' I agreed. 'So Denise gets to be the banker. But tell me this – how do you plan to slip the luggage through the roadblocks without the contents getting a going over?'

Grinning broadly and nudging Louis with his half-eaten sandwich, Lionel blurted out: 'Go ahead Lou, lay it on him.'

'Well,' says Louis in an expansive manner, 'I did forget to add that the people who will be aboard the limousine are conventioners, but ...' he said, holding up his finger for emphasis, 'These are no ordinary conventioners. No sir, each and every one of them is a goddamn judge!'

After a lot of laughs and more planning and debates, it was agreed that we would remain in the city, in individual hide-outs, until the roadblocks were lifted. It would be Louis' job to spirit us out of town so that we could reunite in Montreal and split the loot minus ten per cent for Lou. Tomorrow Louis would scout the city. Using his hotel credentials he'd rent four more places for us to stay; duplicate sets of keys to each address would be made in case it was necessary for one of us to make a sudden switch. The same for the car. Meanwhile, until the heist went down we would all be living at this Water Street address with only one bed and one couch. As soon as Louis left for his place we all drew high cards for sleeping positions; Babear and I ended up on the rug for the night.

Early the following morning Babear and I left to get a look at the bank and get the feel of the area. The city of Saint John is encircled not only by dense forest hundreds of miles in depth, but also by water. The Bay of Fundy carries the world's highest tides, surging in from the Atlantic Ocean twice daily to lap at the mainstreet with a twenty foot tide-mark and flowing back into the sea leaving the fishing boats stuck fast in the muddy bottom. If the law blocked off a few bridges, then whoever was dashing around furiously within the city looking for a way out, would find himself trapped. Our target was in the east end of the city, a suburb with hilly streets and angle-parked cars. It had the look of a quaint village. The three man police force was less than a block away from the bank, a hazard which we seriously considered rendering harmless before entering the jug.

It was crucial that we take control of the bank without sounding an alarm because it was approximately four miles back to the Admiral Hotel, our pivot point. Three of those four miles was along an icy ribbon of road which was completely barren, plagued with hairpin turns, and situated one hundred feet above and parallel to the turbulent river. It was the only usable road in the winter to and from West Saint John; but it was like a single set of railroad tracks in which one was helpless to escape whatever was pursuing. Plunging into the river below was out of the question.

The alarm must not go off. With this in mind I turned to Babear who was behind the wheel of the big Pontiac.

'When we get back uptown I'm going to buy a couple of high-powered rifles and some steel jacket bullets. Remember that time on the country road where two clips stopped that motor dead?'

'Uh-huh,' nodded my friend. 'Like you say, we'll get us a couple of rifles.'

It was midmorning before we parked downhill from the red brick building that housed a large branch of the Bank of Nova Scotia. In the middle of the sharply sloping block it was flanked by a house and a store. Across the street were more houses and stores. At the top of the street were traffic lights, a service station, and a supermarket. The inconspicuous police station was at the bottom of the street and just around the corner.

The main floor of the jug was elevated some ten feet above the slanting sidewalk and reached by a set of stone steps where, a few years later, a bandit coming out of the bank with a sack full of loot was killed by the police, shot through the neck. Two sets of glass doors led into the interior. It was a large square bank and all the windows, front, back, and sides were shuttered by blinds. With the shuttered windows and the elevated floor no passer-by could see what was taking place inside once we made the entry, not even the Brink's guards who would angle park their armoured truck with the back door facing the stairs leading into the jug. All of these factors made the heist feasible. Every second Thursday an armoured truck would pick up a strongbox at the main branch of the Bank of Nova Scotia in downtown Saint John and deliver it here between 11 a.m. 11.25 a.m. In that strongbox was a $110,000 payroll for the CPR longshoremen. Scattered around inside the vehicle would be smaller amounts of money. According to Louis there were only two guards: the driver and a shotgun guard. Incredibly both men would leave the truck after parking and enter the bank together carrying the payroll between them. Our plan was to overpower them as soon as they entered and disarm them, whereupon I would don one uniform and go out and collect whatever else of value was inside the vehicle.

Sitting inside the car and staring at the bank I could feel no bad vibrations. Turning to Babear I said, 'This time tomorrow morning there's going to be some wet drawers in that jug. C'mon, let's go and get those rifles.'

That same evening about 8 o'clock Louis dropped over to the Water Street flat and handed out keys to various hideouts around town. I talked them into letting me keep the one we were in. It was then that somebody suggested we kill the evening with a game of poker. I didn't much like the idea, but I agreed, stipulating that the losing limit be no more than a thousand dollars, to be deducted from the shares after the heist. The game got underway and by midnight I owed about $600. Tired of the cigarette smoke and the boozy talk I bowed out and went to bed.

About two o'clock in the morning the sound of a breaking bottle jarred me out of my sleep and sent me racing barefooted into the kitchen, just in time to wrestle a jagged whisky bottle away from Blackie who wanted to disfigure Lionel with it. Eventually I brought a semblance of sanity to the room and learned that the crazy Indian had lost nine thousand dollars to Lionel, who then refused Blackie's request to go double-or-nothing.

Thursday morning, March 1. I was the first one up and

about. Finding myself in an unusually good frame of mind with none of the usual stomach butterflies, I took this as a good omen. To further enhance my luck, I gently stroked my medallion. By 7 a.m. everybody else was up on their feet, a bit wobbly from the effects of the night before, but still very much alert.

By 8 o'clock all the weapons were spread out on the rug for a final inspection, done with gloves so as not to leave fingerprints in the event that a gun was lost. Even the shells were wiped clean, especially the ones for the automatic weapons. Our arsenal consisted of two ·303 Enfield rifles each with a magazine containing ten shells apiece; a full length shotgun; a sawed-off automatic shotgun; a German machine pistol; a ·44 revolver; two ·32 revolvers; and finally a ·25 automatic. None of us were to wear suits. I was wearing a bulky blue nylon jacket because it would be the best thing for the automatic shotgun and the pockets were deep enough to hold the large shells safely.

By 9 o'clock, Babear and I had left the flat and raced off in the Pontiac to a large factory parking lot that we had picked out earlier. It was an ideal spot to snatch a hot car, one that would not be found missing until at least noon hour. This time I was in the driver's seat and manoeuvring the big car, I parked directly behind a new Chevrolet. Sitting there with a pistol on my lap I watched intently as Babear walked over to the passenger side and popped open the small vent window with a screw driver. It took less than one minute for him to slide behind the wheel, insert the universal switch we had brought along from Montreal, start the car, and drive slowly away with me following at a distance. After gassing up we left the getaway car next to a snow covered athletic field on a quiet residential street, midway between the Admiral Hotel and the heist. We then returned to the Water Street flat to go over the plans once more.

It was decided that I would do all the talking inside the jug because I spoke with hardly a trace of French and we didn't want the police assuming that we were a Montreal gang. Also, because it was imperative that no alarm be given, two of us would have to be stationed right inside the bank when the rest of the gang rushed in brandishing guns,

222

so as to be in a position to rush through a swinging gate and immediately get the drop on the desk personnel at the back of the bank near the vault before they could trip an alarm or shout into the telephone. Blackie and Marcel were assigned that position. The bank had a lot of floor space and a long U-shaped counter which encircled the entire room beginning at the entrance where the manager and assistant manager's offices were situated. As soon as we entered Babear and Lionel would take care of them. It was left up to me to freeze and control the tellers and clients and make damn sure that none of them stepped on an alarm or reached for a gun.

It was cold and overcast but the roads were fairly clear of snow when we reached West Saint John with Babear behind the wheel of the stolen Chevrolet. The first time we cruised past the bank a patrolman was slowly walking his beat, so we went around the block once more and parked at the bottom of the street, which was about a hundred yards from the police station. Blackie and Marcel got out of the car and walked swiftly towards the jug. We waited until they climbed the stairs and disappeared inside, then the car moved rapidly up the street and angle parked off to the side of the front entrance and next to a station wagon with a big man sitting patiently behind the wheel. It was now exactly 10.55 a.m.

'Let's go!' I said as I shifted the heavy shotgun around inside my coat and slid out of the car. Leading the way I moved quickly towards the concrete stairs and upon reaching the top I pulled open the first set of glass doors. Stopping inside the vestibule, I slipped my ski mask down over my face and pulled out my shotgun. Feeling my two partners crowding up behind me I saw Blackie and Marcel glance nervously in our direction, then move away from the check counter towards the swinging gate.

Kicking the doors inwards I burst into the bank shouting, 'Hold-up! This is a goddamn hold-up!' Pushing through the startled customers I vaulted on to the high counter, smashing the glass partition as I scrambled to my feet and pointed the shotgun down at the tellers, 'Touch that alarm and I'll blow your feet off!'

Terrified and staring hypnotically at the bore of the shot-gun they all raised their hands and backed slowly out of their cages. With all my senses on red alert and pacing the top of the counter and pointing my weapon in all directions I could feel my scalp prickling and chills race up and down my spine. If the police were hiding inside the bank and if I was going to be killed, then the time was now. Everybody was frozen into a still position and with my eyes still roving the interior I could feel my heart beat slowing down to a trot as my senses told me that everything was under control.

This time speaking in a calm voice I said (while gesturing with my weapon), 'Everybody put your hands down and relax and nobody will get hurt, not if you do what we ask of you. Now move towards them two gentlemen at the back of the room and they'll take good care of you.'

I jumped to the floor just as Babear emerged from the manager's office prodding a burly man in the back with his machine-gun. As I dispatched the manager to join the hostages I noticed that he was bleeding from a cut on his cheek. Hurrying to my side Babear muttered something about the man trying to play the part of a hero. Then bringing himself under control and looking grotesque behind the hood that was covering his head, he asked anxiously,

'Any chance that somebody tripped the alarm?'

Shaking my head I replied, 'The tellers were too scared to do that.'

'Good!' he exclaimed with satisfaction.

'But,' I added ominously, 'you better check with Marcel. I think I saw someone on the blower when I came in.'

I was emerging from the head teller's cage with a ·32 Colt revolver I had found in the drawer when Babear and Marcel showed up and said that everything was okay. Babear then displayed an identical revolver he said he found in the manager's office.

Gesturing towards the entrance Babear said, 'We'll guard the doorway and watch for the truck and more customers.'

I then made my way back to Blackie who was guarding the two dozen hostages off to one side of the large vault. They were seated on the floor in three rows and the girls seemed shy and continually tugged at their skirts in a nervous gesture. Again I tried to soothe their apprehension by telling them that all we wanted was the bank's money and the payroll. Meanwhile, Lionel was happily looting the teller's cages and dumping the money into pillow cases. For once in his life he was moving unusually fast.

The ponderous vault door was open. Down inside amid the rows of safety deposit boxes were two huge safes that I wanted unlocked. Gesturing to the manager to get up to his feet and follow me inside, I watched him carefully, ever mindful from Babear's reaction to him that he could be trouble. Stopping before one of the safes I said simply, 'Open it please.'

With a determined look on his kisser and with his jowls quivering he shook his shaggy head and growled, 'No, can't be done! The time lock is set.'

Crowding him back against the row of safety deposit boxes with the stubby barrel of the shotgun pressed deeply into his ample belly I snarled, 'Liar!'

Holding his hands high over his head and with perspiration running down his face the man stared intently into my eyes through the slits in the wool, grunted painfully a few times when I pushed the weapon deeper into his guts, and finally coming to his senses he said quarrelsomely, 'I don't know the combination to this one, but the one over there is my responsibility.'

Within a minute the big door swung open to reveal, among other things, more than $21,000 worth of negotiable travellers' cheques. A sharp whistle on my part brought Lionel on the run, whereupon he immediately started loading up. From the manager I learned that the other identical safe (this time with two combinations) was the responsibility of the accountant and the head teller.

Before returning to the vault I had to get the accountant to answer a persistent ringing telephone and get rid of the caller, then he and the head teller quickly dialled the right combinations and in a moment the heavy door swung open to reveal four more safes! Together they opened the first one which contained stacks of currency and again a whistle brought Lionel on the run with his sack. Keeping the accountant with me I let him do most of the work, like calling individual tellers into the vault to open their respective safes and whistling for Lionel when the money inside was exposed. He also answered a few more phone calls, informed me that the loot we were collecting amounted to more than fifty thousand dollars, and that the armoured truck was due to arrive at any moment. He also said that the bank manager was a tyrant with all the employees.

At intervals two piercing whistles from Marcel would inform us that somebody would be coming into the bank, and each time the bookie and I would slide noiselessly from the vault and crouch together behind a counter, my shotgun at the ready. Behind us with their arms folded watching the entire drama evolve were the hostages, whose ranks were steadily increasing. The first to make the scene was the big guy who had been sitting out in the station wagon; he got a kick in the pants when he tried to give Babear a hard time. Later on three middle-aged ladies entered yakking away so persistently that they were half-way across the main floor before they spotted the five hooded figures pointing guns in their direction. A lot of squawking and a flapping of arms and Blackie had three more hostages to look after.

By 11.20 a.m. two pillow cases were overflowing with money. As yet there was also no sign of the armoured truck and we were all becoming increasingly anxious. About this time an old lady in her seventies entered walking with a cane. She was thin and wore a flowery dress and gold spectacles.

'Oh my!' she exclaimed upon seeing us. 'Oh my!'

Hurrying to her side and talking loudly into her hearing aid I said: 'Now ma'am, you just come with me and everything will be fine.' I led her by the arm into the assistant manager's office, sat her down in his chair, ripped out the phone, and told her to stay right there and be a good girl.

'Oh I will! I will!' she said in a tiny little voice.

By 11.28 a.m. we were sweating bullets under our masks and our mouths were so dry we could hardly speak. Those thirty-three minutes were like a lifetime and it would be suicide for us to remain any longer. To hell with the payroll. We decided to leave while we still had the option.

It took another five minutes to herd more than thirty hostages into the vault – a move on our part that was absolutely a necessity if we were to gain that head start in our getaway. No one showed the least sign of panic, especially after the manager explained that there was no danger of suffocating. I promised them all that as soon as we were safely away I would phone the police and explain the situation. The accountant then handed me a notebook which contained the double combination for the vault door and asked me if I would leave it where the police would find it. Assailed with pangs of conscience I swallowed hard and assured him that I would do exactly as he requested. He then turned around and was the last one to enter the vault before Lionel and Blackie put their shoulders to the massive door and pushed it closed with a hollow clank. By the time I placed the book on the spoked wheel of the vault door my partners were disappearing through the front entrance. Quickly I ran over to the office where the little old lady was sitting patiently leaning forward on her cane. A few minutes earlier I had a heated confrontation with one of my partners who wanted me to lock her in the vault with the other hostages, something that I had flatly refused to do. She looked at me with a gentle smile as I loomed over her; I shouted into her hearing aid: 'My friends want me to tie you to the chair, but I won't do it if you promise not to yell for help or leave the office until the clock up there reaches 12 o'clock. Can I trust you?'

Nodding her head very solemnly she said alertly, 'I promise.'

Patting her hand with my gloved hand I turned and rushed out of the bank. The time was 11.33 a.m. and we had spent a record thirty-eight minutes in the bank!

In two minutes flat we were out of that tiny municipality and roaring along that barren stretch of road, fishtailing dangerously on the hairpin turns as Babear expertly fought the wheel. Ice increased the possibility of crashing through the guardrail to the river far below. Lionel remained in the front seat with the machine-pistol while I clutched a rifle in the back seat searching the way we had come for any sign of pursuit. Just eight more minutes and we would be safely off this spooky ribbon of road and in among the cobweb of city streets.

227

Unknown to us the manager had activated a burglar alarm inside the vault which immediately sounded an alert inside both the local and city police stations. However, because it was a night alarm, the law assumed that it had to be just a short circuit and so just one cruiser took its time responding to the call. When the patrolman walked into the empty bank all hell broke loose.

Meanwhile I watched as Blackie and Marcel stuffed all the loot into one large brown suitcase, including our disguises. A few minutes later when we bumped over a small bridge and entered the city proper our weapons (except the rifles and shotguns) also went into the suitcase, leaving us with nothing incriminating on our persons. The switch to the rental car was carried out swiftly and smoothly and again we were underway. Keeping to the side streets we now travelled more moderately towards the downtown section because all around us was the plaintive sound of sirens. With their job completed Blackie and Marcel bailed out of the car on to a quiet street a block apart from each other, with the instructions to go their separate ways to their hideouts.

Nervous about putting all the loot in one spot Lionel suggested taking all the hundred dollar denominations to Louis's place, putting it all in a large envelope and then mailing it to Denise. Babear thought it was a good idea and volunteered to accompany Lionel in order to verify the count, then afterwards they would make their separate ways to individual hideouts. In preparation for such an emergency Louis had sent his girl shopping for the afternoon and had provided keys for the apartment. Louis lived in a cluttered, downtown section among fruit and fish markets and old buildings and narrow streets. Threading the car into an alleyway, Babear pulled to a halt between the rear of a Chinese restaurant and the back of an old wooden apartment building with a maze of stairways and porches. Stuffing packets of hundred dollar bills into a brown satchel and leaving the motor running, they both slid out of the car, knocking over a garbage pail in their haste, and disappeared into a dark hallway echoing with the sounds of children playing games.

Sliding behind the wheel and brushing the perspiration

from my eyes, I manoeuvred out into the heavy noon hour traffic all the while keeping a sharp eye peeled for police cruisers. Reaching a large and picturesque traffic circle with a beautiful park in the centre I was peering through the maze of statues and cannons and shrubbery to try and pinpoint the Admiral Hotel on the far side, when suddenly I ran through one of those suspended red lights! My nerves, already quivering raw areas of anxiety, now reached an explosive pitch inside my skull with the blare of horns and the loud squeal of tyres. Half-way through the busy intersection I decided to continue my flight at the same steady speed while struggling to regain my cool. Surprised that there was no pursuit, I continued the wide swing around the park until I reached the front of the hotel. Spotting Louis watching my arrival through one of the large windows in the lobby I pulled over and parked at the kerb behind another car and turned the motor off. Without another glance in his direction I climbed out on to the pavement and quickly crossed the street and disappeared around the block.

The angry wail of sirens haunted me all the way back to the Water Street flat and it was only when I was safely inside and with the door locked that I was able to breathe easy again. Staring down at my trembling hands I thought to myself 'The hostages must be free by now and I sure hope they're okay.'

The first reports coming in over the local radio stations were in the form of fragmentary bulletins as an excited voice spoke of a ... Daring commando raid ... Roadblocks ... Hostages still locked in a vault ... Later a reporter on the scene was describing how the police couldn't work the complicated combinations and that an executive was being rushed from the main branch to open the vault and free the people inside. The old lady who was left behind in the office was interviewed briefly, saying that for the most part we were good boys and that it would be a pity if the police killed us. Then shortly before one o'clock the people inside the vault were released and I was greatly relieved to hear that no one had panicked and that they were in good spirits.

One teller was giving a reporter her impression, 'The first indication I got that a bank robbery was underway was when the hooded leader came hurtling over the counter at us, waving that big gun.' The manager estimated our take at between fifty and sixty thousand dollars, adding that our obvious goal was the armoured truck.

Along about 1.30 p.m. I was just poking around inside the refrigerator in preparation for making myself a bite to eat when the living-room door suddenly crashed open! Gasping I spun around wild eyed just in time to see Louis standing in the doorway with a bag of groceries in one hand and keys in the other. Seeing me crouching there and the fierce look on my face, his smile faded and self-consciously he quipped, 'Guess I should have knocked, eh?'

'You stupid jerk!' I exploded trembling all over.

Smiling softly he said, 'Sorry old pal, really.' Then perking up he added: 'Good thing I brought some eggs.'

Following his pointed stare my eyes fell on both of my clenched fists in which the remains of two squashed eggs were dripping to the floor. That was crazy enough to make me laugh and soon I was at ease again.

Lionel had called Louis at the hotel to explain the minor switch in plans and to ask him to bring some stamps so they could mail the envelope containing five thousand dollars. Lou said that he would, just as soon as he delivered a bag of groceries to each hideout, mine being the first stop. He apologised for the bum luck with the Brink's truck and said as it was we scored quite a bundle. 'I got rid of the rifles and the shotguns and the suitcase will be on its way to Montreal in a couple of hours.' After pouring himself a stiff drink he left to drive over to Blackie's hideout about a mile away.

On the surface everything seemed to be going according to plan. Nobody except Louis was supposed to have anything on their person or in their immediate surroundings that could connect them to the bank robbery. Since being released from the pen some two months earlier I had been getting very little sleep and had been experiencing too much tension; within an hour after Louis left my place I was in a deep sleep in my bed, one that was plagued with nightmares. I should have stayed awake because right about that time an incredible chain of events was taking place.

Still smarting from his losses the night before in the poker

230

game and worried that since we missed the payroll most of his share would go to Lionel, Blackie decided to hold out on us by stuffing five thousand dollars from the suitcase into his shirt. Marcel saw him and cut himself in for a piece of the action. In addition to the loot they each retained a revolver taken from the bank, I suppose that was in case we discovered their deceit. Instead of each going to their separate hideouts, they decided that they needed each other's company, so together they went to Blackie's flat whereupon a very nosey landlady overheard them drinking and talking about the robbery through a door.

Half an hour later a dozen detectives armed with machine-guns and using a pass key burst into the room and captured them both. Under a sofa pillow the police found a pistol and twenty-five hundred dollars and in the closet a similar amount and another pistol. That clinched their guilt and off they went to the police station.

Learning from the landlady that the place was rented to Louis, the detectives got very excited. They knew exactly who Louis was and so with a small army of police they swooped down on his apartment and took Lionel and Babear into custody, along with five thousand dollars in hundred dollar bills.

Unable to find any trace of Louis' whereabouts the law set up stakeouts at his place, the hotel, and Blackie's flat. It was at that crazy Indian's place that poor Louis walked into the ambush. However in his pants pocket was the cardboard claim ticket to the money laden suitcase; ignoring the gun muzzles that surrounded his head, Lou darted his fingers downwards and coming up with the piece of stiff cardboard he popped it into his mouth! Incredulous, the law stared bug-eyed as Lou began to chew furiously, and by the time they reacted with gunbutts and fists it was too late, Louis had swallowed the whole thing. (Later he told me that the most difficult part was getting the cord string attached to the stiff cardboard to slide down his throat.)

For the moment (as far as the police were concerned) they had custody of all five bandits who robbed the West Saint John bank. Louis, they were sure, was the hooded leader who did all the talking inside the bank. Because there was still

$43,000 missing and those arrested refused to tell its where-abouts, they were immediately locked up in primitive cages in an unused concrete dungeon in the basement of the old police station. Here they were held under heavy guard in-communicado while the law scoured the city in a furious search to find the missing money and weapons.

In the meantime I was dead asleep in a shark infested dream world while the dragnet was slowly and inexorably closing in on me. Even before falling off to sleep I had briefly entertained the thought of what would happen to me if I was arrested in the flat, and decided not to worry about it, concluding that there was no way the law could come up with concrete evidence that could connect me to the bank robbery.

It was midnight and the landlord of the Water Street flat (who ironically happened to be a railroad detective) had just come home from shift work and was tuning in to the late news. What he heard set him scurrying to the nearby tele-phone. Frenchmen!

Shortly afterwards a squad of heavily armed detectives using a pass-key rushed my bed and got the drop on me!

'How do you fit in, and where the hell is the bank loot?' they wanted to know.

CHAPTER SIXTEEN

July 11, 1962: Five days after our arrest the money was found (through the process of elimination) and we were moved to the city jail next door and kept there under extra-ordinarily tight security. So tight in fact that my partners were soon gasping and pleading 'Guilty' so as to get trans-ferred to the Maritime Penitentiary at Dorchester.

Lionel and Babear, having the worst criminal records,

232

received fifteen years apiece. Babear and Marcel picked up a sawbuck and Louis a fin. (Lionel later hanged himself and Louis died in the prison hospital after a long illness.)

Since the evidence against me was all circumstantial, I stayed behind to fight my case in the courts, losing a jury trial in April and finally my appeal early in July.

I was frantic! My dreams were bugging me again. A great weariness engulfed me the first day I was admitted to the Saint John County Jail to await trial on the bank robbery charge. My hands had started to tremble so visibly that I had to hide them. Totally exhausted, I sprawled on my straw pallet and like a man drugged I slept for six days and six nights. It was a strange sleep plagued with eerie images and great violence. One particular dream kept recurring in vivid detail, a macabre scene that I actually witnessed the year before in Saint Vincent de Paul Penitentiary. It was breakfast and I was walking along the bottom range of B-Block gripping my tray when a young con took a screaming nose dive off the top tier. Smashing into the wall radiator his head literally exploded with bits and pieces of his brain splashing all over me!

Alone in the county jail in the early weeks of my arrest, I tried to conjure up a face for the dead con. It was becoming an obsession to picture what he looked like. The nightmares continued to repeat themselves and with each recurrence the face on the plunging figure became clearer, the gaping mouth and horror-filled eyes, but still I couldn't see. Then on the day the jury found me guilty and the judge sentenced me to twelve years that was the night I woke up screaming – the face was mine!

In the morning the sheriff would be transferring me to the Maritime Penitentiary to commence my sentence now that I had exhausted my appeals. However, for the past four months I had been busy planning my escape and now I was ready to put it into action.

It was a warm Sunday evening about 9 o'clock and the jail was deathly quiet except for the odd honking of a horn from the street traffic outside and some cop pounding on a typewriter next door. Earlier in the afternoon some detectives had brought in a new girl sobbing and screaming, sounds which had left me edgy right up to now.

It had taken me months of patience to weaken the locking clasp on the cell door so that it could be sprung with a good solid push, but that would only get me out into the dimly lit corridor, leaving two more locked gates between me and the street. The real test would come when I moved to overpower the two burly guards on duty with my home-made knife. Joe, the big ex-cop, would probably have the brains not to try and be a hero. It was that big pig I nicknamed Pancho Villa who might try and take the shiv away from me, being so ill-tempered and all, but that would be his mistake.

Finally I heard a chair scrape in the office down the hall and watching through the food slot in my steel door I observed Joe step out into the hallway, unlock a steel gate, relock it, and then his footsteps receded up the metal stairway. I had calculated that it would take him not quite ten minutes to make the rounds of the cell-blocks.

It took me almost five minutes to get my door open and by then I was sweating bullets. Moving stealthily along the hallway towards Pancho in the inner office I tiptoed up the short steps into the tiny visiting-room and hugged the wall, slowly inching through the shadows towards the lighted doorway. From where I was standing gripping the knife I could clearly see the big bastard, Pancho, seated behind the cluttered desk on a swivel chair, his size twelve boots propped up on the desk while he read from a newspaper.

'My god!' he cried out as I lunged at him from the shadows. Dropping his paper, he was reaching one hand for the wooden club and also trying to activate the direct alarm to the police station when my fist crunched right between his eyes! It knocked him backwards out of his chair and when he landed in a heap I was right on top of him with the blade of the knife at his bull neck.

'One sound, one move, you're a dead sucker!' I hissed at him watching his eyes for a defensive action.

His face contorted in fear and anger. 'Awright, what the fuck do you want me to do?'

'Roll over and play dead so I can tie you up.'

Racing against time while keeping an ear cocked for Joe's

arrival I pulled rope from my pockets and quickly bound Pancho's hands behind him. That was all the time I had because I could hear the sound of keys as the second guard made his way downstairs – all 210 pounds of him.

'Be very, very quiet,' I whispered to Pancho, lightly tapping his skull with the nightstick as he glared at me.

I posted myself next to the entrance of the visiting-room, a position that enabled me to keep an eye on the office while waiting for Joe to step into the darkened room. Looming ominously on the opposite wall was my distorted shadow gripping the knife in one fist and the club in the other.

I let him walk right past me and came up behind him as he came to a dead stop at the entrance to the office and saw the legs of his fellow guard sticking out from behind the desk.

My words dripped with venom as I pushed the shiv into his back and said, 'If you want to live, do as I say.'

Dropping his keys and flinging up his hands to his face he twisted around making gurgling sounds and started slowly backing towards the wall, his features a mass of horrified jelly.

'Please, don't kill me too!' he croaked, finally getting the words out. 'I'll do anything you say!'

As I slowly advanced towards him, he held his trembling hands palms up towards me as if to ward me off. 'PLEASE!'

Stopping where I was and changing my expression I said in a reasoning voice, 'Nobody is going to get hurt if you'll just lie down next to your buddy so I can tie you up.'

'Sure, sure,' he mumbled, only too happy to co-operate now that he saw that Pancho was still alive.

Throwing away the rope I handcuffed their hands behind their backs and placed leg irons around their feet. Taking the ring of keys I prodded them to their feet and made them shuffle slowly to an empty cell next to the one I had broken out of. Unlocking the steel door I rushed inside and hauled two straw matresses to the concrete floor and ordered them to lay down. Hurrying back to the office I opened the medicine cupboard and took a roll of wide tape and a full bottle of phenobarbitals (a powerful sedative) and hurried back to my prisoners.

'No, no please!' begged Pancho when I tried to get him to

235

swallow half a dozen of the little red devils. 'My heart!'

I hesitated, not knowing if they were snowing me with all their ills. Staring at the goofballs in my hand I could envision the police trying to shake them awake in order to question them, and being unable to do so! The picture of that taking place was enough to crease my face with the first smile in months. But there was the very real danger that if they vomited while gagged they'd choke to death and so reluctantly I replaced the capsules in the jar.

Taping their mouths and eyes, I took the keys to Joe's car and locked the cell door behind me. I then dressed in my civilian clothes. I moved around the jail very carefully so as not to alert the other 80 prisoners or so who were all shaking short bits. Some of them would put the finger on me in a hot second to regain their freedom and all it took was a yell out the window to the adjacent police station. Never trust a wino, was my motto.

All the time I had been hog-tying the guards the female prisoners, about a dozen in all, were persistently sounding the call bell in their dormitory. It was getting on my nerves and so taking a key from the ring I unlocked a sliding panel about chest high in the office.

'What can I do for you ladies?' I said to the circle of faces.

'Where's that fuckin plumber we asked for an hour ago?' demanded a tough looking little brunette with a pencil on her ear and a deck of cards in her tiny hand.

'What are you, honey?' inquired another in a pony tail. 'The peter man?' Seeing my face flush crimson they all laughed.

'No, I'm the candy man,' I said handing them a few hundred goofballs that were in the jar. 'Have a ball.'

There were loud squeals of joy as anxious hands tore the bottle from my hand and more girls ran up to the window. A girl who was obviously pregnant exclaimed with a shout,

'That's the bank robber!'

'He's breaking out!'

'Too fuckin' much!' laughed the brunette, digging her fingers into the bottle.

At least twenty minutes had elapsed since taking control

236

of the jail and I had to get the hell out of there! Unlocking one barrier that led to the street entrance with a key, I had to tape an electric button to activate the current that would open the final door. At last I was free to go!

It was truly a grand summer evening with twilight settling over the beautiful park across the street. People were strolling along in no big hurry and even the cars on the street seemed to be in no hurry. Fifty feet away in front of the police station two policemen were deep into conversation around their motorcycles. Taking a deep breath and adjusting my sports coat, I stepped off the sidewalk and crossed the wide street where Joe's old Ford was angle parked facing towards the park.

While glancing furtively at the two policemen and the female prisoners gathered at the barred window I tried desperately to unlock the door on the passenger side but could not do it. Circling the car I tried on the opposite side and just as I was swinging the door open some dummy on the third floor of the jail yelled out.

'Hey the bank robber is escaping!!'

Glancing through the rear-view mirror as the motor roared to life, I saw the two cops reaching for their guns and more running down the stairs! I would have had to back right up towards them to turn the car into the traffic and that would have been suicide.

'HALT! HALT!' somebody commanded as I pushed the accelerator to the floorboards. With a mighty roar the car leaped the kerb and plunged into the grassy park like an angry lion, scattering people and pets every which way as I dodged a huge cannon, careened off the statue of the town father, ploughed through a flower bed, fishtailed under a water sprinkler, and finally bounced back on to the street in a squeal of tyres. With a renewed burst of energy the car flashed through a red light and soon I was lost in the heavy traffic as the hornets' nest behind me erupted in pandemonium.

Half an hour later I was in a phone booth outside a restaurant in a seedy part of town dialling Louis' girl. There was no way I was going to leave town and get busted at a roadblock.

'You did it!' exclaimed Marge. 'Louis told me you would and that you would call me. Still I can't believe it!' Laughing nervously she added, 'You didn't kill anybody did you?'

'No, everything went okay,' I reassured her. 'You still got that place to stash me?'

'Yes, I promised Louis I would help you and I will. I'll call my girl friend now, then we'll drive over and pick you up.'

I gave her my address explaining that I would be standing just inside the front doorway to a run-down apartment building.

'Give me forty minutes,' she said.

'Make it twenty.'

'All right then, twenty minutes.'

The street I was standing on was slanted like a toboggan slope with the apartment building being at the bottom. Behind the wooden building and towering over the four-storeyed structure was a street and houses. That's how hilly the immediate area was.

Almost half an hour passed since the phone call and I found myself getting more and more anxious. Suddenly I gagged in disgust as five police cars swung around the corner and came to a screeching halt ten feet from where I was concealing myself! All the car doors flung open simultaneously and out scrambled the law armed with machine-guns!

Turning on my heel I bounded up the first flight of stairs expecting my spine to disintegrate from a hot blast of lead.

'Stop or we'll shoot!!'

In ghastly panic I could feel my eyes going crazy with the all-consuming need to escape. Rushing headlong I managed to keep a landing between me and heavy footsteps below, never giving them the opportunity to get a shot at me as they bumped into objects in the darkened hallways.

Reaching the fourth landing I again punched out a light with my fist and this time I raced to the rear of the building as tenants nervously poked their heads out of doorways. Yanking a door open I found myself on a wooden balcony with the stars overhead. Directly below was a black void, a sheer drop of sixty feet, while fifteen feet straight out was the slanting roof of a house nestled in the side of the hill. Gripping the railing as a great burst of shouting erupted behind me, I shuddered at the thought that my nightmare was at hand, the one in which the con plunged to his death over the top railing. If it was prophetic, then I would die.

'Don't shoot yet – you'll hit somebody!' The voice screamed as I teetered precariously on the railing before jumping . . .

Down I plunged into the inky darkness. My knees buckled violently as I crumbled on to the roof of the house. I rolled dizzily head over heels, fell a short distance on to the roof of a garage, and then spilled into a narrow slanting walkway.

It took me too long to regain my wits and scramble to my feet. I was still out of wind. Already figures from the street below were rushing up the narrow slot after me! Hemmed in on both sides there was only one direction I could take and that was straight up to the street level above.

I was just a few feet away from the exit when a bright flash stung my face and a loud roar sent me sprawling backwards into the brick wall. Blinded I staggered about as figures rushed me and wrestled me to the ground pounding me with their fists and gun barrels until I could no longer move.

'JAILBREAKER RECAPTURED IN JIG TIME!' was the way the local newspaper put it the following day. Two more years were tacked on to my sentence as I went numb all over.

CHAPTER SEVENTEEN

July, 1962: After I had busted out of the county bucket in Saint John the staff there didn't want me around anymore, but getting rid of me proved to be something of a problem.

Chained hand and foot, they hustled me into a sheriff's car for the two hundred mile drive to the Maritime Penitentiary at Dorchester. There my escorts were aghast to learn that the warden wanted no part of me either, so they had to wheel around and drive all the way back to the jail while I sat grimly in the back seat.

Within hours the local Saint John radio station was carrying news reports about my being the first prisoner refused the hospitality of their local penitentiary. The city fathers didn't think it was funny and so somebody got on the blower to the Commissioner of Penitentiaries in Ottawa. It was decided that I would be transferred to Kingston Penitentiary for safe-keeping.

Handcuffed and under heavy guard, I was placed aboard a commercial flight at Moncton. From there I was flown non-stop to Montreal. There we switched to a smaller plane for the last leg of the journey. It was a warm evening when we circled a small private airport outside Kingston and landed.

Parked in the shadows of the small white building was a dark station wagon. Inside the vehicle were two uniformed guards waiting to deliver me to their walled fortress to vegetate for the next fourteen years. Dragging my chains along the tarmac I glanced longingly at a sexy girl in the small crowd watching me and it made me want to stop and scream.

Bitter and volcanic I truly felt that I would go stir-crazy if the opportunity to escape did not present itself. In that state of mind it did not take much to trigger my temper. I was inside those walls only four days when some power tripping punk informed me with a shove that I was sitting on his private chair in the TV viewing-room. Instinctively I decked him with a right hook, a blow that left his nose a bloody mess. The following day some of my old friends located me working out in the weight pit and Honky then told me that this tall blond guy who worked in the kitchen was bad-mouthing me, claiming that he was going to kill me with a shiv for lumping his partner. At the evening exercise period I was told that Eddy Hop was in the gym watching television and that he had a knife on him.

Reacting to the threat, I picked up a short bar and a few minutes later I was confronting the guy, Harsh words were exchanged and then a violent fight broke out between us with chairs flying and prisoners scrambling madly to get out of our way. But the time the lights came on and the goon squad rushed into the TV room, Eddy Hop was on all fours and his kitchen whites could no longer be distinguished as such, because his head was split open as if by an axe and the blood was oozing all over the place. My buddies had by now pulled me into the crowd of milling cons because I was splattered with gore from the encounter. The shiv and bar had been scooped up from the floor and immediately stashed. I looked too suspect to be able to truly disappear amid the crowd and a bunch of screws spotting the blood swooped down on me, but when they grabbed me by the arms I reacted by shoving them away violently and raising my fist to them. Seeing that my jungle defences still had the better of me, they cautiously backed off.

Just then Honky shouted, 'Look out Roger!' Looking like a nightmare, Eddy Hop had moved up behind me with a metal chair. Ducking I took the blow across my back and came up from my crouch with my right fist cocked and caught him flush on the mouth, a blow that squashed his lips and sent all six foot four of him crashing into a pile of chairs. Pissed off at the guards for having caused my defences to sag I again shook my fist at them and shouted, 'Don't come near me again!'

Some of the blood that was covering me was my own, as Hop had cut me over my left eye. After Hop was transported to the joint hospital and things quietened down an old jail-wise keeper sent the goon squad away and gently talked me back to my senses. Off we went to the cooler where I was stripped and searched; then decked out in coveralls, I was lodged in a dungeon-like cell and told that the male nurse would be down to stitch me up. By this time I was in a state of extreme depression, thinking that I was better off dead than living like this. But I was a survivor and thoughts like that never stayed with me for long.

Hop was as mean as they come and although he possessed a superior IQ and an attitude to match, he had to be dumb in the ways of the prison jungle to go around blowing in the wind that he was going to kill me the first opportunity he got. More cons got filled in from just rattling their sabres than any other way. Although I felt badly about what had happened there was still a current of anger running through me that the bastard wanted to kill me over something that didn't concern him. As this was a Friday, I would not be appearing in the warden's court until Monday, so that gave me a few days to prepare my defence.

The warden's court was situated just inside the entrance to the hole and guarded by a battery of screws as if it were an army command post. I spread my legs and placed my hands against the wall for rough hands to shake me down for weapons and then I was ushered into a small room with a barred window. Here I was ordered to stand at attention before a white line that separated me from the warden seated behind a desk and flanked by the deputy and a male stenographer. Over their heads loomed two flags and a picture of the Queen, while lining the walls were big bruisers ready to pounce on me should I make a threatening gesture towards the 'Colonel' as the warden was called. Reading from a charge sheet he cited the accusations against me, half a dozen in all, including wounding another inmate and threatening two guards.

'How do you plead to these charges?' inquired the warden.

'Guilty, but with an explanation, sir,' I replied in a clear voice, mentally preparing my snow job and hoping that Eddy Hop had received my message that morning in the hospital.

'It's true, warden, that I slugged the person in question, but only with my fist and only after I was mistakenly attacked by him.' I then went on to explain that I was seated behind Hop and that sombody behind me barred him and spinning around, blinded by his own blood, out of his mind with anger, he attacked me thinking that I was his aggressor. I said that I too became unstable and that I panicked when the guards grabbed me and that I did not assault them intentionally.

It was a good story and one that caused the warden to tap his swagger stick uncertainly in the palm of his hand. 'Hmm,' he mused. 'Well let's hear what the victim has to say,' Picking up the phone he dialled the hospital.

I was waiting out in the hallway when Eddy Hop, supported by an orderly, shuffled into view wearing a striped robe. His hard face was unshaven, his lips swollen, and his head was swathed in white bandages. All in all he was quite a grotesque sight. As he disappeared into the room I tried to obliterate his image from my mind because I was being assailed by severe pangs of conscience. At the same time I was hoping that his own conscience would cause him to adhere to the inmate code.

Five minutes later I was called back into the room and told to stand beside Hop, who towered over me.

'Caron,' said the warden, clearing his throat. 'Hop here substantiates your story and so I am going to give you both the benefit of the doubt by dismissing the charge against you.' He was pointing to me with his swagger stick when he said that, adding ominously, 'But by God, Caron, if you've lied to me concerning this mess I'll entomb you in the hole. Yes, by God I will.'

Eddy Hop was returned to his hospital bed, displaying no signs of wanting a rematch. Released back into the population I immediately devoted all my energy and imagination to discovering a chink in the prison's seemingly impregnable armour.

Just one week later I was again responsible for disrupting the good order of the institution. It started with a nosey old screw making the 11 o'clock security check of the tiers. Passing cell C-2-7 he flashed his torch through the cell bars on the form beneath the blankets, started to walk on, then with a quizzical look on his seamy face he stopped and this time he flashed the light on the head, noticing that the features showing were unnaturally pale.

'Hey, lad?' he inquired in a hoarse voice so as not to disturb my neighbours. 'Hey, are you sick?'

Getting no reply he hurried down the range to the dome below and picking up a phone he dialled the hospital

243

orderly: 'Better get down here right away, there's a prisoner on 2-C who's paler than he should be. I think he may have slashed himself!'

Moments later gathered in front of my cell were a handful of guards. The gate swung open and a slim nurse stepped inside, stooped to shake the form beneath the blankets and staggered back with a cry of terror as the head rolled free!

Immediately the cry went up 'Prisoner missing!'

The switch-board inside the keeper's hall came alive with calls. Police were notified of the possibility that I may have had time to scale the wall and my description was given. The warden was alerted and he in turn gave orders to call in off-duty guards to search the institution high and low for me. Inside the prison armoury at the front gate shadowy figures with light gleaming off badges lined up anxiously to arm themselves with a variety of weapons. Meanwhile a ripple of unrest spread throughout the inmate population as hushed voices in the gloom of the cell-blocks whispered that they could see blue figures scurrying across rooftops and sliding down manholes to reach the underground sewers, and through the windows in the workshops flashlight beams were flickering everywhere.

On the high, grey walls the guards shifted their rifle straps as they blinked into the heavy mist coming in off the lake, manoeuvring their powerful searchlights to rest momentarily on the search parties as they moved slowly through the ground fog. It had been five years since a prisoner had managed to escape from his cell and they knew that such a man had to be dangerous. From over the wall the eerie sound of a fog horn could be heard as the RCMP patrol boat cut slowly through the waters of Lake Ontario, their spotlights trained on the outside walls of the penitentiary.

Meanwhile, cramped and concealed on a narrow shelf in the washroom out in the big yard I lay under a large piece of waterproof canvas, stiff and sore and cold, yet not daring to move a muscle for fear of giving myself away. To the casual observer it would seem impossible that a human form could be hiding beneath the crumbled canvas used to cover the baseball diamond on rainy days. In fact I heard several search parties echo those very words while using the urinals below my place of concealment, too lazy to make the hazardous climb to the shelf to find out for sure. Miserably aware that my dummy decoy failed me and that it was just a matter of time before they discovered me, I was nevertheless too stubborn to give myself up. Let them bust their butts finding me. Wrapped in a bundle at my feet was a forty foot braided rope and a padded three-pronged grappling hook, plus a dagger and a wooden gun. When I left my cell at 6 o'clock for two hours of recreation in the yard I harboured qualms about the plaster dummy head because I hadn't had time to apply a second coat of skin pigment. My plan had been to lie low in the yard until the shift changed at midnight and the number of manned towers were reduced to three. I was then going to scale the south-west tower by catching the guard rail with my grappling hook and climbing, fully expecting to draw fire before I could slip into the water with a log concealed there by the coal gang. Fuck them! Let them find me.

It was 2 o'clock in the morning when the triumphant cry echoed across the prison grounds, 'We got him!'

With my hands on top of my head I was paraded at gunpoint into the keeper's hall where the warden himself unlocked the gate. Greeting me with a 'Good evening!' and telling me that he didn't blame me for trying to escape with the time I was shaking, he then got deadly serious and straightening up militarily he pronounced sentence right on the spot. I was to be mummified, not in the regular segregation block, but rather in the hole for a minimum of TWO YEARS! Cringeing inwards in horror, I nevertheless kept my face deadpan as I was led away.

The hole was a square white building connected to the dome by means of a tunnel. Near the entrance were two offices, one was the warden's court and the other was for the screws on duty in the cooler. Beyond this alcove was a locked barrier and wooden door that gave access to a miniature cell-block containing twenty wooden doors, ten facing ten. Behind those grim doors with peep holes were prisoners serving up to thirty days on bread and water. Down here everything was damp and gloomy and escape proof.

Above the cell doors was a circular catwalk and an

observation window in the high ceilinged cells for the guards making their rounds at night to peep in. Just inside each doorway was a tiny space followed by a steel barrier with a food slot, and beyond that was the drum itself, some five feet wide and ten feet long. The bed consisted of a concrete platform ten inches off the floor with a lumpy mattress and two army blankets, no sheet or pillow. A strong light encased inside a screened box high up by the ceiling burned day and night until you wanted to scream. It was almost impossible for any light rays to seep through the security window some ten feet up the back wall; to do so it would have to penetrate two sets of window panes, two heavy screens, two sets of iron bars, and finally a thick sheet of Plexiglas that blocked out any fresh air. My clothing consisted of coveralls.

I had cell No. 9 and the walls were covered with dried blood and angry words scratched into the concrete. The cell pulsated with bad vibes from those who had suffered there before me, and especially from those who could not go on and had hung themselves with a blanket. I could almost feel an anguished presence in the cell telling me to somehow discover a ray of hope or else I would perish too. All sense of reality was lost in that dungeon where the will to go on was quickly extinguished in both the weak and the strong. – If a person did not have a goal to fight off the despair and that gut-eating loneliness he was lost. Pacing the floor like an animal in a cage, I wracked my brain to come up with a ray of hope before dawn.

In charge of the cooler during the day shift were three creeps who we thought must have got their training work in an abattoir, because they seemed heartless and devoid of any compassion for a fellow human being. I guess that's why they got the steady shift in the first place. All three had a perverted sense of humour and loud and foul mouths. Their idea of a joke was to place a hot plate on the floor in front of the cell of some poor guy who had been on bread and water for a month, and fry some bacon and eggs. The ass-beat rack was also down there and they were the ones who administered the paddle, which was something they seemed to enjoy very much.

The keeper in charge was an old hard-line screw hired

when probably the only qualification was army service. McGruder was a man about fifty, with craggy features and a white crew cut. He was tall and lanky with a protruding pot belly. He looked like he enjoyed pounding a prisoner while his two goons pinned the guy down. I believe he drove one of my friends to hang himself.

The second was built like a gorilla – even looked like one, and talked through his nose. He slouched when he walked.

The third was young, in his twenties, hired for his brawn and the black belt he held in judo. Dark and swarthy, he swaggered when he walked and bragged of his toughness. He appeared very much at ease in that sort of occupation. Like McGruder, he would never tackle a con alone who could handle himself. Cloyne soon became the most hated guard in the institution and he thought that was something to be proud of. Cloyne was eventually fired for his brutality and not long afterwards was sentenced to a year in reformatory for blowing out someone's bedroom window with a shotgun.

By sunrise I was curled up in a ball on my hard bed and so lonely that I thought I was going to die, but I had a plan that might possibly get me out of the hole and into the psychiatric ward. From there I would have a good chance of escaping over the wall. My scheme was to put on a crazy act – by no means an original idea because cons in every prison throughout the world have tried it. I was going to have to put on a tremendous act to convince McGruder and his two goons, as well as the warden and the shrink that I was psychotic. They knew all the tricks. I decided to be more cunning than the average con and so instead of firing my food tray at them and telling them that I was on a hunger strike because they were poisoning me I'd let *them* advise *me* that this was what was happening (sort of reverse psychology). Otherwise they would just chain me up and force feed me with a tube every day until I relented. Guards are a paranoid lot who can't stand to be snowed – they think it reflects on their intellect if they're tricked, and they get mad.

At 7 a.m. the wooden door squeaked open and in walked Cloyne with my breakfast tray. Depositing it on the food

247

slot he growled, 'Jug-up! Get over here and get your tray.'

Blinking and speaking softly I replied politely, 'No thanks, I'm not hungry.'

He gave me a penetrating look and then shrugging his massive shoulders he grabbed the tray and kicked the door closed. A moment later the door next to me could be heard opening and I could visualise some hungry con reaching for the food. Then I heard Cloyne's growl, 'Back off sucker! Just bread and water for you.' There and then, I was committed.

By the end of the second day it was obvious that my three keepers had me under close scrutiny from above and below. I had just politely refused my sixth meal by pleading that I wasn't hungry. From the beginning I did nothing but lie listlessly on the slab of cement that was my bed and stare up at the ceiling with hopeless eyes. Like three dimwitted bullies, unable to fathom my strange behaviour, they tried to taunt me into badmouthing them so they would then know how to cope with me, but I maintained my cool and kept up my zombielike composure, making it difficult for them to get overly mean with me.

Five days later I still had not eaten a bit and was still answering that I wasn't hungry. Snorting in confusion and scratching his big belly, McGruder would sputter, 'You better not be feeding me manure, boy!' Then he would slam the door and stomp off in frustration not knowing what to do.

A week of not eating and I didn't have to play the zombie any more because that's what I looked and felt like as a black pall of depression settled over me. I was finding it difficult to remain alert as my stomach was convulsed with cramps, my lips were dreadfully parched, and my voice sounded like a death rattle. But I knew that I would die before giving up what I had started. It now sounded preposterous each time I croaked out that I wasn't eating because I had no appetite. I particularly hated it when one of them, after offering me my tray would choose the choice parts, and like a noisy hog he'd gobble it himself with gusto, smacking his lips, and talking through his nose, telling me that I was missing a great meal!

On the eighth day my three keepers barged into my cell

armed with stubby blackjacks and a rubber feeding tube with the crude intentions of muscling me into eating.

'Go ahead!' I croaked. 'You know I won't eat your poisoned food and now you're going to choke me to death!' I then started chewing on the tendons of my left wrist in an insane effort to open an artery, but the flesh stretched like taffy.

'He's crazy, grab him!' shouted McGruder, and they pounced on me and pinned my arms to my side. The brief struggle left me drained of energy and again I lay back like a corpse. The goons left my cell and I heard someone say, 'Get the doctor.'

Soon the portly Croaker and a male nurse were squatting down beside my stone pallet probing by body as I lay there with closed eyes.

'How long has it been since you've eaten?' The Doc wanted to know.

'Breakfast,' I answered in a gravelly voice.

'And before that?'

'Every day,' I replied, taking note of his startled expression.

'What in hell is going on here!' spluttered the doctor in exasperation as he straightened up glaring at McGruder who was standing there with keys gripped in his hand and a shocked expression on his own face. 'Has this inmate been eating or not?'

Spluttering in embarrassment McCruder ushered the doctor and the nurse from the cell, locked the barred gate, and then as he was closing the wooden door I heard him exclaim in anger, 'What I told you is so, doctor. That boy in there is crazy!'

When I heard McGruder say that, I just closed my eyes with a great sigh of relief, convinced that I had hooked the stubborn sonofabitch! From that moment on he was committed to convincing the authorities that I was a mental case.

On the twelfth morning the white-haired psychiatrist and two of his assistants crowded into the stuffy cell and squatting down beside me heard me repeat that I was eating and that everything was all right. In the background I heard

249

McGruder snort and exclaim: 'See, I told you he was loony. I just don't want his kind down here.'

That afternoon, the head nurse, and two inmate giants, squeezed into my cell and lifted me onto a stretcher and carried me off to the East cell-block with McGruder's words still ringing in my ears: 'You never know what them crazy bastards might do.'

'Welcome to the snake pit, Roger,' said big Moose, the inmate orderly, as he and hulking Tuffy transferred me from the stretcher to a hospital bed in a large cell on the second floor of the psychiatric ward. I knew them from the old days. Moose was a likeable giant with jug ears, rather slow-witted, but popular all the same.

'Guess you could use something to eat, right?'

Opening my eyes I looked up into Tuffy's battered face with the busted nose twisted to one side. Tuffy was an old boxer who had obviously taken some terrible beatings in his ring career. Smiling, I gave him a slow wink.

'For sure we better start you off with a bowl of soup and maybe a piece of toast. Okay?'

To this I nodded my head enthusiastically.

While Tuffy was gone to get the soup I looked up at big good-hearted Moose sitting on my bunk and in a hoarse voice I asked him that ageless joke about him and his partner Foxy. 'Is it true what the newspapers said, about you and Foxy?'

With a roar of indignation Moose shouted, 'You know that's bullshit!'

Lying back contentedly on the soft pillow I thought about the days when we used to rib poor Moose about Foxy's version of what happened in the bank: 'I came charging into the jug behind Moose yelling for everybody to get their hands up in the air, and would you believe it, that big lug was the first one to reach for the sky!'

The East cell-block was a long, concrete, three-storeyed structure with ranges of cells back and front. The bottom floor contained a range for segregation and another for protection cases. The two ranges on the third floor were reserved for old-timers and those prisoners who liked it quiet. The middle floor also contained two ranges of cells, plus

250

offices for the psychiatric staff and the clerical help. There were twenty-four drums to a range each containing the bare facilities, bed, toilet, and sink with cold water only. Each ward was ten feet wide and about one hundred and twenty-five feet long. At one end was a locked barrier: the dividing line between the staff and the patients. Fronting the open grilled cells were large windows with ledges to sit on and look at the view – the top of the wall.

The drums in the psychiatric ward remained unlocked from 7 a.m. until 1 p.m. Patients had the choice of sleeping, reading, watching television, playing cards or chess, or sitting around in groups in a cell or on the range shooting the breeze. As for extracurricular activities, such as popping pills, indulging in home brew, or even a little illicit sex, all of that was available too. Bossing each ward were two tough inmate orderlies whose doors were always unlocked, and whose cells were lavishly decorated and curtained off. In fact it was here where most of the parties were held.

In those days the ward was a real loony bin where everything could and did happen. Some of the most dangerous prisoners in the entire institution were patients up there and they often had hair-trigger tempers.

Both the medical and the custodial staff seemed powerless to do much more than keep a semblance of order; this was done by handing out tranquillisers like candy, in the hope of slowing the patients down to the point where they didn't kill each other. In one two-week period one inmate hanged himself from his cell bars, one guard had his nose broken, and another guard had his leg busted in two places while grappling with a patient. All of this was not the fault of Dr Abrams, who carried a tremendous load, including an outside practice. There was neither the professional staff, the space, the co-operation of the Penitentiary service, nor for that matter the interest of the public. Retribution and banishment were the catch words then, certainly not rehabilitation or cures. Most of the basic work was carried out by staff nurses whose only qualifications seemed to be first aid certificates and a solid streak of callousness. Screws in white coats were what they were, for the most part, cowards who taunted patients into a suicidal act and then laughed collectively about it afterwards. Little wonder that the patients reverted to animal behaviour whenever their basic needs went uncared for. The basic idea was to keep the bugs separted from the normal cons in the population. They did have one modern cure-all, but it was used more as punishment than anything else. They called it 'Electro-convulsive-Therapy".

They gave me a week to regain my strength and then I was informed that I would be compelled to take shock treatments to justify my remaining a patient. If I refused, I would be transferred back to the hole to finish off my two years of solitary. Accepting what I thought might be the lesser of the two evils I ended up getting jolted into oblivion on Tuesday and Thursday each week.

My first encounter was the spookiest of all. Seated mutely on a plain wooden bench facing a plain wooden door in a shadowy hall way were five sorrowful patients, including me. Suddenly the door snapped open to silhouette the fatherly-looking doctor, decked out in a white frock, who crooked his finger at the chunky guy seated to my right.

Like a puppet on a string the inmate rose silently and faded into the room. The door closed quietly behind him.

The rest of us went on staring gloomily at the floor while nervously awaiting our turn. Ten minutes later the door again snapped open to reveal our mate unconscious on a stretcher! Fearfully we all pressed back against the wall as the two hulking orderlies wheeled the stretcher silently past us to a recovery room.

The moment that I dreaded was now at hand; I stared hypnotically at the doctor crooking his finger at me. Fervently pressing my hand against my shirt and feeling the comforting outlines of my medallion I entered the brightly-lit room and stared with hostility at the operating table, searching for restraining straps. I felt a measure of relief at find none. Briskly the doctor ordered me to lie down on the table and roll up my right sleeve. In a moment two of the nurses were administering to me, one rubbing alcohol in the crook of my arm while the other dabbed glue on my temples to hold fast the electrodes for the current. Wires were attached to my head and a stout stick placed between my

252

teeth. A sharp needle was pushed through the flesh and into a vein.

'Start counting backwards from one hundred, slowly,' ordered the doctor as he squeezed medication into my blood system. My voice was barely audible by the time I ticked off 'ninety-two'. That was when the switch on the machine was activated! My brain seemed to explode inside my skull as I bit down convulsively on the stick and my body jerked about spasmodically on the table. A few more jerks and I suddenly went limp.

I came to three hours later in the recovery room with a bad headache, feeling as weak as a kitten. In addition to that my throat was parched and my neck muscles were very sore. If their purpose was to drive the devil from my soul then I was more than willing to tell the shrinks that they had succeeded and not to submit me to any more shocks. In actuality the doctors were just as mystified as I was as to what the shocks were really supposed to accomplish. All they knew for sure was that it looked good on paper, while admitting that there was a grave element of risk involved. Was it not the mysterious brain they were messing around with?

Within one week of my admittance to the ward I had devised an audacious escape plan. On the far side of the cellblock where I was a patient was the prison wall or should I say from our height, the top of the wall. The approximate distance from the barred windows to that wall was twenty-five feet, easy throwing distance for a grappling hook! No one had ever tried such an escape route before and I felt that the odds were stacked in my favour. The real danger would come from the guard towers a hundred yards to the left and a hundred yards to the right, because even at that distance with all the bright lights at night, they'd spot me crossing over and pick me off the rope without even taking aim. The thing to do then was to wait for the first heavy snowfall, which could be expected the following month. In the meanwhile I could pave the way by cutting the thick bars on the last window on the range which would be situated behind the television set. Because all this was in the open and thus tricky I enlisted the help of two of my neighbours who were

253

keen on escaping. Together we would make the necessary diversions and sounds to mask the window operation. Slow and easy, we would all the while accumulate whatever escape material we needed.

The two cons who dealt themselves in were considered by the prison staff to be psychos, unstable personalities who would kill in the blink of an eye. These guys talked about violence like some people talked about sports. Having both been in a series of asylums, their arms and torsos were covered with deep, self-inflicted scars; floating around inside their bellies were a variety of metal parts, swallowed over a period of years as a form of protest. They were also profusely decorated with joint tattoos which advertised their rebellion. Both of them were smart and popular, but so filled with hate they could never stay out of jackpots. They were both patients in the psychiatric ward (via the segregation route) for suspicion of setting a diddler on fire in the big yard.

Billy, in his mid-twenties, short, stocky and dark, had pleasant features and was good-hearted to his pals. He was serving twelve years for blowing a man's leg off with a shotgun blast during a robbery. He had a lengthy record.

Morris was the third man in the party and a close friend of Billy's. Serving twelve years for robbery with violence he was the more unstable of the two. Average height and weight, sandy hair, bony face and shifty eyes, Morris had a weakness for pills and home brew. His character was such that you could never truly let your guard down when in his company, it was an instinctive thing.

It took us two weeks to complete the opening on the window, camouflage both bars that were cut through (except for a sliver), and replace the putty around the window pane we had to remove. A few days beyond that and we finally possessed all the necessary escape equipment we'd needed to regain our freedom. Friends constructed a three-pronged hook in the machine shop and smuggled it up to the ward in a milk can. Pieces of braided rope arrived by the same method from the mailbag department and we had our three suits from the tailor shop and the home-made shivs. Because our cells were always being searched by

254

squads of screws, this equipment had to be laboriously removed in order to create a large enough cavity, and then the debris had to be dumped down a ventilation shaft. It was nearing the end of September and we estimated that we would be doing our high-wire act within thirty days – the first evening snowfall.

Most of my leisure time was spent sitting on the window ledge in front of my cell gazing up into the visible patch of sky, just daydreaming. I have never been one of those people interested in sitting around in groups, or even with a close friend, exchanging experiences or philosophical opinions. I have tried to be more sociable because I know I can make more friends and contacts that way, but I quickly revert back to my solitary ways. I just cannot open up.

It was the second Tuesday in October that the shadow of death decided to take designs on me. The guards and the orderlies had just busted up a fight between myself and a local tough who thought of himself as a killer and a crusher. The patient's name was Punchy, a husky guy in his late twenties with a lantern jaw. He was too mouthy and nosey for his own good, poking into our escape plans like that, trying to tell us what to do. Our clothes were torn and we were splattered with blood. Because I had clearly got the best of him he was shame-faced in front of all the patients. The guards had their orders to separate us and this they proceeded to do by giving me a bed change to B Ward, which faced the heart of the prison. Punchy was con enough to realise that the escape plan was being jeopardised and quickly volunteered to go to B Ward in my place. But like hockey referees, the guards would never change their minds once they had made a decision.

Big Moose was the head orderly on that side of the building and try as he might he was unable to secure a bed change for me back to my old ward. All that first day I spent brooding about my stupid bad luck, getting into a fight because my temper got the best of me. By the following morning I had come up with a scheme that would leave me in a position to join the escape attempt when the time came. The far ends of A and B wards (where the televisions were situated) were connected by a dark tunnel that enabled the guards to

255

make their nightly inspection tours without having to back-track. At each end of that twenty foot tunnel was a locked barrier, but the box lock was old and not too complicated, so I decided to make a crude key. Having made up my mind to a course of action, in two days flat I had fashioned a workable hook from a bedspring that unlocked both barriers. Anxiously we monitored weather forecasts, fervently wishing for that first snowstorm, be it daytime or evening.

October 10, 1962: It was a Sunday evening and all that day Big Moose kept feeding me reports from the other block where a wild drinking party was underway in Tuffy's cell. The tomato brew was powerful and the pills they were popping helped to reinforce the macho images they had of themselves. Already one poor slob had been hammered out and a young kid had been conned into letting one of the guys cut a tattoo on his penis. They were thirsting for blood and kept getting on Punchy's case and belittling his super tough guy act by pointing out how I had decked him. By 9 p.m. Punchy was roaring like a tiger and bragging that he was going to dump me first chance he got.

Bloated on bug juice his joint partner, Morris, slurred, 'Why wait 'til later, ol' buddy? You ain't scared of him, are you?'

'Yeah, why not get it on right now,' added Billy in a conspiring voice. 'We got the hook for the back gates.'

More juice and more taunts and suddenly Punchy lurched to his feet and sticking out his lantern jaw declared loudly, 'Dig out the shivs because Punchy boy is getting it on!'

Called to the rear barrier from where I was seated in front of the television set, I was greeted by Billy and Morris. I could only distinguish their faces from behind the bars while the tunnel farther in remained in total darkness.

'What's up?' I inquired, peeved that they were using my escape key.

A shadowy network of bars spilled across the face of Morris as he got closer to me, whispering that his friend Punchy wanted the satisfaction of saving face by fighting me with knives!

Reaching out I gripped the bars as icy tentacles crawled

up and down my spine. Saying nothing I peered past the two until I was barely able to make out the silent form of Punchy deeper in the shadows, midway between the two barriers. Anguished over the thought that a fight was sure to screw up our planned escape. I pointed this out to them.

'Fuck the escape!' interrupted Billy. 'Punchy is our jailhouse partner and his rep is more important than our freedom.'

They were too drunk to reason with and I had too much pride to just walk away and let the creeps power trip, so like the prize fool that I've always been I nodded for them to unlock the gate. I silently warned myself to keep a close eye on them because they were backstabbers and the odds were that I was walking into a gold-plated trap.

My voice did not betray my emotions as I stepped inside, asking, 'How is this going to work?'

Pulling back his shirt and displaying two long bladed shivs Billy said in his drunken voice, 'When you two face off in the middle I'll hand you each a shank and you can go at it.'

I found myself moving forcibly towards where Punchy was waiting with a face filled with hate and came to a stop directly in front of him. It was weird because I didn't want to fight! I was feeling very sad and very sick at heart, but my manhood was being challenged and like a primitive beast I always instinctively attacked.

I was waiting to be handed a shiv when Morris, standing slightly behind me, snarled, 'Give it to the frog!'

I sprung around and unleashed a solid blow that struck Morris square in the eye and sent him sprawling into Billy. Realising my mistake I swung back around to face Punchy, but I was a split second too late as more than a foot of naked blade punched a hole deep into my left side, breaking the lower rib, rupturing my spleen, and coming to a stop directly under my heart! Excruciating pain flooded my whole being as my vision went misty red and my breathing started coming in short gasps. Face to face as in a slow motion nightmare, we stared into each other's eyes, his twisted with cruelty, mine with agony. Desperately trying to prevent him from withdrawing the blade, I grasped the wrist that held the knife handle and said to him in a strangely calm voice, 'We're scratch and now leave me be.'

Sensing that he had defeated me he started puffing out with great ferocity at having me at his mercy. Exclaiming triumphantly as he withdrew the blade from my stomach, 'It's going to take more than that to make us even!' he then took a looping swipe at my face as I staggered backwards and the sharp blade caught the side of my nose, rupturing it like a balloon.

Falling back against the wall clutching my bloody intestines in my hands, I was overcome with waves of shame because I had been rendered too helpless to fight back.

'Kill me,' I said lurching towards him as blood squirted straight out between my fingers and more flowed down my face from my mangled nose. 'Kill me, creep!'

Suddenly overcome with panic he raised his bloody dagger threateningly towards me, crying out, 'Get out of my fuckin' way, let me past!'

With my nose flapping loose and the blood flowing freely down my face and throat, I fell against him and spat a glob of it in his face, 'Kill me!'

Like it was molten lava Punchy clawed wildly at his face and then dropping the shiv, he shrieked, 'Get away from me!' With a mighty shove he flung me back against the wall and raced madly past me on to the illuminated range and out of my sight.

Drained of emotion and weakened, I slid down the grimy wall until I was sitting still clutching my guts in my hands, fascinated that my insides could push through such a small hole. I was convinced that I was dying and I didn't want the process to be reversed because for the first time in my life I could sense a great and strange contentment that I had never known before. I was drenched in gore and the blood rushing from my nose was choking me and making me cough. Everything was a misty red and there was a buzzing in my ears.

'Hey Roger? C'mon out of there!' The voice was far off and I tried to close my ears to the sound because it was intruding. 'Roger? Roger?' Opening my eyes it was like looking through a very long gloomy tunnel with shadowy figures swaying towards me. It was Tuffy and Moose! Reluctant to come into my dark cave because they feared the unknown, they wanted me to come to them; but I didn't want to.

Suddenly looming over me was Big Moose, his face displaying shock and horror. 'The asshole screws are too fuckin' scared to come on to the ward, Roger, so they sent me and Tuffy to lug you to the hospital. C'mon, pal. Don't be like that! You're gonna die.'

Somehow by supporting most of my weight they got me to my feet and out on to the range, slowly lugging me towards the locked barrier at the far end where a group of guards was waiting.

Leaning against the cell bars and crowding up against the window ledges were my neighbours and they all seemed to be saying the same thing, 'Hang tough, Roger . . . take it cool man . . .' It seemed like a hundred miles to the barrier and I could not distinguish any of the faces around me.

Now we were descending some flights of stairs and voices were saying, 'Take it easy! Watch it!'

The cold October air cleared my head a little as we slowly crossed the yard to the hospital a hundred yards away. Each time a cry escaped from my lips I'd say, 'Sorry.' It seemed so terribly important for me to die bravely. At each occurrence Tuffy or Moose would exclaim in anguish, 'Let it go! Don't smother it, you'll feel better.'

Like a beacon light the hospital door was yawning open and white coated nurses were waiting to receive me. Now that most of the initial shock had left me the pain was now becoming almost intolerable and I was inclined to double up more and more. By the time that I reached the short flight of stairs leading up to the hospital entrance my feet were dragging and my two big friends were supporting me like a rag doll. From there everybody pitched in to carry me up the stairs and deposit me on a stretcher and I was clear-headed enough to notice that even the guards were getting drenched from the blood that was gushing from me, yet they didn't seem to mind. The stretcher was wheeled into a bright operating room while still more guards rushed off to get the institutional ambulance. Faces gathered around me, male nurses were applying heavy bandages to my face to stem the blood. Still more bandages were placed under my hands so that I could press down on my bulging intestines. A few feet away I could hear somebody talking to the General Hospital, supplying them with details, my blood type, and expressing their opinion that I might bleed to death before reaching the hospital.

Finally the joint ambulance arrived at the hospital door and in a blur of motion the ceiling above me flashed past as I was loaded into the vehicle. Just before the doors closed I heard Moose and Tuffy wishing me luck and a nurse saying coldly, 'Looks like we lost this one.'

The ambulance emerged through the front gates of the penitentiary in a loud squeal of tyres, then with a tremendous lurch and a great roar it raced off through the dark streets with the siren screaming. Its human cargo was thrashing about in delirium as the guards struggled to hold the stretcher in place, because by then the monstrous pain was chewing away furiously inside my belly. So as not to choke I continued spitting out blood.

Screeching to a halt at the emergency entrance amid a large crowd of visitors leaving the hospital, the ambulance quickly backed up to a platform, the doors were yanked open as doctors and nurses reached for the stretcher. A sea of faces bent over me, probing, dabbing, cutting away all my clothes, and jabbing needles into me. A commanding voice ordered me to remove my hands from the wound, and I tried, but my fingers remained fixed in a death grip. A priest bent over me asking if I wanted him to pray and I mumbled something about not letting them take my medallion away. The stretcher was being pushed rapidly along and everybody was still probing away at me and then somebody said, 'Here, help me pull his hands away.' Everything went black.

When I regained consciousness nearly twenty-four hours later it was like I was returning from a very long journey studded with endless detours. Blinking against the perspiration I let my eyes move around the strange room until they focussed on the nurse talking to the guard in the doorway. Groaning aloud as the memory of what happened came flooding back to me I once again wished that I were dead.

When I again opened my eyes I saw with relief my Mother, sister and brother gathered around my bed. Mom was gently sponging my forehead and making clucking sounds at my bandaged nose from which a tube extended to a stomach pump. 'Thirsty!' I croaked. 'Thirsty.' There was a rattling sound and then I was sucking on a piece of ice. I was hurting and I was lonely and my hands found those of Susie and Gaston and I squeezed with all my might like a drowning man. Shortly after that my strength ebbed and my hands fell loosely to my sides.

On Wednesday afternoon two city detectives and a prison official showed up at my bedside to question me about the knifing.

'Who stabbed you?' they wanted to know.

'Nobody.'

'Come again?'

'I did it to myself because I wanted to die.'

'Is that going to be your version?'

'Yes.'

'Won't change your mind?'

'No.'

The prison representative glared down at me and belittled the inmate code of silence by pointing out there was too much violence inside the walls, arguing that if I helped to prosecute my attacker K.P. would be a safer place for my fellow numbers. Again I reaffirmed that I had inflicted the wound on myself.

'Stick to that story,' he shouted at me, 'and we'll see to it that you end up in an asylum for the criminally insane!'

The very next day the local newspaper and the Toronto Globe and Mail headlined the story: 'INMATE CLAIMS WOUNDED SELF!'

The following Sunday after my 'accident' the doctor removed me from the life supporting systems, including the long rubber hose down my throat so that I was able to drink and eat a little for the first time in eight days. In a four and a half hour operation my spleen had been removed and my nose neatly sewn back together. All of which left me with a Frankenstein-like scar on my belly a foot long and crudely stitched together. Below the slit where the knife had entered was another hole the Croakers had made to permit the wound to drain through a rubber tube that was still sticking out of me and fastened with a safety pin. My whole upper torso was heavily bandaged and pulled together with small sticks. My stomach muscles were so crushed that I couldn't possibly sit up in bed without help, and there was a twenty-four hour guard on me.

Neverthless within half an hour of being disconnected from the life supporting machine, the goon squad was there to take me back to that walled-off blasphemy in a wheelchair, informing me that I was to recover from my wound in the prison hospital. A mournful groan escaped from my lips at the thought of being treated in that awful place that was constructed more than a century ago. The concrete cells had no lighting and only rusty buckets for toilets and at night bats flew around the cell-blocks. Obviously someone was mad at me.

I was flat on my back in the joint hospital only a few hours and already claustrophobia was making me squirm and sweat. I didn't mind the pain that was threatening to engulf me so much, but what was bugging me the most was the feeling of helplessness, knowing that I couldn't rise out of bed by myself. I yelled for the head nurse and when he eventually showed up outside of my barred cell I requested a transfer back to my old drum on the psychiatric ward. I explained that I could receive the same medical treatment there and that I had friends who would take care of me. Turning a deaf ear to my plea he just walked away leaving me muttering to myself in the gloom.

Not long afterwards they were all gathered around the front of my cell watching aghast as I ripped and tore at the bandages until the gruesome wound was bare for all to see. Digging my fingers into the incision I cried out in despair, 'You get me up to the bug ward right now or you'll be sweeping up my guts with a dustpan!'

'Don't be a fool!' yelled the hospital administrator. 'Let me call the warden first.'

By the time he got back the goon squad was gathered in front of my cell ready to move in on me. Suddenly I heard the deputy warden's voice ordering them back as my mother and sister showed up at the barred gate! 'We went first to the General Hospital but you were already gone. Oh Roger, I can't believe this!' she cried out covering her face as she saw the blood bubbling through the wound from torn stitches.

'Susie,' I groaned in agony. 'Please tell them to get me out of this tomb or I'll go berserk!'

My mother was crying as Susie turned on the deputy warden with such indignation that he threw up his hands and said, 'OK, OK, we'll send your brother up to the Psychiatric ward.'

Just as suddenly the short special visit was over because the Croaker was on his way in to patch me up.

Right after supper Big Moose and Tuffy showed up with a stretcher and transported me over to my old ward and settled me into a cell in front of the television set, making me as comfortable as they possibly could. Poor Moose, he just couldn't do enough. All the guys on the tier were equally eager to help. Not so the psychiatric staff, they were as cold and inhuman as ever. I was crestfallen to learn that the escape plot had been discovered the morning after the knifing. A massive shakedown for the missing shiv had led to the discovery of the cupboard stash, which in turn eventually led to the window bars that were sawed through. Billy ended up in the cooler because of the contraband found in his drum, Morris swallowed a spoon, and Punchy was mysteriously sprung back into the general population. I immediately started wracking my brains for another escape route.

CHAPTER EIGHTEEN

October 26, 1962: True to his word, and just a few weeks after the prison official threatened me, I was on my way to Penetanguishene, a maximum security asylum for the criminally insane!

The two hundred and fifty mile trip was made through a raging snow storm, and having heard frightful stories about that bug house Alcatraz, I wished throughout the long journey that the government vehicle would crash and kill me and my keepers. I was convinced that it was the end of the line for me.

Perched on a high ridge and surrounded by dense forest, the brick building gave me the creeps as I shuffled painfully towards the entrance, dragging my chains through the snow as the two Kingston guards supported me. Unlocking the main gate for us with a long key was a hollow-cheeked attendant looking as if he had been resurrected from the dead.

The asylum operated differently than a penitentiary where an inmate was or could be a somebody, and most important of all have a definite release date to look forward to. Here all the patients were sentenced to indefinite terms and were all treated alike, that is to say as mindless zombies. In Penetang the shrinks were god-like figures in white coats whose very presence on the wards reduced most patients to the point of tears. Panting like house dogs they would clutch at the doctors' coats ready to cringe in terror or leap with joy. As for the attendants, they were more callous than the average jail guard, unfeeling goons who handled emotional patients by strangling them unconscious with a towel (a popular method in high risk mental hospitals known as the 'sleeper').

I was in the institution only a few weeks when the sleeper was used on me after I was caught sawing the bars in my cell. As additional punishment I was carried bodily up to the Violent Ward and tossed naked and freezing into what they called a therapeutic cell, better known as a padded cell.

All around me were human vegetables rendered 'tame' through the use of frontal lobotomy operations in which neurosurgical drills killed a part of the brain that was thought to trigger violence. In reality they were reduced to bona fide zombies. The more subtle method of reducing violent activity was through the use of experimental drugs which were given to the patients on the violent ward four times a day. The pills came in all sizes and colours and you were severely punished if you were caught spitting them out. One old timer in Penetang who had been a patient for thirty-five years told me that there were patients on the violent ward who had been driven crazy simply because they had refused to go along with the programme. He said one guy was still up there eighteen years later reduced to a raving maniac.

All the while I remained in the isolation box I remembered all the old man told me, especially the pill gimmick. The first two weeks I was made to swallow twelve pills a day, half were medication for my wound, while the remainder were bug pills. The result was massive muscle spasms every thirty seconds, from the top of my head on down to the tip of my toes, so violent that I was unable to rest or even think clearly – all of which left me very shook up. Nor was there such a thing as hiding the little devils under my tongue because the attendants made damn sure each pill was swallowed. However from the old timer I learned the sleight of hand trick of popping them up my nostrils and afterwards blowing them in the toilet. Still I had to fake the spasms everytime a shrink came nosing around.

All that winter I was kept in that ice box sleeping on the floor and eating off paper plates with a wooden spoon. My toilet was a hole in the floor and I had no drinking water. Scared half to death that I would be driven mad like my neighbours who growled, cried, and screamed all night, I made sure that I kept a tight reign on my wits and morale. One nut would chant over and over in a sing-song voice 'that he didn't want to get well'. However the one that made me jump out of my skin was the guy with the piercing whistle always yelling 'TAXI!'

During this lock-up period I gave an attendant a black eye after he poured coffee over my hand and again I was given the sleeper and also placed in a straitjacket.

Early in March I appeared before a panel of so-called experts whose job was to determine if I was 'sane or insane'. To come to this momentous conclusion they bombarded me with tricky questions for more than an hour. To my great relief I came though it all with flying colours. I was then transferred to a normal ward to await transfer back to Kingston Penitentiary. The cell they moved me into had been occupied a few hours earlier by a patient who hanged himself!

CHAPTER NINETEEN

March 15, 1963: It was like a spring day and with the centre lanes on the 401 highway bare of snow, the blue government vehicle was able to get solid traction as it streaked along at high speed. It was mid-afternoon and my two escorts seemed to be in an obvious hurry to get back to the penitentiary. The blond driver, who was a keeper, always did everything in a big hurry, be it bragging or arguing or playing his tough guy role. Seated squarely in the back seat next to me in civilian clothes was another loud mouth who was a big wheel in the K.P. psychiatric ward. He was a tyrant who in his tough guy role terrorised both staff and patients and tolerated only those who were willing to be his lackeys.

Here I was, ready to run the biggest bluff of my life in a bid to regain my freedom, a desperate move that counted on cool heads, and the prison administration had to send two clowns to take me back. Tucked away inside the folds of my heavy coat was a plastic imitation ·45 automatic pistol with all the moving parts so realistic looking that it had to be handled to be detected as a bogus. Before leaving the asylum I had managed to retain the gun through two separate frisks, which does not say much for my escorts.

Approaching the first turn-off that led into the city of Toronto, I noted that we were travelling at 70 mph. Moving my shackled feet and hands slightly made a noise which caused my guard to turn his pugnacious face in my direction. Whipping out the gun I jabbed it between his eyes, commanding in a firm voice, 'Freeze!'

'Oh God, don't!' he shrieked, his features turning to jelly as he impulsively threw his arms lightly around me and buried his face in the folds of my coat! Not trying to disarm me and making the strangest sounds, he continued to hide his face as I poked the gun at the driver, ordering him to pull over.

Letting out a startled yell he threw up his hands and the next thing I knew we were spinning around like a top on the icy side of the road, ripping out the side of a steep snow-bank, and coming to a jarring stop under an overpass. Propelled head first over the front seat with my two escorts on top of me screeching and beating the dashboard with their blackjacks, I found myself in a very uncommanding position and in utter disgust I said quietly, 'Awright! Awright! Game fuckin' over.'

(I learned many years later that the one in the back seat bragged to all who would listen that it was his wartime secret service experience that got him out of that tight spot, and enabled him to get the best of me! Also the gun I used, the plaster dummy head, the braided rope and grappling hook, and the dagger that wounded me are all on display at the Canadian Penitentiary Museum in the city of Kingston.)

Upon my arrival at the gates to the penitentiary I was given the bum's rush straight down to the cooler by McGruder and company with the warden leading the way. Entombed once more and facing a two-year banishment from the general population I wondered how I was going to survive without the incentive to escape or attain an early parole, both of which were impossible to achieve from down

267

there. Everything was so dismal that for the first few weeks I often thought of suicide, but gradually I slipped into a murky dream world and the thought of dying down there retreated. The three uniformed goons down there were their usual petty, sniping selves. In a way they gave me the incentive to make the grade, because every time they opened my door I got the impression that they were noticeably disappointed to not see me hanging from the bars. I could just picture them wise-cracking over my corpse and saying that I wasn't so tough.

I was segregated under section PSR 230 of the penitentiary rules and that meant that they had to give me three meals a day and a library book to read, but apart from that I was shafted every which way. I had no pillow, mattress or sheets, and wore coveralls in lieu of regular clothing. The No Talking rule was strictly enforced. I had no contact with direct fresh air nor did I see anything other than the interior of my drum. The brightly burning light inside the security box up by the ceiling would in time become an instrument of torture. It was on day and night, until I was forced to burrow beneath my blankets to get away from the all-consuming glare. But hiding like that was not permitted, so after being warned several times I was put on report, and the warden took my blankets away for three days.

If it wasn't the light glaring down at me, then it would be the screws, sneaking up to the catwalk and peering down through the observation port. After a while when I saw the face of a guard up there glaring down at me I'd think of him as something other than human, more like he was a light bulb too. It made me shudder.

In order to keep mentally and physically alert it was necessary for me to exercise each and every day. I would do push ups, dynamic tension, spot running, and shadow boxing; but more than anything else I would pace the floor, to and fro, hour after hour, five short steps – pivot – five short steps – pivot – swiftly and unconsciously fast. The day finally came that I was doing it so effortlessly that I had the feeling of travelling in one continuous straight line. It was my only outlet for burning off all the daily anxiety that built up dangerously in me. I was also trying to exhaust myself in the hope of being able to fall asleep that night. Often I'd walk at least ten hours out of twenty-four. Others before me had done the same thing and there were grooves in the concrete to prove it.

Only when I was asleep could I truly escape the reality of grinding out the days down there, and I guess during the first few months I really abused that privilege. There came a day when I couldn't go under long enough to refresh my brain. That made me frantic and I paced and paced like an addict, trying harder to exhaust myself so I could sleep. But like all addicts I had to extend myself more and more. It was frustrating to realise after a while that I couldn't even escape in sleep.

I knew there were three other cons in their twenties segregated down there under maximum deadlock. Ralph, a bitter, bespectacled, sharpwitted guy, was extremely anti-establishment. He had already spent seventeen months down there because it was suspected that he had stabbed a guard to death in a dormitory washroom. Fortunately for him he had only a few years left, and could see an end to his suffering.

Next there was Big George, a well-known Montreal underworld figure who was rumoured to have killed a lot of people. George was presently serving a twenty-five year sentence for bank robbery and had been transferred to Kingston from Saint Vincent de Paul. Tall, gawky and stooped, he had a hollow face and crazy eyes and when he talked fast, spittle would form at the corners of his mouth, giving him a frightening appearance. Everybody was afraid of George, especially the police and the guards. He looked like a kill-crazy psycho, but actually he was a real brainy guy. He was in 'seg' for shanking another con.

Our fourth neighbour was also a guy transferred from Saint Vincent; he was shaking a twenty-five year bit for knocking off a jug. Jacques wasn't a big guy. Wiry and swarthy-looking, with dark hair always hanging over his face, he was good-natured and very talkative. He was also quick to anger, as one of the belly robbers in the joint kitchen found out when he had power-tripped once too often and Jacques had sliced him up a bit. George and Jacques

269

were segregated about two months before I arrived from Penetanguishene.

The only way we could communicate down there was by way of our special telephone. This was done by bailing out the water from the toilet bowl and carrying on whispered conversations through the sewer pipe that connected the twenty cells. Because there were still a few inches of water remaining throughout the pipe system our voices carried clearly, but not to our keepers. Nevertheless we rarely got on the phone during the day unless it was something really important, because it was too easy for McGruder and company to nab us if they should open our door suddenly. But at night it was different because normally we could hear the screws coming in through the locked barriers to make their hourly rounds. To be sure, whenever a newcomer was admitted on a bread and water trip, we'd get him on the phone later in the evening and squeeze him dry of information.

One afternoon a con came down and immediately got us four guys on the phone to inform us that President Kennedy had just been assassinated. Now this was really big news and we all got rather excited.

'Oh man, what a goddamn shame!' exclaimed Ralph in surprise. 'I really dug that man; he had class and guts.'

'Yeah,' I breathed the word out softly. 'Guess the Russians are going to be happy to hear that, especially after Cuba backing down on the question of missiles.'

'Ten will get you nothing that the Russians knew all about the bump, say six months in advance,' speculated Jacques.

'I wonder how much the trigger man got for his end?' Big George wanted to know.

Just then a roar interrupted our little gabfest. 'Flush them fuckin' shitters! Now! You wanna go on bread and water?'

Staggering away from the toilets we didn't wait for McGruder to finish as we hit the buttons in unison, refilling our bowls with water, shaking our heads in amazement that the belly-crawling creep would go so far as to bail out a toilet and listen in on us!

Other intruders on our telephone line were rats: great big sewer rats so bold that they would sometimes jump out of

270

the toilet and into our cells. Mostly they just made a pest of themselves by splashing through the pipes while were were trying to talk; sometimes there would be a whole herd of them.

'C'mon. Move it!' we'd shout and away they'd gallop.

Poor George was terrified of rats and wouldn't even sit on his toilet for fear that they might castrate him. Jacques was just the opposite; he used to con rats out of his toilet to kill them. One day he captured a little mouse and really became fond of it as he set out to tame it. He called it Whiskey. It used to sleep with him at night, snuggling in his neck or his armpit.

Cloyne one day got a flash of Whiskey. Not long afterwards the terrible trio showed up in Jacques' cell to shake him down.

Cloyne spotted the mouse wiggling inside Jacques' coveralls and let fly with a vicious punch that squashed Whiskey to death against Jacques' chest. The scream of hatred that our friend cut loose chilled us to the bone – it was so full of suffering. He attacked the three goons with a fury, but he was outnumbered. Afterwards they stripped him naked and tossed him into the Chinese Cell, a special, barren, cold cell designed to make a con feel so alone and lonely that he just wanted to die. Jacques did lose the will to live and not long afterwards he was transferred in bad shape to the Psychiatric ward in Saint Vincent de Paul, where he hanged himself from the cell bars. It was too bad that he did not live long enough to hear of Cloyne's humiliating downfall, from a guard to a con with a number.

George started going stir bugs too. We could all see it coming, especially when he took up the Bible and started preaching to us. When fellows like George did that it meant that they were at their wits' end.

Still later George became paranoid, convinced everybody was out to get him, including his friends. He refused to talk to anybody and became dirty and shaggy-looking with his black hair spilling over into his face – very spooky looking. He lived directly across the hall from me and whenever our keepers would unlock our wooden doors to feed us, my friend would grunt like some wild thing and then hide

271

around the corner of his cell, peeking weirdly out at me until the doors closed again. Another strange habit George had was taking his cigarette and carefully burning the eyes out of people's photographs in every library magazine he received. That shocked even us! He ended up in an asylum.

Eventually Ralph was transferred out to another penitentiary where hopefully he could start anew. For several months after that I was the only one segregated down there and Christmas of '63 was only a few weeks away. Guys would come down there on bread and water and ring me up on the phone to complain that they had to be down there for a few days or a few weeks, asking me how they were going to do it without cracking up! After a while they'd ask me how long I'd been down there and when I told them they would get very embarrassed.

I had long ago lost my appetite and about twenty-five pounds of body weight went with it. Because there was always a neighbour on a bread diet down there, I'd save what I could from my food allotment, and send it over later in the evening. I'd do this by unravelling part of my woollen socks and using a tough material to make a line I'd fire it out under the door and into the cell of some hungry guy.

Apart from losing my appetite, I also lost my concentration to read, not to mention my ability to sleep. I still exercised and paced the floor, but now more than ever I was slipping off into dream worlds for increasingly longer periods. Although food turned my stomach I drank a quart and a half each meal of that hideous hickory concoction called joint coffee.

Maybe that was playing havoc with my nerves, which were now stretched to the breaking point. The slightest sound near my cell would bring a blood curdling scream out of me, sending me bouncing off the walls and shaking for minutes afterwards. Being in a fog all the time and staring off into space is what did it mostly. The sudden invasion of sound would explode inside my brain like a bomb, blasting me back to reality.

My hearing became phenomenally acute. This may sound incredible, but I felt that if I saved some bread from my food tray and left it on top of my sink until late in the

272

evening when things got really quiet, I would hear crackling sounds, like somebody walking on dry leaves, for several hours as clear as could be. I believed I was hearing the bread drying up!

But it was the gorilla who took the greatest delight into scaring me into climbing the walls of my cell. Always pussy-footing around and observing me through the peephole, he would wait until I got spaced out and then with a brutish grin boot my door with great force! I'd come right up off that concrete pallet with arms slashing, eyes rolling, and my mouth twisted open in one long shuddering scream.

Sometimes a new guard would be sent down, probably on some pretext like, 'Here lad, take this library book into the prisoner in cell No. 20'. As soon as the screw approached the tiny cell block, the other guards waited quietly in anticipation.

Each time my door was hauled open it made a sharp sound so when the unsuspecting screw pulled on that door he'd be greeted by the loudest bloodcurdling scream he had ever heard. Dropping the book or whatever and clutching his heart he would stagger towards the office in a state of shock, only to be greeted by howls of laughter from the keepers of the zoo.

Meanwhile, back inside my cage, I'd be struggling to pull myself together and bring my muscle spasms under control, hating the creeps that much more.

The night shift, not to be left out, would also get into the act while passing along the catwalk late at night. Observing me through the port as I paced the floor below as effortlessly as a cat, they'd rap their knuckles sharply against the Plexi-glas, just loud enough to send me into a violent convulsion, my scream driving my neighbours straight up out of their sleep.

Sometimes my reaction was so violent that I would hurt myself or make myself sick. Towards the end of my stay some of my friends out in the population complained to the inmate committee, who in turn complained bitterly to the warden.

Even without the screws bugging me I was still climbing the walls of my cell daily from an assortment of other sounds. By then even though I'd hear the guards approaching my door, I was in such a deep fog, that I would simply 'forget while I was remembering'. One night I was just lying back on my pallet reading a book, and having no pillow I was using my arm as a cushion. I soon forgot about my arm as it went dead on me. Sometime later I got an eerie feeling that something menacing was behind my head. I swung my eyes around, spotted this hand – and screamed! I just went berserk, smashing my fist into the walls and bellowing in rage. By the time the screws galloped on down to my cell to see what the hell was happening, I was calm once more, but in an extreme state of bewilderment, studying my hand like I had never seen it before.

Strange happenings were commonplace down there, like that evening in November, when an electrical storm knocked out the light. For the first time in eight months my cell light went out! What a fantastic and indescribable feeling of joy that was: total darkness. I couldn't even see my hands before my eyes. Enveloped in inky darkness I immediately became intoxicated with a flurry of emotions and wild flights of fancy. Standing in the centre of my floor I raised my arms up towards the grimy window, illuminated briefly by brilliant bolts of lightning. Laughing, I imagined myself to be in a balloon high up in the turbulent heavens, bobbing and weaving and playing tag with the elements. I was Mercury, messenger of the gods, leaping up and away from my coffin-like cell, powerful beyond belief! It was a fantastic mind trip that lasted almost half an hour until the emergency lights suddenly came on and I was dashed against the rocks, a castaway. Depression settled in.

In my tenth month there one of the eeriest experiences in all my life took place, and even today I am not certain if I was hallucinating or if it was authentic. I heard it for the first time around eleven o'clock on a quiet night. It was bitterly cold and I was buried deep under my blankets. At first the sound was very faint – I mean the sobbing, a young girl's sobbing – and so thinking that my ears were playing tricks on me I lay very still and held my breath. I heard it clearly: heartrending sobs! There was no mistake, and to be sure I got out of bed and prowled my cell, every nook and cranny, shivering in the cold, looking for a plausible explanation for the eerie sound. It lasted for half an hour and then gradually stopped, giving me the distinct impression that the poor girl had cried herself to sleep. For the rest of the night I just lay there with my eyes wide open, kind of in shock, wondering if I was going nuts.

The second night it happened again at the same time, the same young girl crying her heart out. This time I was more or less able to isolate the sound as coming from the air shaft that pumped a semblance of heat into my cell. When I sat on the floor with my ear pressed against the hollow wall there the sobs were louder and much more distinct. At first I was greatly relieved thinking that what I was mistaking for a human voice was simply something mechanical, but then my experience told me that nothing other than a human being could make those sobbing sounds, and that it had to be a young girl. It was just too distinct and real! Nor could I believe that the screws had placed a tape recorder down there in the tunnel; they were too lazy for that; besides the trap door was right outside of my cell and I'd have heard them clambering around in there.

When the sobbing went on for eight nights, I concluded that it was a girl crying herself to sleep, and that like me she was very lonely and distressed, which was why I was able to tune in to her moments of greatest anguish. It came to the point where I became so emotionally involved, that I actually tried to soothe her with words, explaining that I understood how she felt, but that I couldn't help her. Then came the night when the tears stopped forever, and I felt a profound loss.

I know that the reader is going to believe that my mental state at that late stage was fragile and I tend to agree, but let me leave you with this bit of information. Almost straight across the street from me was the prison for women, a frightful institution where new arrivals often cried themselves to sleep in their cells, especially for the first week or so. Furthermore, less than a thousand yards away from the building in which I was held captive along the same lakeshore, was the Ontario Mental Hospital for male and female patients. Also a terrifying place to a young girl, especially alone late at night.

CHAPTER TWENTY

March, 1964: After decaying in solitary for a year I once again emerged into the light of day, again in chains, to be transferred to another prison some fifteen hundred miles away because a warden found me a threat to the orderly running of his institution. When I arrived at Stoney Mountain Penitentiary in Manitoba by plane I was like something out of the wilds, edgy and enormously underweight, and gripping tightly my only possession: five ragged scribblers containing a mass of notes. This was my entry into a strange new world of self-discovery, a subconscious and compulsive effort on my part to better understand why I was trying to destroy myself in such a painfully slow manner. Jotting down my mercurial inner thoughts on paper was totally alien because I hated writing and could barely spell dog and cat; but within me was a compelling force that drove me to scribble and scribble on scraps of paper like a drowning man hanging on to a buoy. I was totally unaware that this early, primitive effort would eventually evolve into thousands of pages of manuscript.

It is anger that will kill a man in prison. It makes him sick and crazy, and that's when the system breaks him. He has got to have control over his emotions and keep in touch with reality, or anger will cause him to do things that are against his nature.

The first year that I was in Stoney I was so touchy that I struck out with both fists each time a loudmouth provoked me, punching with such devastating effect that I became

276

somewhat of a legend. In one morning I had five fights. One day a notorious stool pigeon slashed my best friend with a dagger and instinctively I wrestled it away from him and drove it through his chest! Later that same night, realising what I was becoming, I was struck with such a pang of conscience that I fell on my knees in my cell with a gurgled scream, and by way of punishment cruelly mutilated my left arm with a razor blade, swearing fervently that I wasn't going to hurt anyone again.

June, 1965: I graduated with high marks from bricklaying school after a one year intensive course and received my diploma. At this time I was also elected by popular ballot as Chairman of the Inmate Grievance Committee, which was the highest accolade in the inmate hierarchy. I completed the term successfully.

August, 1966: Circumstances beyond my control forced me into a duel with a hated prison psychopath. After rubbing my lucky medallion I plunged a pick-like instrument deep into his chest, just as he released a lethal arrow-like shaft at me from a spring-loaded gun fashioned in the machine shop. He recovered later in a city hospital and maintaining the inmate code he refused to testify against me. Nevertheless the warden buried me for six harsh months in the cooler on suspicion, and I really do think I would have gone crazy if I hadn't been permitted to scribble away in my increasing pile of notebooks.

CHAPTER TWENTY-ONE

February, 1967: I was fast becoming the most travelled and unwanted prisoner in Canada, as again I was plucked from solitary, eyes blinking, dishevelled, and shivering in the midst of a snowstorm. Hustled aboard a jetliner in handcuffs

I flew the seventeen hundred miles to Montreal, and was locked in a small cell in the segregation block at Saint Vincent de Paul. Two days there and the kid next door to me hanged himself; three weeks later an older prisoner further down the range also hanged himself from his cell bars, livid welts from an earlier attempt still clearly visible around his neck.

Appearing before a routine inquiry board the day after the second hanging I was sullen and trembling so violently that even my teeth were chattering. The deputy warden gave the order to release me on the spot.

Waiting to greet me with open arms in the main prison population was my old partner and friend Claude, easily the most popular guy in the institution. All macho, he was so recklessly brave that I sometimes thought he harboured a death wish. He had just finished serving four long years in the segregation block for his part in the kidnapping and murder of a custodial guard who was shot five times in the back by his rescuers!

Spring, 1968: My kid brother Gaston who had joined the American Army a few years earlier to fight in Viet Nam, had returned to Canada on furlough after being declared 'Soldier of the Month'. He came to Saint Vincent and was granted a special visit inside the walls by the warden. Here he met and chatted with all my best friends and looked poster perfect in his sergeant's uniform. The guys loved him and it was a proud day for me.

CHAPTER TWENTY-TWO

October, 1968: My quiet behaviour while in Saint Vincent de Paul so impressed the authorities that they eventually granted me a transfer to Leclerc, a medium security institution situated in a nearby field and not far from a busy expressway.

There were no visible gun towers and high grey walls and the exercise yard had a lush carpet of green grass to walk or lie on. If you peered out through the fence you could see the world passing by. Here the emphasis was not on security and retribution, but rather that old-fashioned word Rehabilitation. At first it was hard for me to get used to the lax atmosphere and just one guard supervising where normally in a 'max' there would be a dozen badmouthing creeps doing the same job. Here most of the inmates had healthy minds because they were encouraged to think and act for themselves, and as a result the staff treated them as individuals, not just numbered robots.

For several weeks I remained strangely apprehensive and paranoid, half expecting to be confronted by a goon squad and told that it was all a mistake, that I hadn't earned the right to be in a medium security environment, and that I was being shipped back to the pen. For this reason I did not display any open joy, telling myself that if I acted happy all this would be rudely snatched away. So I remained tense and alert expecting anything and everything.

Another alien pleasure was being permitted to stay out in the recreation field even after dark. To be allowed to approach the fence without armed guards shouting threats at me, to feel the moon and stars gazing down upon me, to feel the soft grass underfoot, and to gaze longingly at the traffic zooming by in the distance, all that was pure ecstasy. However the most comforting feeling of all was knowing that I was trusted not to betray a trust and scale the twelve foot fence.

No bulletproof glass separated me from my visitors – fantastic! Now for the first time I was able to hug my mother and sister and hold and play with my little nephew Todd. He was a beautiful and gifted little boy with the blondest hair, bluest eyes, and fairest skin. At two and a half he had already won a baby contest.

June 1, 1969: At the age of thirty and deeply scarred in body and mind, I walked through the front entrance of Leclerc clutching my book manuscript and two stuffed penguins. I was now a parolee armed with a bricklayer's diploma and a grim determination never to return to a life of crime. This time around I was positive that I could make the grade with my family standing firmly at my side. Blinking in the bright sunshine I hurried towards the parking lot where my kid brother was waiting to take me home.

CHAPTER TWENTY-THREE

November 8, 1969: This is one date in my life that I will never forget for all the grief and bad memories it brought me in my efforts to go straight. Everything was going well for me in Cornwall. I was making decent wages as a bricklayer. I had a comfortable apartment, a secondhand convertible, and although I was still solitary in my ways I stayed close to my family and relatives, and had a steady girlfriend. But I kept receiving long distance phone calls from mysterious characters, who having been furnished with my qualifications as a gunman, wanted to bring me out of retirement to do a special job for them. An emphatic 'No'! was usually enough to get them off my back.

But not one smooth-talking creep, who was pressed for money and in possession of a blueprint to a perfect heist. Lorne finally resorted to a treacherous trick to get me to travel to Toronto so that he could get me to feast my eyes on all that money, letting me see for myself how easy it would be for a guy with my experience.

Looking like the smooth salesman that he was, Lorne was running off at the mouth real fast until he noticed with alarm how livid I was getting as I sat in the front seat of his Buick in a downtown section of Toronto.

'Honest to gawd, I'm sorry Roger for snowing you but I was told that if I could get you to see for yourself what a

280

cinch heist this is, you would forget that lunch bucket crap and do it for me.' Licking his lips and pointing to a grey building across the busy street with a shaky finger he added, 'It's all stacked in there right now, just waiting for the Brink's truck to pick it up. I was told that you could take it all by yourself while I drove the car.'

My first punch smashed his sunglasses and after that he covered his face while hollering for me to stop! He kept pressing the horn and that was what brought the cop down on us. Unknown to me, there was a satchel in the back seat containing a blueprint, a balaclava, and a holstered ·38 calibre revolver. When that was discovered we were both arrested and charged with conspiracy to rob.

With my record it was too much for the police to believe that for once in my life I was innocent, especially when the other creep ratted out and laid all the blame on me. For eight long hours in a small back room at police headquarters I was put through the grinder by a relay of detectives in an effort to get me to sign a confession. I hung tough, signed nothing, and won their wide-eyed respect – but not my release.

One year and two trials later (the first one ended in a hung jury) I was finally convicted on a conspiracy to rob charge and given the unheard of sentence of twenty-five years! The police convinced the judge that I was a professional gunman. It was as if I had fallen into a bottomless pit and was struggling desperately to find a grip that would stop my headlong plunge, crying out in rage that I was innocent, refusing to believe that no one could hear me.

To my rescue came a frail legal genius straight from his classroom in the Faculty of Law at the University of Toronto – a God-like figure to his students, and a respected legal adviser to the government. He was an Irish rebel with a pocketful of pipes and never any matches, a walking memory bank who couldn't even recall where he parked his car. A little big man to whom justice was a goddess not to be misused by bullies, Professor Morton believed in my innocence and waiving any fee he bore down on the Appeals Court with all his influence and legal expertise, grimly promising to regain my stolen freedom.

281

I was transferred from Toronto to Kingston Penitentiary to await the outcome of the appeal, a ponderously slow process. While in KP I became embroiled in one of the most nightmarish riots in penal history. The date was *April 14, 1971*. It was on a Wednesday around 10 p.m. when the repressive and dehumanising conditions inside the 140-year-old cauldron finally reached the point where the lid blew off. The explosion was recorded half-way around the world. It was a plot that only Satan himself could have spun over the six hundred prisoners in full control of the cavernous dome. A colossal beehive overturned and overrun by prisoners running amok. Intoxicated with rage and pent-up frustration, they vented their fury with inhuman strength on the locking bars to free their neighbours. They bent them like so many pretzels, ripping three hundred pound gates right off their hinges, using the barriers to barricade the exits. Amid wailing sirens and gunshots, we smashed everything in sight, glutting ourselves on the carnage we wreaked.

Everywhere insanity reigned. The army, threatening to bypass the barricades by blasting through the cell-block walls and attacking with machine-guns and fixed bayonets, were on one side. On the other were hundreds of pirate-like figures armed with long spears, clubs, and firebombs ready to meet this military might head on, reminding them that despite their superior weaponry some of them would die too. Six guards held as hostages on the top tiers had their hated uniforms torn from their quaking bodies and replaced with ill-fitting prison denim. In a reverse role they were locked into cells by their convict keepers and told if the army attacked that they would be the first to die. Helicopters with government officials landed inside the grey walls at all hours while a committee of prominent citizens debated prison conditions in a desperate effort to stave off a bloody massacre on both sides. One of the main driving forces on this four-man committee was my own lawyer, Professor Morton. He was also the only man who had the bravado to step over the sandbagged machine-gun nest and walk in among the rioters – a veritable hornets' nest, in which inmate leaderships were changing as fast as the new demands.

282

Meanwhile, I was three hundred feet overhead on a narrow catwalk, busting out windows to hang out white sheets with scrawled messages for the TV cameras across the street. For ninety two spine-tingling hours the negotiations went on and on while the gut-eating tension, lack of food and sleep, reduced us to near savages. We struggled in the tornado-like ruins to survive, squatting over bonfires and cooking scraps of meat like cavemen. Wolf packs were roaming everywhere, looking for food, sex, or just thirsting for blood. It was cold with all the broken windows so everybody had to scrounge makeshift clothes, making ponchos out of blankets, and even using dark, ankle-length cassocks pillaged from the chapels. Drag queens swished around in the flashier garments, causing fights and giving themselves to the victors. During the last twenty-four hours Satan again took control of our minds.

The bloody climax was so primitive that it left even the most hardened criminal gasping in awe-stricken horror, as fourteen diddlers, rapos, and stool pigeons were tied with chains to chairs in a circle in the centre of the dome. Under ghostly illumination they were ritualistically tortured while hundreds of convicts lined the four circular galleries pounding rhythmically with steel clubs on the hollow railings like jungle drums. By daybreak twelve of the 'undesirables' were horribly mutilated and in critical condition; two others were dead. Dead, because according to the inmate code they deserved retributive 'justice': one had viciously raped two little girls, while the other had 'disciplined' his children by burning them on a red hot stove.

At sunrise, just moments before the army was to set off their explosions and attack, settlement was agreed to by both sides. The six hostages were released and the four day riot was declared over and done with.

However, for a third of us, who had responded to our names and numbers being called over a loud-speaker and had emerged from the ruins with our hands on top of our heads and submitted to a shakedown at the point of bayonets, our nightmare was just beginning. Placed aboard special buses with an escort of police cruisers we roared through the prison gates, the sirens driving back the crowds,

283

and raced off through the countryside at top speeds. Our destination was a brand new multi-million dollar, electronically-operated human warehouse called Millhaven.

Waiting for us at the rear loading ramp were Millhaven's finest, a double line of pot-bellied guards armed with clubs. With our hands and feet shackled we could only shuffle down the long hallway as the clubs rained down upon us, crunching through bone and muscle, releasing a torrent of blood.

One month later while still licking my wounds in my cell I heard over the radio that the court of appeal had quashed my twenty-five year sentence and ordered a new trial! A loud cheer went up from my neighbours because they knew that I was serving an impossible sentence for a crime that I was not guilty of committing.

In July in Toronto my third trial in two years on the same old charge lasted for two emotionally charged weeks as Professor Morton, his equally effective colleague and three assistants, Sheldon, Gunter, and Nadia, dazzled the courtroom with their combined brilliance and zest for hard work.

Under their expert cross-examination the police who were witnesses against me and my co-accused were caught in so many inconsistent statements that their stories just didn't hold up anymore. The most shocking disclosure came when my defence obtained a statement made two years earlier by my co-accused, in which he confessed to being a cat burglar who had personally looted eighty-seven private homes.

In acute embarrassment the detectives could give no reason why the creep had not been prosecuted on any of those burglaries. To the jury and everyone else in the courtroom it was perfectly obvious that the charges had been withheld as enticement by the police to get the Judas to sink me in order to save his own skin. Thus when my lawyers got the opportunity to cross-examine Mr X (as my co-accused was referred to in the newspapers), they proved him to be not only a despicable Judas, but also a treacherous perjurer.

It was 2.30 a.m. in the second week of my trial that the jury returned a verdict of 'Not Guilty'!

Although my innocence was vindicated the lengthy judicial grinder had left me deeply scarred and too emotionally drained to rejoice. Instead I just sat there mute and trembling. Professor Morton removed his cloak and draping it around my shoulders sat at my side talking softly; he asked me to forget about the past and to look forward to the future.

CHAPTER TWENTY-FOUR

July 22, 1971: Grabbing a seat next to a window, I looked down at the platform where my two friends were waving good-bye to me and my heart went out to them. Gunter and Nadia were as yet untainted by cynicism and indifference. Professor Morton had asked them to see me off in case I got hassled by the detectives who had lost the case.

The train gave a lurch and slowly moved off as my friends faded from sight and I closed my eyes. The swaying passenger car and the powerful hum of the diesel engines lulled me into an almost hypnotic state as we ate up miles of track. Suddenly my eyes flew open and staring into the mirror-like window where the night was flashing past in a kaleidoscope of vivid colors I lashed out with the back of my hand, breaking the crystal on my watch! Shivering violently, I wrapped my arms tightly around myself, despairing that I would never rid myself of those hideous spectres lunging wraithlike at me, always mocking and grinning cruelly at me with their mutilated features and bloated tongues. I didn't kill them so why bug me? Times like that made me wonder what it would be like to have a mind so soggy with alcohol that I wouldn't be able to remember anything. . . .

The train wouldn't be pulling into Montreal until daybreak. Meanwhile I became aware of a strangely beautiful girl in her twenties seated across from me, sneaking glances at me from beneath honey-blonde hair that cascaded around her dark eyes like candy floss. Her features were exquisitely

285

delicate and her body was the sort bikinis were designed for.

Still uptight and restless in my seat I made my way to the rear of the car where I rented a pillow, then on second thought, I obtained an additional one. On the way back to my seat I offered the lady across from me the extra pillow which she accepted, stretching languidly like a cat and purring her appreciation in a throaty voice that caused my heart to pump wildly and words to stick in my throat.

Again I tried to sleep but her sensuous voice continued kneading my memory. Turning my attention to the darkness of the night outside my window I was careful to keep my fantasies centred around her. From time to time light reflected my face in the window as the train clattered along, stopping at every sleepy town along the line. Somehow or other I cut the back of my hand on my busted watch, just enough to make things a bit messy. Almost like magic the lovely blond was applying plasters to the cuts.

To look at her and to hear her voice, you would never suspect her toughness. Pamela had once served time for passing counterfeit money; once she shot a man who threatened her. Her cool intellect and fierce loyalty made her invaluable to certain underworld organisations as a courier, something she had been doing since she was sixteen. By the time I was coming into her life she was only twenty-six and burnt out on the whole scene, tired of travelling and living in hotels half-way around the world, always looking over her shoulder. She told me about herself and her dreams of opening a small boutique, settling down and taking care of her ten-year-old son. She complained that she smoked too much, and although she drank moderately, she was heavily dependent on 'uppers' (like those starlets in 'The Valley of the Dolls') and this, too, she wanted to be rid of. The more we confided in each other, the closer we felt. Soon we were holding hands, touching one another's face and hair, and kissing so softly and tenderly that our lips barely touched.

Pamela was catching an early morning flight at the Dorval Airport outside of Montreal. When the train stopped at the tiny station a chilly dawn was just breaking into the light of day as I helped her down to the wooden platform with her bags, turning them over to a taxi driver. She wanted to see me again.

'Call me in Toronto on Sunday,' she said, sliding her arms around my waist, 'and I'll drive up to wherever you're staying. Okay?'

Kissing her longingly while holding her face in my trembling hands like she was the most precious diamond in the world, I answered, 'Please be there.'

'Oh, I will!' The train came to life and I had to leap aboard. 'Don't forget my phone number,' she added.

Smiling down at her I cried out, 'I won't, not ever!'

In Montreal the very first thing I did was to visit the offices of the John Howard Society. They handled parolees and since I planned to live and work in the city I requested to be a part of their case load. However, after a few phone calls to Ottawa, the young caseworker informed me that it was his opinion that since I had just served twenty-two months in custody, and the fact that I had only nineteen months of parole left to be served when I was arrested in 1969, that the parole term was now terminated. According to him I was free of those invisible chains, free to travel wherever I wished!

That same day I rented a hotel room directly over a night-club operated by a friend of a friend. Jimmy couldn't do enough for me; he even offered me the choice of his many go-go girls. With Pamela still fresh in my mind, I settled for sitting at the bar and watching the girls gyrate seductively on stage. While waiting for the days to pass until I could call Pamela, I spent my time walking through the streets of old Montreal, visiting the Expo grounds, and talking to my family on the phone.

Pamela was in my arms late Sunday night and for the first time we made love together, just as tenderly as our encounter on the train.

The next day we decided to take a vacation and with this in mind I called Claude, my old bank robbing partner in Quebec City. I hadn't seen him since his release from Saint Vincent de Paul Penitentiary in 1968. I had heard through the grapevine that he was living high and that his pleasure was still fast cars and beautiful women.

'Hey, Wop!' his voice roared over the line, kidding me as always about my bastard French. 'Christ, it's damn good to hear from you. Say, heard you were jacked up on a beef out of Toronto?'

After explaining to him that I got sprung on the charge and that I was in Montreal with my girl, he laughed happily and roared out an invitation to be his guest.

Dawn was breaking when we zipped across the steel bridge leading into Quebec City and wheeled into a restaurant for coffee and toast. In response to my phone call, Claude pulled into the parking lot in a squeal of tyres so loud that I almost upset my cup. He was behind the wheel of a powerful sports car with that suicidal grin of his. Seated royally at his side was a magnificent Dobermann Pinscher, as fierce and shiny black as the devil. Impatient as always, Claude honked the horn madly and beckoned us to follow him while revving the motor. I was no sooner behind the wheel of Pamela's red convertible than he tore off like a bat out of hell, wheels spinning and rubber burning, and that damn Dobermann sitting straight up and enjoying every second of it.

I didn't know where he lived and so I had no choice but to match his speed! We were soon doing ninety miles an hour. Poor Pamela just sat there, trying to be cool while clutching her little white poodle Bridget, who whining like a frightened child huddled inside her coat. The streets were deserted but I still cursed that mad fool for making me race after him. Finally we roared into a highrise development and fishtailed to a halt! Even before the car came to a halt in the lot, I was out the door and rushing towards Claude and with an angry shout wrestled him to the ground. Cursing and pounding mightily at each other, we rolled around in the dust as that mutt of his growled fiercely, trying to squeeze through the car window. Next thing we knew Pam was looming over us with a pop bottle gripped in her tiny hand saying, 'Hold him still honey . . .'

'No Kitten, no!' I laughed, rolling on top of Claude. 'We're just horsing around.'

Claude thought that was funny as hell, that my girl was going to clobber him, only he didn't know how serious she was! Anyhow, they hit it off well even though one couldn't speak English and the other didn't speak French. However little Bridget, who had only one eye, didn't like Claude, probably because he was always teasing her with his dog Satan.

Claude was living with a sensuous blonde called Renee, almost a copy of Pamela, except that she had a lot of tart in her and flaunted her wiggling fanny. Claude on the other hand ruled her with an iron fist and she seemed to really dig that. They were living in her pad and since Claude's apartment was empty it was agreed that Pamela and I would live there while staying in town.

All four of us had a terrific time visiting the beaches by day and the nightclubs by night. It seemed that everybody in the city knew Claude or wanted to know him, including the local police. (At the time he was out on bail for having allegedly stolen money in his car which the law claimed was his share of loot from a recent robbery.)

I was proud of Pamela's self-control. She gave up her pill habit the day she came away with me. She was talking about marrying me, even if I decided to carry a lunch bucket; that was saying a lot for a girl like her who had known only luxury since she was a teen. She was like a little kitten but I treated her like a princess, even combed her hair, but she knew that my strong feelings for her could go to sub-zero in the blink of an eye if she gave me cause not to like and respect her anymore.

In a way we were both going through an emotional transition. The fact that Pamela found herself falling in love with me made her feel very strange, very unsure of herself, because she had never been dependent on anybody her whole life. She was used to manipulating men as if they were paper dolls. Being off the pills also made her feel insecure. In her purse was a thick address book filled with connections and kingpins throughout North America. She used to say teasingly that she could be dropped anywhere in the world, and so long as she had that little book, she would never be stranded. I came to see that book as a buffer between us and I would tell her that when she burned it, that would be the day she accepted me totally. Meanwhile all the time we were together in Quebec City I was torn between going straight or heisting a jug with Claude. I remembered only too vividly what happened the last time I tried carrying a lunch bucket for a living. Pamela felt guilty when she saw me pace the floor, knowing that I was thinking that I had to go out and rob banks in order to lavish the loot on her.

'Roger honey,' she'd plead with me. 'Everything is swell! Don't go getting yourself killed!'

'But Kitten I can't go on sponging off Claude and you!'

I was convinced that they thought I was 'burnt out'. And in a way I was, because the idea of picking up a gun again left me feeling very sad and depressed. Nevertheless, I couldn't help feeling that I might soon lose Pamela if I didn't soon go out and prove my manhood. I wanted to bring Kitten a suitcase full of money so that she could be a princess again.

Towards the end of our third week together Pamela became increasingly edgy and melancholy and I suspected that she was taking uppers on the sneak. She was also receiving mysterious long distance phone calls about which I never asked anything. Sometimes I'd catch her looking at me kind of funny or else she would rush over and hug me exclaiming, 'Roger I'm no good for you! I'm bad luck, honey.'

Then came the rainy night in August when Claude and I were returning from a trip to Montreal. Letting myself into the apartment I could hardly wait to grab her up in my arms and tell her the good news about how in a few days I was going to be rich, that the two of us were going to be rolling in dough. But the apartment was dark and not even Bridget was there to greet me. Next to the telephone was a short note saying that she felt that she was a jinx for me, and that eventually she would lead me to my destruction!

'I love you honey. You'll always be my special guy. I love and respect you . . .'

With thunder and lightning erupting overhead I walked in the rain, a void as black as the chasm in my heart, searching the parking lots of our old haunts looking for her red convertible, especially the motels with the thought in mind that some man had lured her away from me with pills. Drenched to the skin and with my hair plastered to my forehead, I was on my way back to my apartment along a dimly lighted street lined with cheap booze joints. Emerging from a tavern were three young toughs, walking shoulder to shoulder, whispering and laughing, obviously intent on muscling me off the sidewalk for kicks. Instead of stepping down on to the road I met them head on. I suckered the first guy a tremendous punch, splitting his cheekbone. The second I also punched but the third one ran away. The first two, bleeding and unsure of themselves, had their fists raised against me.

Panting with rage I slowly advanced saying, 'You better get lost because . . . I'm CRAZY!' I then pummelled a telephone pole with hard crunching blows that split my knuckles and caused blood to squirt.

'C'mon!' yelled their buddy from up the street. 'C'mon! He's nuts.'

With Pamela gone from my life I told Claude that I didn't feel like going on the heist he had planned for months, and to get someone else. He told me to take care of his girl and that he'd see me in a few days. The very next day Renee and I were watching the television news when she screamed! Claude and his partner Leo had run into a massive police ambush, and were writhing in horrible agony in front of the broken windows of a small-town bank. Brink's bags lying beside them contained almost two hundred thousand dollars. Fingered by the creep who obtained the getaway car for them, they would have been killed except for the bullet proof vests they wore. Even so Leo lost a leg and Claude's was shortened by a few inches leaving him with a permanent limp.

First Pamela and then Claude – I thought I was going to crack up. The friends my buddy had left behind knew how rough I was taking all this and they looked after me, making sure that I didn't sink too far into depression.

CHAPTER TWENTY-FIVE

September, 1971: Three weeks after Claude was shot up I got a long distance call from Professor Morton. In a voice filled with anxiety and concern he explained to me that the National Parole Board was in the process of issuing a warrant for my arrest! He urged me to travel to Ottawa on my own and give myself up to the authorities there, that it had to be a red tape mistake, and probably all it would take to rectify the error was a few minutes of conversation. But I knew differently! Once that ponderous legal machine started throwing out sparks in your direction, you were in trouble.

Giving myself up went against all my survival instincts, but I was sick, and I was tired, and I just didn't feel like running anymore. I went to Ottawa, telling myself that it was all a mistake, that maybe, just maybe, the machinery would find a way to correct itself.

In Ottawa I was taken into custody and locked up in the old city jail, with the warning to be patient, that when the investigation was over I'd most likely be released, maybe within ten days.

And so I sat brooding in my coffin-like cell with absolutely no plumbing and no lighting as the seconds ticked into minutes, and the minutes into hours, and the hours into days, and the days into weeks, and the weeks into months . . .

It was there that Pamela located me, but I no longer trusted her with my emotions after she had left me, and so I closed my heart to her.

I was in the Ottawa jail over two months when I received a telegram from Pamela's girl friend in Toronto, informing me that Kitten had slashed her wrists and was in hospital.

292

That night for the first time since I was a little boy I cried in my cell.

CHAPTER TWENTY-SIX

November 26, 1971: I was greatly relieved to find myself re-instated on parole (with the stipulation that I live in Ottawa). Nevertheless, I had sweated out eighty-six long days in the bucket on a bogus beef, with four and a half years of parole still to be served hanging over my head.

The document that had triggered the arrest warrant was from the Criminal Intelligence Branch of the Ontario Provincial Police in Toronto. It claimed that I had been planning to hijack two armoured trucks travelling from Toronto to Ottawa. That was pure bullshit! Nevertheless, it was instrumental in putting me back in jail. Fortunately, the parole service demanded some additional back-up information and months later, when none was forthcoming, the board members signed my release.

This made the second time in two years that I was put through the judicial grinder on a bum rap. I couldn't help but think that it was futile for me to even try to go straight.

And when I looked back over my past, all that dead time, all that anguish, all the waste of my life that I could see there, I felt as if I was bursting with a fierce compulsion to fill the ugly void with something meaningful so that the mirror would quit accusing me of being a total failure. That is why I habitually returned to crime upon each release from prison, not really for the money, but like a compulsive gambler who tries to recoup his losses the only way he knows how to prove that he wasn't a fool after all.

Once again with a mind full of conflicting emotions about all the tomorrows in my life, I ventured into the outside world with another pocketful of freedom. As before I had the option of accepting my losses at the judicial wheel of fortune, investing my new found freedom in the lunch bucket brigade, or I could wager it again against awesome odds that I could rip off a fabulous score. To give up bucking the odds at that stage in my life and thus admitting that I was a dismal failure could drive me to drink or even suicide. However if I was able to pull off a million dollar heist then the horror of all those wasted years would not have been in vain. There lies the proverbial carrot that keeps the prisons of the world overpopulated.

My parole officer insisted that I live with an uncle who owned a grocery store in the city, at least until I got established. It was here that Pamela contacted me on my second day out saying that she wanted to live with me again. I had been severely burnt by her once and I was grimly determined there would never be a second time although I knew I loved her.

'Honey,' she pleaded all syrupy and cuddly. 'Don't keep shutting me out like this!'

'I'm sorry, Kitten, but you scared me off.'

'Will you meet with me? I'll drive down and we'll just sit and talk.'

Nervously I agreed to see her the following evening at the cocktail bar in the Holiday Inn.

Pamela drove down from Toronto and was at the Inn one hour before I got there. The brightly lighted bar was crowded but very subdued and Pamela was easily the most beautiful woman in the elegant room. Her hair created a golden halo around her perfect features as she coolly watched me approach and then reached out for my hands, smiling warmly.

Sitting down and pointing to the row of drinks in front of her I said softly, 'You turning alcoholic on me?'

'If you hadn't showed up I might have been tempted to drink them.' She squeezed my hand and laughed while explaining that the drinks had been sent to her table by admirers around the room.

Later we went to a restaurant and then retired to a motel where we talked through most of the night. I felt too defensive towards her and too betrayed to do more than hold her tight. It was impossible for me to totally forgive her, although I really wanted to, but the vibes just weren't there.

In the morning she drove me back to my uncle's store and hugging me feverishly she drove off leaving me standing in the cold snow ...

One week later on a bitterly cold evening I was out walking the downtown district when on an impulse I entered a night club to get warm and ordered a screwdriver from a bosomy barmaid. Business was slow and the smouldering beauty behind the bar was talkative and friendly with a natural affinity for stray dogs and lonely strangers. She reminded me of an Indian princess with her tawny skin and long black shimmering hair parted down the middle. She was a very sensuous woman with the most beautiful eyes and a smile and bubbling personality that caused everybody to like her on sight.

Her name was Louise, she was French and the divorced mother of a beautiful little girl eighteen months old. She was also the mistress of two big dumb lovable mutts called Nanook and Papoose. Nanook was the mother of the pup and Louise had brought them home with her from up North where she worked for a while with the missionaries teaching school to Indian kids. Poor Louise, smart while being dumb, always weeping at sad movies and strangers' funerals. She was twenty-seven years old and had worked as a barmaid and cocktail waitress for ten years and yet she didn't smoke or drink!

As soon as she learned from me that I had been locked away in prison for the better part of my life her Florence Nightingale instinct surged to the forefront and she took me to her home to mother me. Within a week I had moved into her townhouse with my meagre belongings – the first man to do so since her painful separation from her husband, whose name was also Roger.

I think it was my obvious affection for her daughter Ann and the two dogs that made Louise love me from the very beginning. We found peace and pleasure in each other's company, excluding everybody else until soon the glow of togetherness moulded us into a fun-loving family. With

295

them, I observed my first Christmas in the outside world in seventeen years and we had a grand time erecting a tree. After it was all decked out, I just sat there on the rug admiring it and bragging to lovely little Ann who didn't understand a word, but who politely squealed with joy and jumped up and down with the dogs.

Later that night a loud crashing sound brought me bolt upright in bed and rushing downstairs I nearly cried when I found my Christmas tree in one big heap. Peeking at me through the carnage with doleful eyes were Nanook and Papoose whining fearfully and begging me to understand that they meant no harm.

'C'mon, sourpuss, smile!' laughed Louise, flinging herself at me in her flimsy baby doll. Together we fell to the rug rolling around and hugging and kissing while the two mutts crawled out from beneath the branches to lick our faces and wag their tails.

We were always having fun like that, acting more like children than responsible grown-ups. Seeing as how both dogs were female, that left me the only male in the house and so I'd refer to the whole gang as my four dumb broads. Louise had made affectionate slobs out of the two dogs and it got to the point where they could only 'Woof!' instead of 'Arf!' Ann was also spoiled rotten, as Louise herself was, and so it was up to me to enforce a certain amount of discipline in the household. The first rule was that the big mutts couldn't sleep in the upstairs bed anymore. The next rule was that Ann couldn't play grown-up at the crack of dawn with a mixing bowl and all the ungodly ingredients trying to make pancakes while Nanook and Papoose looked hungrily on. The most important thing of all was to get Louise in the habit of being tidier and not leaving her things trailing all around the house. Sometimes as punishment I would assign all four of them to a different corner of the living-room and make them stay there until they promised to do better. The first week I cleaned the house from top to bottom and even washed the dogs in the tub and that was a sight to behold! Louise was always falling asleep on me while watching television and so one day after seeing this commercial about the miracles of Geritol I went out and bought a bottle. After gathering all four girls in the kitchen I made them open wide and pinching their noses I fed them each a spoonful amid a lot of gagging and wry faces. I did it for their own well being and yet the ungrateful bunch conspired to hide the bottle on me, never to be found again!

We all got along just great and our idea of having fun was bundling up warmly and skating on the Rideau canal with the dogs hauling Ann on a toboggan. Other times we'd all cram into the car with lots of blankets and sandwiches and roar off in the snow to the local drive-in theatre. I also registered Louise and myself at a beautiful health club where all the recreational facilities were at our disposal. While I lifted weights she would visit the pool. Watching Louise in a bikini was enough to take any man's breath away!

Like a little kitten she loved to play goofy games, some of which almost drove me nuts. For instance I could never drive up to the house in the evening without her jumping up and down excitedly and pleading, 'Oh, Roger please! Let me go inside and hide on you.' With those big beautiful expressive eyes staring into mine I could never refuse her anything. She was only one hundred and ten pounds and yet it was uncanny the places she could squeeze into. I wouldn't have been surprised to see her pop triumphantly out of the breadbox on the shelf. The look of astonishment on my face was her reward as she'd squeal with delight and throw her arms around me.

Right from the beginning I used to call Louise my little Funny Face and later when Donna Fargo came out with a sad song of that name that clinched it because the girl in the song was Louise.

In spite of being very happy, only a small part of me was truly alive while the rest of me brooded darkly. The feeling that there was something missing in my life kept attacking me like a bad case of rheumatism.

By late January I had singled out a large Air Force Base not far from where I lived. Inside the guarded base was a trailer bank right next to the military police barracks that handled the massive payroll. I was sure that I could heist it with just one back-up partner and get away with more than half a million dollars!

Two factors were missing to make it a success – dry pavements and a gutsy partner. The first would arrive in early spring, the second I would have to search for.

Ironically it was while visiting a lifer friend in Millhaven penitentiary that I met my prospective partner in crime. We had our ladies with us as fronts and upon seeing each other they made a big happy scene greeting each other as old friends having worked together as cocktail waitresses. Naturally this led to me and Rolly shaking hands and shortly after that we concluded that we had a lot of things in common. He was a fiery red head who dressed mod and was bubbling over with courage. Having just been released from a joint out west on an AR bit he was hungry for action because he had expensive tastes, including his girl who was a bunny in a club in Ottawa. Rolly, who was in his mid-twenties, was not only brainy but also dangerously impulsive and sometimes too hot-headed for his own good. Loyal beyond belief he liked to be surrounded by friends most of whom belonged to a karate club in Hull, Quebec.

By early March everything concerning the Air Force Base was falling into place and it was just a matter of waiting for good traction for our wheels because it was going to be a lightning raid. In the meantime we needed some working capital and the experience of working together so we decided to knock off a local jug.

Even on a quick grub stake like this I insisted on checking things out to the last detail – something that Rolly didn't have much patience for. Each banking section is covered by a phantom police car with the occupants armed to the teeth patrolling that area in the hope of getting the jump on guys like us. My method of unmasking a ghost car was by visiting the local police station at night and jotting down all the licence numbers of the unmarked cars. The next day it would be just a matter of carefully checking out the parking areas around a number of banks until one of the plates tallied. After that it was easy to keep on the goons.

It was these cautious habits of mine and my premonition for danger that saved our lives one cold Friday evening as we slowly drove into the parking lot of a large shopping plaza. The place was teeming with cars and people. The new

298

bank stayed open until 8 p.m. to accommodate the shoppers.

'Let's get out of here!' I suddenly exclaimed. 'Go-Man!'

Later at a restaurant Rolly was greatly peeved when my only explanation for my strange behaviour was that I smelled a trap. Bitterly disappointed he drove back to his apartment while I returned to the scene in my Couger convertible to sniff around.

The plaza was crowded right up against a huge sprawling college and a mass of other buildings all connected by a maze of roads and laneways that could easily conceal a platoon of soldiers. I had been nosing around in ever widening circles for more than an hour when I suddenly uncovered the first ghost car in a dark lot at the rear of a nursing residence. They had cunningly dug out a narrow corridor through a ten-foot snow bank that gave them a straight beeline to the side entrance of the jug five hundred yards away. The bushwackers were everywhere, including the rooftops, with high powered rifles!

Later that same evening at a noisy discotheque where his girl worked as a bunny, Rolly profoundly apologised for doubting my state of mind. I was convinced that had we gone through with the play we would have died in a hail of bullets. However our grave mistake was in sloughing the whole thing off as an isolated ambush set for any bandits unlucky enough to blunder into it. At that hour on a Friday night there were only three banks open for business and it was logical for us to come to this conclusion. Nevertheless we decided to cool our heels for a week before striking again at the opposite end of town during regular banking hours.

With a burst of speed Rolly pulled the Pontiac away from the intersection, wheeling it though the entrance of the plaza parking lot and around in a looping U turn, coming to a halt beside the door leading into the bank. With the motor still running we hurried in, pulling our ski masks down and withdrawing our guns.

'Everybody on the floor!' I shouted. 'This is a hold-up!'

There was a flurry of movement and nervous squealing as employees and customers did as they were told. Rushing towards a room at the rear I kicked open a door almost expecting to be met by gunfire. Empty. Rolly was filling the

299

bag with loot and having problems with an hysterical teller who was so nervous that she didn't remember locking her money drawer then putting the key in her pocket. I was counting off the seconds. The silent alarm would have been activated when we burst in. At 28 seconds Rolly yelled, 'Got it!' and rushed past me. I followed, warning everybody to stay right where they were. Rolly was already behind the wheel when I slid in next to him pulling off my hood and laying my gun on my lap.

'Let's go!' I said. Just then a blue Mustang came out of nowhere and crashed into my side of the Pontiac, throwing me violently against the dash. Dazed, I groped blindly for the gun that had fallen to the floor; the driver of the other vehicle was desperately trying to shoulder his door open. Like a slow motion nightmare my fingers found the gun and were curling around the butt, when Rolly croaked, 'Up front!'

I turned my head just in time to see a white car veer off the boulevard and smash recklessly into us! When a third vehicle made contact with our rear bumper the gun was again lost.

And so was I! Sprawled on the hood of our hot car was a policeman disguised as a bearded hippy, his shotgun pressed up against the windshield, mouthing curses and dire threats. Emerging from the scrap pile, we were ordered to place our hands up against the windows of the bank, while shotguns and rifles pressed our spines.

We were busted by a crack squad of OPP officers from the Criminal Intelligence Special Services Branch whose headquarters is in Toronto. They had arrived on assignment in Ottawa a few weeks earlier in great secrecy equipped with sophisticated listening devices and a mind-boggling array of disguises. Their orders were to get me, dead or alive.

CHAPTER TWENTY-SEVEN

March 21, 1972: Never had the security of a city jail come under such intense attack in so short a time as that of the Ottawa jail. My partner and I started cutting bars and digging holes almost from the day of our arrest. When the superintendent had a nervous breakdown and was hospitalised, it was decided that Rolly and I should be separated and held under tighter security while awaiting trial.

The Brockville City Jail, where I was taken, was an old fortress that hadn't seen any escape in forty-two years. I was placed in an iron cage the like of which I had never seen before. The sides, back, and front consisted of rows and rows of iron bars like a monkey cage. Even the roof was iron bars so that I would have been able to swing from one end of my cell to the other without touching the ground. The bunk was a steel cot; there was no plumbing. There was not even a light bulb.

Sunday evening, August 9th: The jail was very quiet as prisoners filled their water buckets before being locked into cells for the night. It would be a perfect night to escape, I thought. There was going to be a thunder storm and only three guards were on duty.

Sharing the tiny cell-block with me were two others. Doug, a handsome blond kid in his mid-twenties, was shaking real rough time; only a few hours earlier he had nervously volunteered to join me in my escape attempt.

Suddenly, I quit pacing the monkey cage and told Doug, 'It's time!'

Licking his lips nervously, he asked, 'How about Scotty?'

The newcomer looked at me expectantly.

'We're busting out. You can stay behind or you can join us,' I said flatly.

He laughed nervously. 'You wouldn't be putting me on, would you?'

By way of answer I strode to the corner of our cage, got down on one knee and ripped out two bars we'd cut. I removed my blue denim shirt in order to squeeze through the small opening. Tucked in the waistband of my prison jeans was a small wooden revolver. The iron bars we would also take with us.

'He doesn't want to come, Roger,' said Doug sadly. 'Says he's got a wife and kid.'

'It's okay, Doug. Don't worry about it,' I said, squeezing his shoulder reassuringly. 'But are you sure yourself you want to go?'

'Yeh, Rog. I'll go crazy here.'

'Remember, you've got a wife and baby, too,' I reminded him so that he would know precisely what he was getting into.

'I know. But I still want to go.'

Bathed in perspiration and dragging in lungfuls of fresh air Doug and I stood just inside the front entrance of the jail searching the town square. Behind us the guards were tied with shoelaces. We stepped out, locking the door behind us.

'Easy, Doug, easy!' I whispered, keeping a wary eye on the strollers and passing vehicles. To break into a run now would give us away. It was a quarter to ten and the guards would soon be discovered missing. We had to be on the highway before roadblocks were thrown up.

In the parking lot Doug slid behind the wheel of a Volkswagen, flicked on the motor which purred nicely but when he tried to throw it in reverse to back away from the wall there was only a grinding of gears.

'Can't find reverse on this fuckin crate!' he cried out in frustration. For long panic-filled minutes he continued to mesh gears while I stared up helplessly at our cell-block, half expecting to see someone show up yelling for the police.

'C'mon!' I said impatiently. 'We'll lift it right around.'

We drove agonisingly slow, stopping for every red light and flinching at the sight of a police cruiser. Raindrops were just starting to splatter against the windshield as we got on to highway 401.

'Do we go straight on to Montreal or do we cross over at Prescott?' asked Doug, anxiously crouched over the wheel, concentrating on the dark, rain-swept highway.

Fiddling with the radio, I didn't answer him for long seconds. The international bridge was less than twelve miles away. Not even the police would credit us with having the unmitigated gall to slip into the USA in a stolen guard's vehicle!

'Yeh, we'll cross,' I said finally.

'Jesus!' he exclaimed, gripping the wheel tighter.

I tried to shut out the faces of three young kids I had seen back at the jail when we were breaking out. They had been so impressed by us it bothered me. Each one was a reflection of my lost youth.

'How much bread have we got?' asked Doug, to break the silence.

'A little over three hundred dollars. Enough to help us break our trail.'

The closer we got to the border the more apprehensive we became. We had no way of knowing if the alarm was out and if roadblocks were waiting ahead. At 10.30 we pulled off the main highway on to a winding drive that was brightly lit and bordered by lush green grass and bramble bushes. Suddenly the Canadian Immigration building appeared. Further on was the bridge; beyond that, the American immigration and freedom.

'Keep going, Doug,' I coached. The poor kid was almost frozen with fear and so I gripped his elbow to give him strength, worried that he might panic in front of the border patrol. He didn't even respond when I told him to take out the guard's wallet with its ownership papers and driver's licence and so I stuck it in his hand.

Doug came to a very jerky halt at the US immigration booth, far enough away from the building so that the officer had to rush out in the rain to look into the car. Close by were two highway patrolmen seated in their cruiser, talking but not looking at us. I felt the outline of the wooden gun under my pant leg.

'Where're you boys off to?' inquired the young border guard, rain dripping off his hat. He made no move to look at the ID which Doug was proffering in a grim-faced manner.

Leaning over my partner, I plastered a big grin on my kisser and replied, 'Just going across to visit a couple of chicks we met at a dance last week.

Grinning, he asked, 'Hot stuff?'

'Nothing to write home about,' I allowed.

'Well, if you boys see a stray one be sure to bring her back,' he winked and stepped back and waved us on.

Poor Doug was so relieved that he poured on the horses a bit too energetically. The little red Volks reared back, gave a powerful lurch and then zoomed off into the night with its two occupants whooping it up with elation and joy.

One hour later we arrived in Massena, N.Y. where we wanted to get rid of the hot car. We zipped into a parking space behind a large downtown building which unknown to us was the local police station. We learned later that the car sat there for thirty-one days undiscovered.

Crossing the street, we entered a crowded cocktail lounge, picked out a quiet corner and sat down. When Dougie ordered a drink from the pretty waitress I decided to celebrate my freedom by doing likewise.

Jail habits are hard to break because Doug was sitting across from me rolling a cigarette with tobacco from a rumpled pouch. Reaching out I knocked the makings from his hands.

'Hey!' he exclaimed in surprise.

I grinned and pointed to the cigarette machine beside the juke box.

'Oh!' he said sheepishly, getting up and reaching for change in his pocket.

We hired a taxi to take us all the way to New York City where we rented a room in a cheap hotel.

The view from the window showed me two harness bulls pinning a black kid up against a barber shop and busting the blade on his switchblade knife. And I thought we had just left the jungle behind!

We spent the next five days getting to know our part of

304

the city, especially the banks. This time I felt there was something missing. I felt sad and moody all the time. The thought of obtaining a real gun and robbing a bank depressed me even further. But we would soon be running out of money.

It was up to me to do something. The only thing I knew well was robbing banks. I kept wishing that I was alone and then the responsibility of doing something wouldn't be so great.

Doug was always complaining about having left his wife and newborn son behind. I offered to pay his bus fare back to Canada but he'd shake his head, saying that he'd rather send for them after we got some money. I couldn't ditch Doug until we had knocked off at least one jug and I could give him his share of the loot. Meanwhile, he was paranoid that I might leave him and he never strayed far from me. I really think now that if I had been alone I would have gone out and got myself a regular job.

On our fifth day I decided to call Pamela. I wanted her to dig into that little address book of hers and furnish us with some New York telephone numbers of people who could supply us with guns and passports.

It took all of one day to track her down through her answering service.

'Honey, just give me forty-eight hours to put my furniture in storage and get a few errands done,' she promised, 'and then we'll be together again, this time for always!'

Towards the end of August, Pamela told me in a concerned voice that she was out on bail for 'gun possession' and that she had to appear in court in September. She was willing to be declared unlawfully at large in order to stay with me but that would have been irresponsible and so I pounced on the opportunity to have her return to Canada. It was for her own good and would relieve me of the responsibility of keeping her out of an American prison as my accomplice.

'I'll have my lawyer ask the judge for a two month trial postponement and we'll be together again in less than a week,' she hoped.

It tore my guts out to watch her leave and the black pall

305

over my head got stormier as the loneliness flailed away threatening to lay bare my inner insecurity.

Two days later I made the grim decision to rob a bank with Dougie. Strangely enough, the moment that I decided, I felt a warm glow of strength come over me. I visited a nearby gun store and asked the clerk to show me a beautiful, deadly-looking .38 calibre snub-nose Cobra from a display case.

The moment he laid it in the palm of my hand I started to perspire and tremble. It was exactly as if I was gripping a squirming serpent. Revulsion crept up to my throat as my fingers tightened around the handle like a vice until my knuckles shone white.

'Are you ill?' asked the clerk in sudden alarm.

Dropping the revolver, I spun around and walked out of the store, sucking deeply of the fresh air.

It was a bright warm day as Dougie and I parked at the side of a new bank in a large plaza near the county line outside a city. It would be disastrous to be stranded on foot there as the area was surrounded by corn fields.

I was armed with a toy pistol; Doug carried a small satchel. Although scared stiff, he was determined to go through with the play.

A sign on the double doors of the bank warned that the jug was protected by hidden cameras; nevertheless, we weren't masked. We had only taken the trouble to apply a liquid to our finger tips giving them a plastic coating which would leave no fingerprints.

Everything went off smoothly. I quickly got control of the employees and customers, forcing them to lie on the floor so that the crowds passing outside would not see them. All the while cameras were filming our every move; nevertheless, the police obtained no mug shots of us. Unmasked, I patrolled the floor with the bogus gun concealed against my pant leg, looking casual to anyone glancing in. Dougie was awkwardly scooping up loot from the tills, using up many precious seconds.

I probably appeared icily cool but my insides were an inferno of conflicting emotions. For the very first time during a robbery, I was plagued with powerful doubts about my actions. The whimpers of fear from my mini-skirted hostages every time I walked too close to them hammered the doubts home. They viewed me exactly as if I was a wild beast that had escaped from its cage in the zoo.

This image of myself came as a sudden and tremendous shock, causing me to recoil at the scorn I was beginning to feel for myself. I was thinking that I had no right to frighten people like that.

'Let's get out of here!' blurted Dougie as he rushed up holding out the satchel for me to see all the green inside.

'You go ahead,' I advised. Backing slowly towards the exit my eyes roved over all the prone bodies and I felt a powerful compulsion to say something, to apologise. Shaking off these alien thoughts, I realized suddenly that we had taken up almost two full minutes. I spun around and pushed open the bank doors to be greeted by the sight of two sheriff's deputies twenty feet away scrambling from their cruiser with shotguns!

I made a snap decision. I would decoy the cops away from Dougie sitting inside the stolen vehicle so that he could at least get away. I dashed towards a row of store fronts and burst into a hairdressing shop where a dozen ladies were seated under dryers. I reached the rear exit and glanced over my shoulder. A lawman was staggering under a white sheet like a ghost in a cat house while his partner tried vainly to negotiate past a fat lady.

I sprinted across an asphalt drive amid wailing sirens and leapt a watery ditch. Expecting to be blasted apart as I scrambled to my feet, I regained my balance and disappeared into a forest of giant cornstalks.

CHAPTER TWENTY-EIGHT

September, 1972: Numb with loneliness, hollow-cheeked, my hair dyed red, spooked by the terror-filled eyes of my most recent victims and paranoid about the police, I travelled unwaveringly towards the Canadian border. I stumbled on by night, terrified that I might be found, an anonymous stiff on a garbage heap in some alley thousands of miles from home, away from my family, from Kitten and from my unfinished book manuscript.*

On the 8th of September I slipped across the Detroit border and straight into the waiting arms of Pamela. Two days later we were in a Toronto motel room studying a map around midnight when suddenly the door and windows smashed inwards with great force and we found ourselves staring down the muzzles of guns.

Pamela was charged with aiding in my escape but the charge was later dropped. However, she did serve a reformatory sentence on other outstanding charges. Released, after six months, her pill habit was gone. Determined to go straight and give more time to her handsome son, she invested in a small boutique. Nearly working herself into nervous exhaustion, she is today the owner of a string of thriving shops and a highly respected businesswoman in her community.

* Ed. note: The reference is to this book.

CHAPTER TWENTY-NINE

November 21, 1972: I was leaving Millhaven Penitentiary, the maximum security, multi-million dollar nightmare – scene of riots, grief, murders, unfeeling guards, the political punching bag that has been branded a human warehouse by the warden himself – jinxed from the first day it swung open its doors to receive inmate refugees from the 1971 Kingston Penitentiary riot.

Electronically the many doors slammed open and then shut as I shuffled through them chained hand and foot, three detectives escorting me forwards, until finally we reached the chain link fence topped with barbed wire that surrounded the 'Mill'. Again a gate slid open and shut behind us. We waited, enclosed on all sides by chain fencing. Finally the last gate slid open, manipulated by a guard high inside the main gun tower. Tethered to the base of that tower was a black four-legged incarnation of the devil himself, lunging with teeth bared and saliva dripping from his jaws. The patrol dog, I reflected, for all its ferocity, was just another victim: treated inhumanely and conditioned to behave viciously.

I was being returned to Ottawa for sentencing on the Ottawa bank robbery. Eight years had been added for jailbreak and parole violation and now I was worried that a life sentence waited me.

In the crowded Ottawa courtroom I stood in the dock, facing the judge, a prosecutor and my lawyer. Outwardly calm, inside I was churning with anguish.

Everybody it seemed was bent on assassinating my character on this day, or at least assassinating the individual that emerged from my police record. Each verbal swipe struck home with the impact of a whip. I wanted to raise my manacled hands and cover my ears and scream that they were wrong in their conclusions, that I wasn't the mindless robot they were so cruelly dissecting as if I was part of a biological experiment that had gone haywire. I wanted to find the words to convince them that I was a human being just like everybody else in the courtroom, and not some criminal psychopath who preyed on society like a killer shark. The transcripts show even my own lawyer taking pot-shots at me in addressing the judge:

' ... I would admit that, on first reading, it's one of the worst records that I am sure has come before your Honour, and certainly in my experience, one of the worst that I have ever seen. There are, however, certain factors about the record which are interesting, and that's that, with the exception of the charges at the age of 16 in Cornwall, Ontario, most of the convictions registered arise out of escapes from various institutions. I believe that there have been six escapes to date ...

HIS HONOUR: I have counted six.

Yes ... and that during the course of these escapes, there are various charges of theft of auto, break and enter and theft, which are charges arising out of the actual committing of the escape itself. ... This is not to condone, of course, the escapes; I would like to refer to them later.' Near the middle of his submission he allowed, 'This is a very bad record in many respects. There is a lot of big time given on it.'

My lawyer went on outlining my record, then said,

What's interesting is that that record purports to be the life of Roger Caron ... What's interesting about Mr Caron is that he has spent almost all of his life from the age of sixteen, over half his life, in gaol, and while on the surface would appear not to have been benefitted, there is the fruits [indicating my manuscript for this book] of eight years' labour, for what it's all worth.

There contains on these pages the work of an illiterate man, if we go by his standing of education; and to read this is to read a chronicle of penal history ... It is the story of a young man who finds himself in gaol, who finds himself adhering to the code of the prisoners, who finds himself leaving gaol with the white pallor of prisons, of really fighting for survival. It is a story of work gangs, unbelievable punishment and isolation for meaningless little things. It is the story of a man who lived through our penal system in the days when its sole aim was to break down a man so that at the end of it a tailor-made cigarette was a supreme gift. And that's how it worked.

At Kingston they used to say once the big door clanged behind you, you went for three months of the blue fog when you didn't get cigarettes, when you didn't get exercises [sic], when you didn't get to see anyone else; and the idea of that was so that you would be placed in the prison population at about the same level of consciousness as the rest of the blue-shirts. They didn't want you coming in remembering what it was like to go for a beer; to have a girl. What they wanted to maintain was discipline, the requirement of the individual was to put him into a state of semi-consciousness, and that's what he is a product of. And while I am not saying that he is not to blame, at the age of 34, I do submit that he is a product of that system, and because of that, we are to blame because we maintain such a system, and to expect a man to come out after all of those years, maybe a bit better than when he went in, is fine, but to expect of so many of those men that they could come out completely rehabilitated was the most illogical and ridiculous thing that we ever had, so we have had the changes because the old way didn't work.

And Roger Caron is an example of how it didn't work. His record of escapes is logical and to be expected when taken in light of the circumstances. They reflect someone who is trying to get out, just as he tried to escape from the harsh reality by what he has done to his body. He bears the scars of eighteen years of depression, and in those deep depressions he did things to himself that we think impossible, but he carries those scars, and I submit that those scars are reflected in his mind.

After my defence came the prosecutor and after him came the judge who said:

'I have to keep in mind, of course, the protection of society. I have tried to find something that would give me some hope for your rehabilitation, but I certainly haven't been able to see anything. You have been convicted of armed robbery. This is the fourth or fifth . . . I have thought about this a great deal, and I can tell you that my first inclination was to put you away for life.'

Later the judge stated, 'I can understand the problem: You may have got off on the wrong foot when you were sixteen. You may have rebelled against society since that period of time. That may be your problem. You simply won't accept – and perhaps I can't tell you you have to accept – the shackles of society, but I can say you have done nothing in the last sixteen years to change whatsoever. Every time you have been out, it has been a question of armed robbery or some other crime. That disturbs me a great deal.'

Then came the sentence: 'Well, I think the needs of society and your own needs would be faced fully if I were to sentence you to a consecutive term of 12 years in penitentiary. That appears to me a total of nineteen and a half years for you, Caron. Again, what you do with that, that's your affair, not mine, but please don't say that any Judge just sits here and decides things. I don't just sit here. I also stew about these things, and I have given you as much thought as I have given anybody else.

MR CARON: I appreciate it, thank you; sure.

HIS HONOUR: Remove the accused please.

—Whereupon the prisoner is removed and the Court is adjourned sine die at 3.22 p.m.'

The Latin words *sine die* which mean 'without a time being set for further consideration' conveyed a terrible sense of finality with no hope for appeal. To me it sounded like a death knell. SINE DIE! For five long years those damning words scoured away at my conscience. SINE DIE! It clawed and whispered in my ear with the sound of a death rattle as I struggled to stay afloat in the quagmire of steel, cement, and stone. A world of caged men, muffled sobs, and long shuddering screams that echo throughout the night. SINE DIE!

In my dreams I became a vegetable and the guards were planting me in the prison yard.

'What type of vegetable do you want to be?' they snickered.

'A turnip!' I shouted with a cry of despair. They joined hands and danced around me, chanting 'You're a fuckin turnip and we'll water you once a week!'

SINE DIE! Stay awake, stay on point, write letters, make the judge understand that I am bad, but that I am not a criminal psychopath. I am a human being with heart and soul and conscience that is battered and soggy with regret. I have paid my weary pound of flesh. Now all I seek is to be at peace with myself, but I fear that I am becoming a vegetable, Judge, because I am losing the feeling of touch, and to love and be loved in return one must have the feeling of touch.

SINE DIE! You have banished me, Judge, shamed me so, and in doing so you have brought me face to face with my inner self. I don't want to believe that I was all those things that were said about me in your courtroom that fateful day. If they were really true it would destroy me; I would not want to live. I have to learn how to tell my story to the world in the fervent hope that it will do some good, warn others of folly. There is so much to learn, so much forgiving to ask. That is why I write letters to you, Judge, hoping to win your respect and your trust, for you are the people, and the people are the judge.

EDITOR'S NOTE

Many people, including the judge who sentenced him, have been trying to help Roger establish himself. In January 1977 he was transferred from the very tense and explosive Millhaven maximum security institution to the medium security of Collins Bay, which operates in a more humane atmosphere although there are gun towers and guards, too. In April 1977 Roger appeared before the Parole Board seeking a conditional release; a decision has been postponed for a year. He has now been inside for five straight years.

It was a joyful man indeed who phoned his editor one day to say that he was going to be allowed out for an afternoon to attend his widowed mother's wedding. He is already well into his second book, for a career in writing; he would like also to open a shop to sell the fine handicrafts produced in prisons. He is clearly on his way to a new life, a 'Go Boy' who will finally make it – with our blessing.

GLOSSARY

ace – dollar
badmouthing – threatening verbal attack
bucket – county jail
bingo – riot
blower – telephone
can – safe
bug – homemade water heater for making coffee
bug juice – depressant drug
bitch – habitual criminal
bug pass – a prisoner who is not responsible for his actions
case a joint – look over a place with a view to robbing it
chunk – hand gun
C-note – one hundred dollars
cooler – solitary confinement, the hole
CNR strawberries – prunes
cranking up – injecting a hypodermic needle
croaker – doctor, physician
damper – solitary, the hole
deuce – two dollars
dissociation – solitary confinement
diddler – child molester
double-doored – from both ends
ducket – to be placed on report
drum – cell
drag-queen – man decked out in woman's clothing
doing the dutch – committing suicide
digger – solitary, the hole
dummy – bread
fence – one who buys and sells stolen goods

fin – five dollars
fish – newcomer
good-time – time off for good behaviour
hack – guard
half a yard – fifty dollars
head shrinker – psychiatrist
horseman – Mountie
horse – smooth block of wood with string attached
inside – in prison
java – coffee
jointman – prisoner who behaves like a guard
jo-jos – bulky coat with no pockets
jug – bank
jug-up – meal time
jailhouse merchant – prisoner who sells two-for-one
kite – a contraband letter/note
lugger – a contraband carrier
Limbo Room – place where corporal punishment is administered
mark – sucker, someone who is gullible
mover – somebody that is ambitious
NG – No Good
OP – Off Privilege, restricted
outside – on the street, *i.e.* not in prison
pete man – safe cracker
prison wolf – guy that likes girls on the outside, boys on the inside
piece – gun
pick man – guy who picks locks
patch – to put the fix in
range – open area outside cells
rounder – guy who knows his way around the underworld
sawbuck – ten dollars
shank – knife
six man – lookout
stand point – to be on the alert
sand – sugar
shiving – a knifing
sine die – indefinitely
Sky-Pilot – priest

snow job – a fallacious but convincing story, the runaround
sweet kid – a boy who teams up with an older inmate
scratch – money
spike – hypodermic needle
scoff – food
shafted – double crossed
stir bugs or stir crazy – mentally deranged from confinement
tank – holding cell
tits-up – dead
topped himself – committed suicide
yard – one hundred dollars

Now Available in Paperback

DOUBLE TROUBLE $2.95

DOUBLE TROUBLE is both the story of Anthony Michael Peter Gabriel, and the most penetrating study ever published of professional football in Canada.

Tony Gabriel:

- sticky-fingered tight end for the Ottawa Rough Riders
- former Hamilton Ticat and key contributor to the Cats' 1972 Grey Cup win over Regina
- the only player in the CFL to sue his team
- three-time Schenley Award winner (in a seven-year career!) for Outstanding Canadian playing in the CFL
- **DOUBLE AWARD WINNER — CFL 1978 MOST OUTSTANDING CANADIAN PLAYER and CFL 1978 MOST OUTSTANDING PLAYER**

Against a background of his own amateur and professional careers, Canada's football superstar discusses the game with a frankness seldom witnessed. He gives football fans the inside info on the game — player contracts, trades, salaries, locker room gossip, pressures to win, the agonies of defeat, and the reasons why Canadian ball is superior to the American game.